**W9-BQM-109**

*Shakespeare and Our World*

ALWIN THALER

# Shakespeare and Our World

THE UNIVERSITY OF TENNESSEE PRESS / *Knoxville, 1966*

TO
*Roderick Page Thaler*

# *Preface*

THE ADDRESSES AND STUDIES here collected are, almost without exception, concerned with if not actually keyed to Shakespeare's impact upon his aftertimes and so upon our world. This is the special theme of Part I of this book. And this theme reappears, in varying degrees, in the studies of dramatic technique of Part II and of literary influence in Part III. This is so because, by and large, they exhibit Shakespeare's special mastery of an ageless technique and his influence upon other writers, other times. Looking before and after, these chapters touch upon problems of craftsmanship or even of ethics or religion which are timely because they are timeless. It is my faith that vital literary study must be concerned about the past *and* the now and hereafter. The materials of my earlier chapters, at all events, especially belong to our world because they were originally written for oral delivery to university or town-and-gown audiences, for such occasions as the recent Quadricentennial, an honors day lecture, or the like. For the most part, they are here printed as originally delivered. Some of my listeners wished to see what they had heard, and more formal treatment might have produced less matter without more art. I have, however, cited chapter and verse wherever this seemed useful.

The closing chapter of the book brings together and reorganizes, in response to persistent demand, my findings on its subject in several earlier studies long out of print.

Though only Chapters I, V, and VI are entirely new, the others are so in considerable part, for all these have been re-written and substantially augmented. I hope that all may gain by their juxtaposition.

For permission to draw upon copyrighted and other published materials, I am especially indebted to the Harvard University Press, the University of Florida Press, and to the editors of the *Publications of the Modern Language Association of America, Tennessee Studies in Literature,* and the *Shakespeare Quarterly*. Aid and comfort has been given me, without stint, by friends and co-workers among whom I gratefully name Professors A. C. Sprague, Nevill Coghill, James Gray, Kenneth Curry, Kenneth L. Knickerbocker, the late Walter Morris Hart, and especially my comrade of old, Professor John C. Hodges, and my wife.

# Contents

PART ONE

*Shakespeare and Our World*
Lectures and Addresses

# 1

## Mingled Yarn

### Shakespeare's "Middle of Humanity"

WHAT I HAVE to say here turns on two key passages from Shakespeare. The first is from the fourth act of *All's Well That Ends Well*, an anonymous "second lord" speaking:

The web of our life is of a mingled yarn, good and ill together. Our virtues would be proud if our faults whipp'd them not, and our crimes would despair if they were not cherish'd by our virtues. (IV.iii.83–87)[1]

The second passage is from the fourth act of *Timon of Athens*. Timon, one-time friend and too-generous patron of every man, turns misanthrope after his fair-weather friends have failed him. While digging for roots before his seashore cave, he finds gold— "yellow, glittering, precious gold" (IV.iii.26). This he abhors and rejects; "On what I hate I feed not" (IV.iii.306). Thereupon he is scolded by Apemantus, a "churlish philosopher":

The middle of humanity thou never knewest, but the extremity at both ends. (IV.iii.300–301)

It is a familiar fact that some of the least of Shakespeare's people say the best things. Unnamed servants or gentlemen, a captain or a second lord—out of their mouths come forth humor, wisdom, charity: "The web of our life is of a mingled yarn, good and ill together." Often, by a glorious failure in mere realism,

---

[1] All citations from Shakespeare in this volume, unless otherwise noted, are from the text of George Lyman Kittredge, *Complete Works of Shakespeare* (Boston, 1936).

the supreme realist-idealist makes even the least of his characters speak as only he himself could have spoken. He must have known that this was not folly but wisdom. Good poems are not made by fools, as Joyce Kilmer himself very well knew. Certainly not according to the Elizabethans. In their moments of deepest insight they looked upon the true poet as a creator, under God. "We Englishmen, with the Greeks," wrote Sir Philip Sidney, "call [the poet] a maker. . . . Neither let it be deemed too saucy a comparison" to honor his work as second only to that of "the heavenly Maker of that maker." In this spirit I approach my subject for the celebration of the four-hundredth birthday of our greatest poet. Unlike Shakespeare, I shall, in all humility, attempt a kind of lay sermon upon my Shakespearean text. He, the master dramatist, did not sermonize. For our time and purpose, however, we may be allowed to ponder seriously the implications of Shakespeare's timeless theme. I think it is as vitally essential for us as for the troubled and glorious time of the English Renaissance. Not as antidote or balm but as hope and conviction with which to confront our fears, our revolutionary strains and agonies, our dreadful violence, our tremendous potential for good and evil, we need to cultivate in thought and works Shakespeare's healing faith in the middle of humanity. In these perilous times, while seeing or reading or listening once more to his stories, his characters, the music of his verse, the pointing of his prose, we cannot fail to profit and delight afresh from the tales he tells, from his irresistible humor, his joy in life, his own wonderfully humane weakness in strength, his compassionate understanding.

His middle of humanity is no convenient trimming for expediency, no cheap compromise with mediocrity. It is almost an article of faith. It sees, tolerantly, both sides of the vexed problems that afflict mankind. More important, it sees, however dimly in trying times, the divine spark in the human spirit seeking its own level, records its immortal longings, conceives, as Hamlet says, thoughts beyond the reaches of our souls. Like King Lear, it recognizes this spirit, steadfast in earthly defeat, as God's spy here below: seeking, however brokenly, fulfillment, excellence, perfection. Four centuries after Shakespeare, this seeking, this humane quest, goes on. I quote from Thomas Hardy's *Tess of the D'Urbervilles*: "It is the touch of the imperfect upon the would-be perfect that gives the sweetness, because it is that which gives the humanity." From Shakespeare's middle of humanity, therefore, we may find a better way to face our own world. From his work we can learn something of the tolerant, open eye and the loving heart of one who knows but ever struggles against the raw violence of extremes, seeks humane balance, kindly understanding of men and things, and, however poignantly aware of the inextricable commingling of good and evil in our world, fights instinctively, victoriously, by the irrefutable logic of events and character in his plays, against evil, for good.

I do not mean to blink the darker shadows in his view of life: his quick awareness, for example, of the sudden stab of rancor; of back-wounding calumny, foul slander sharper than the sword; of the unpalatable draught of our mortality, the innumerable battalions in which sorrows come; of all the mystery of suffering and of evil. Nor would I exploit him as a copybook moralist. Dr. Johnson, a wise man and a noble but not infallible critic, found fault with Shakespeare because he did not, Johnson thought, sufficiently stress moral values nor consistently vindicate "poetic justice." On the other hand, the historian A. L. Rowse, Shakespeare's latest biographer, finds "moralizing tags . . . everywhere . . . in the plays." Shakespeare, in fact, steers between these extremes. He seems to have known that the facts of life do not invariably vindicate poetic justice, and that art does not readily tolerate an overplus of moralizing tags. The function of artists is to add to the sum total of the world's joy, beauty, truth, and compassionate understanding. Artists—and Shakespeare in particular, as I read him—teach but do not preach. The evidence will speak for itself, for I shall presently have something more specific to say concerning some of the plays: of his early work culminating in *Romeo and Juliet,* and of *The Merchant of Venice* and *The Tempest* to represent, respectively, the middle and the close of his career as dramatist. These plays I have chosen in order to pass in rapid review what everyone knows but, for our purposes, may bear to recall: the astonishing range and variety of Shakespeare's achievement in his chosen art, and the remarkable consistency but also the maturing depth of his thinking, his understanding of the heart of our human mystery. However unavoidably hasty, my discussion will be concerned with the plays as plays. I shall touch upon their stories, characters, poetry, ideas, especially their meaning for our times. Before turning to Shakespeare's early plays, however, I must make clear two general presuppositions basic to my presentation.

First, I wish to emphasize the fact, as I see it, that, in spite of the dramatic objectivity of the plays—wherein Macbeth and Othello, Rosalind and Cordelia and the rest, each speaks in his or her own voice, not necessarily in Shakespeare's—it is possible, with reasonable care, to sift out some recurring undertones, inflections, and reflections of their creator. What was Shakespeare's own view—if not always his own way—of life? For our purposes this, surely, is an essential question. Second, I would urge the pertinence, the abiding validity of this view of life, for us. A quick glance at a few of the most critical problems of our time will at least justify the question whether a fresh awareness of his insights and his charity might not now help our troubled world.

The quest for Shakespeare himself must follow one or more of three familiar but not altogether easy paths. The most alluring but not the safest way, in spite of Professor Rowse's engaging "certainty" that his historical method has now solved all its puzzling turns, is the broad, beautiful highway of Shakespeare's sonnets. "With this key Shakespeare unlocked his heart," says

Wordsworth's sonnet; but Browning replied "If so, the less Shakespeare he!" Was Browning, then, the less Browning, when, dropping *his* dramatic objectivity, he spoke in his own voice in "One Word More," say, or in the "Epilogue to Asolando"? Certainly, Shakespeare's fellow poet, the noble Sidney, tells us that when he sonneteered he looked in his heart and wrote. We know that Shakespeare dedicated his non-dramatic poems, *Venus and Adonis* and *The Rape of Lucrece*, to his generous patron, the Earl of Southampton. Was Southampton, then, "the only begetter" of these sonnets, or at least their chief inspirer, and, aside from the dark lady, their major, pervasive subject? Though such scholars as Kittredge and Dover Wilson regard his "title" as "no stronger than" the Earl of Pembroke's, "perhaps not so strong," Mr. Rowse's claims for Southampton cannot be ignored. Nor can the fact that though many of the sonnets clearly belong to Shakespeare's early work, their immediate dates remain quite uncertain. The great sonnets—"When to the sessions of sweet silent thought/I summon up remembrance of things past"; "Let me not to the marriage of true minds/Admit impediments"; "That time of year thou may'st in me behold . . . Bare ruin'd choirs where late the sweet birds sang . . ."— these sonnets were certainly written from the heart. They *are* Shakespeare. But others are unmistakably conventional in theme, easily recognizable literary exercises in the manner of Petrarch and most of his continental and Tudor followers. Mr. Rowse's very interesting speculations, therefore, are also very hazardous. There is little solid ground under his attempt to force the great majority of the sonnets into a schematically sustained revelation of events and personal relationships between Shakespeare and Southampton during a closely dated period of their conjectural careers.

On much safer ground is Mr. Peter Quennell, another Quadricentennial biographer, who thinks the sonnets "tell us comparatively little of the poet's life" but "much about the character of his mind." For this is the safer ground of our second path in the quest to find Shakespeare himself: the oft-repeated pointing of the sonnets toward imagery, moods, themes, favorite ideas which coincide with those ever recurring in the plays. These insistent recurrences make assurance, as it were, almost doubly sure. When we recognize in the sonnets and in the plays a poignantly identical emphasis, for example, upon the ravages of time and change and decay—in the sonnets: "Time's thievish progress toward eternity," "summer's lease" of "all too short a date," "beauty . . . no stronger than a flower"; and, in the plays: King Henry IV's meditation, "How chances mock/And changes fill the cup of alteration"—however conventional the theme, this powerfully cumulative reiteration assures us that we are hearing Shakespeare's own voice. The new critics say in effect: No, only the single document, the individual poem, counts. But the best of their allies, Professor Wolfgang Clemen, though he too puts first the all-important "particular moment," the immediate context of any given passage, admits that Shakespeare does emphasize certain "motifs and imagery" which "hint . . . as to his personal preferences."[2]

A third way to find Shakespeare himself is not least important and could bear clearer demarcation than it has usually had. It is not only the indelible tracery, as already suggested, of his recurring thought, his reiteration of certain favorite fundamental ideas, but also his recurring, maturing convictions as to the worth, the meaning of human life, of the miracles by which it is conditioned, the mysteries by which it is encompassed. One major illustration in each case must suffice. I trust they will indicate how these fundamental ideas, and even more these convictions, are brought home to us by the concluding logic of events and of character, especially in the ending of the great tragedies.

2 *The Development of Shakespeare's Imagery*, Dramabooks (New York, 1962), pp. 2, 16.

One fundamental theme of Shakespeare's, as we have seen, is the mystery of good and evil. Our text from *All's Well*, concerning the mingled yarn of our web of life, anticipates Milton's famous saying in the *Areopagitica*: "Good and evil we know in the field of this world grow up together almost inseparably; and the knowledge of good is . . . involved and interwoven with the knowledge of evil. . . ." Previously, Shakespeare (in a Hamlet mood?) had turned the idea upside down and all but denied its validity, in the wittily nihilistic paradox propounded by the Prince of Denmark to Rosencrantz and Guildenstern: "There is nothing either good or bad but thinking makes it so." In a not dissimilar vein Emilia, toward the end of *Othello*, offers shallow would-be comfort to poor Desdemona: "Wrong is but a wrong i' th' world, and, having the world for your . . . own, you might quickly make it right" (IV.iii.82–85). So again King Lear, with a moving difference—not with levity but wisdom, even in madness, taught by suffering; with a poignant emphasis upon the tragic relativity of good and evil:

Change places and, handy-dandy, which is the justice, which is the thief? . . .
Through tatter'd clothes small vices do appear;
Robes and furr'd gowns hide all. . . .
None does offend, none—I say none!
(IV.vi.156–158, 168–169, 172)

This is like Lady Macduff's sad comment in *Macbeth*,

in this earthly world . . . to do harm
Is often laudable, to do good sometime
Accounted dangerous folly. (IV.ii.75–77)

The other side of the coin is stamped upon the lines of one of the great sonnets:

O benefit of ill! Now I find true
That better is by evil still made better,
And ruin'd love when it is built anew
Grows fairer than at first (Sonnet 119)—

lines which have been said to be perhaps the most truly Christian passage in Shakespeare. So, once more, in a memorable passage in *Henry V*, wherein the king, before Agincourt, comforts his brothers with the reflection that hardship has its compensatory stimulus to noble action:

> There is some soul of goodness in things evil,
> Would men observingly distill it out;
>                              . . . admonishing
> That we should dress us fairly for our end.
> Thus may we gather honey from the weed
> And make a moral of the devil himself. (IV.i.4–5, 9–12)

Not to make a moral but to serve the true purpose of tragedy, certain convictions of Shakespeare, if I read them aright, are stressed again and again in the endings of his greatest plays. Professor G. B. Harrison, in a widely used modern edition of the plays, describes *King Lear* as "a tremendous and pessimistic drama, of which Gloucester's words form the most fitting motto: 'As flies to wanton boys are we to the gods,/They kill us for their sport.' " Some years ago I heard a university president address a far-western student assembly in a similar vein. He listed Shakespeare among the great pessimists, along with Schopenhauer, Nietzsche, Swift, and Mark Twain. Now I think the case for Swift and Mark Twain may be arguable, but I am convinced that the president and the professor are wrong as regards Shakespeare. The ways of wanton boys to flies are not the ways of God to men at the end of *King Lear*. As the story and the persons of the play turn out at last—that is, by the *final* logic of events and character—"The gods are just, and of our pleasant vices/Make instruments to scourge us." Gloucester and Edmund and Lear and Cordelia die but not without hope, Gloucester "smilingly . . . twixt joy and grief," and even the villain, Edmund, with one good he meant to do to the credit of his guilty soul. Lear, before the end, had taught himself and his child Cordelia to pray and to take upon themselves the mystery of things as if they were

God's spies. He dies, as Bradley eloquently noted long ago, in the hope that Cordelia lives: "Look on her! Look—her lips!" There is no final, utter darkness here, nor in *Othello*, or *Hamlet*, or *Macbeth*. Othello will find redemption: through his bitter repentance and through Grace. Hamlet learns before the end that there is a special Providence in the fall of a sparrow, that ripeness, "readiness is all"; and flights of angels sing him to that rest in felicity from which he bids Horatio absent himself a while. And the ending of *Macbeth*, no tale told by an idiot, signifies that though the wages of sin are death, one who, like young Siward, dies for God's cause, standing up, "with his hurts before" (on his forehead), may serve hereafter as "God's soldier." Tragedy, it has been well said, is "Man's answer to this universe that crushes him so pitilessly." Its end, writes E. V. Lucas, is "so to portray life that its tears become a joy forever." Certainly this is hard for those "innocents" who, as Shakespeare knew, "scape not the thunderbolt." But this, by and large, is the end, the upward-looking conviction of the great tragedies. We cannot hope to know all the answers. Even Job could not argue successfully with God.[3]

I can take time for but the briefest specifics to illustrate the pertinence for us, the immediacy, of Shakespeare's outlook upon human life. Roughly, let us say, our world's afflictions—political, nationalistic, racial, and social-economic—have three major sources. First, the sheer pressure of poverty, of absolute want, for the submerged many on other continents, and, alas, on parts of our own. Second, world-wide chaos, the spread of dictatorial despotism, the threat of mob tyranny—in Africa and Asia, not to press nearer home—growing out of the dislocations, the disorganization wrought by our world wars, hot and cold, and by the all too sudden breakdown of "colonialism." Third, the intolerance and the hatreds—religious, racial, economic, political,

[3] See below, pp. 42–45.

nationalistic—engendered or re-engendered ever since Hitler's time by the new order, or rather by the new disorder, the barbaric, untutored, undisciplined chaos of our world scene. "I hate him for he is a Christian," says Shylock. In glancing, later, at him and other principals of *The Merchant of Venice,* and also at *Coriolanus,* we shall see something more of Shakespeare's dealings with this theme of intolerance and hatred, religious, racial, political. As for the world-wide problem of the poor whom we have always with us, I mention, for what they may be worth, but two Shakespearean passages. One, which ironically commends itself to some of our statesmen, is Mark Antony's shrewd recollection of Caesar's political kindness to the poor: "When that the poor have cried, Caesar hath wept;/Ambition should be made of sterner stuff." The other side is stressed in Gloucester's somewhat late attempt to do good and distribute when he gives his purse to poor Tom, and in Lear's confession of earlier failure as he enters his storm-swept hovel:

> Poor naked wretches whereso'er you are
> That bide the pelting of this pitiless storm,
> How shall your houseless heads and unfed sides
> . . . defend you
> From seasons such as these? O I have ta'en
> Too little care of this! Take physic, pomp,
> Expose thyself to feel what wretches feel,
> That thou mayst shake the superflux to them
> And show the heavens more just. (III.iv.28–36)

Shakespeare has much to say, much for us to think about as regards the other, perhaps the gravest of all our ills, the world-wide chaos due in large measure to the failure of discipline, degree, and order consequent upon war, revolution, and the endless threat of wars. I suggest that of Shakespeare's many plays that deal with war and its aftermath, one especially deserves attention now. Again and again, Shakespeare gives both sides: something at once, for example, in *Othello* and *Henry V,* of the romantic pomp and circumstance and the patriotic-nationalistic fervor, but also of the seamy camp followers and the treachery of war. In the *Henry VI* trilogy especially, he pictures the bloody atrocities, the outrageous mob tyranny engendered by civil war. *Troilus and Cressida*, further, presses home, especially in its famous speech on the failure of degree and discipline, what happens when Achilles and lesser men sulk in their tents and all things go awry. Closer, however, to our immediate concerns than any of these is the tragedy of *Coriolanus*—of Coriolanus himself, the arrogantly uncompromising patrician, lover (according to his lights) of Rome and of his wife and little son and his mother and friends, mighty warrior and impossibly incompetent politician. Let our extremists of every stripe and color read and re-read the tragedy of *Coriolanus*! It is a complex web, like all its kind; certainly no smugly over-simplified preachment or copybook object lesson. Still, this tragedy is good medicine for war-mongers ("Let me have war, I say. The wars for my money!"), for those who pocket up war profits and smoothly reckon up the credit balances of war economy ("To-morrow . . . we shall have a stirring world again. . . . we shall ha' means to vent/Our musty superfluity"). The play should be required reading for all extremists of the left and the right, all demagogues and hate-mongers, all the no-compromise, no-holds-barred promoters of racial hatred and the class struggle of the poor against the rich and the in-betweens, of the black and the brown and the yellow against the white: all the bitter, determined old men and all the dangerously undisciplined young ones, all the rabble-rousers of all ages, who, whatever crisis may confront our country or our world, hoist the flag or tear it down, at home and abroad, not as patriots but as provocateurs; rabble-rousers who have not scrupled to exploit and to sacrifice innocent children in mob demonstrations, church bombings, school closings and boycotts, nor to incite mobsters, black and white, to riotous looting and murder.

For this long preamble to my tale I plead that these are public concerns which again and again cry out for attention and for rational, constructive action. It remains to sketch something of the rationale of Shakespeare's humane middle way, of the maturing of his powers as exemplified especially in *Romeo and Juliet, The Merchant of Venice,* and *The Tempest.*

All the world loves *Romeo and Juliet,* the beautiful tragic romance of Shakespeare's youth. It is as popular today on stage and film and television as its numerous and curiously assorted off-spring have always been, from Otway's somber *Caius Marius* and Rostand's pleasantly fantastic *Les Romanesques* to Broadway's recently sad and merry *West Side Story* and *Romanoff and Juliet.* In its own time our play was probably the latest and crowning achievement, with only *A Midsummer Night's Dream* as a possible rival, of Shakespeare's journeyman years as actor, playmaker, and director—if one may judge from Hamlet's later directions to the players. The consensus of scholarly opinion is that during these crowded early years, from approximately 1590 through 1595, he wrote, besides the narrative poems and many of the sonnets, some twelve or thirteen plays: five comedies (*The Comedy of Errors, The Two Gentlemen of Verona, Love's Labour's Lost, A Midsummer Night's Dream,* and, possibly somewhat later, *The Taming of the Shrew*); five or possibly six history plays (the three parts of *King Henry VI,* plus what Polonius would have called the "historical-tragical" *Richard III* and *King John,* and possibly also *Richard II*); and two tragedies (*Titus Andronicus* and *Romeo and Juliet*). In quantity, variety, and brilliant though uneven quality, this was an outpouring of creative power rarely matched in the history of the arts (or at least of artists who lived to attain maturity) except perhaps by that other giant of the Renaissance who lived just until the year of Shakespeare's birth: Michelangelo. To see *Romeo and Juliet* in perspective, we had better glance first at Shakespeare's preceding plays, in their several kinds.

To my previous mention of the earliest histories—the *Henry VI* trilogy of England's civil wars of the Roses—I would add only that the serio-comic Jack Cade scenes of 2 *Henry VI* deserve early re-reading almost as much as *Coriolanus*. These are the scenes in which all the books are burned, all the lawyers killed (together with other obstreperous non-illiterates) and all the laws and "the Parliament of England" are made to issue from the mouth of Cade, the mobster chief of state, in the all too familiar modern manner of Hitler, Nkrumah, and company. Skill in characterization grew as this trilogy progressed; 3 *Henry VI* prepared the way for *Richard III*. This, of course, is a sensationally colorful historical melodrama overcharged with Tudor prejudice against its Yorkist-Marlovian-superman protagonist. Its Richard Crookback, however, is the first authentic Shakespearean hero-villain. First and last there is poetry in his deviltry. Paradoxically, his murderous drive makes even his numerous victims come alive. By and large this play is triumphantly good theater, though it is less thoughtful, far less subtly varied in realistic psychological interest and lyric intensity than the slightly later *King John*. But *Richard III* in its turn had scored a marked advance over Shakespeare's earliest experiment in tragedy, *Titus Andronicus*. A tremendously effective horror play, though, curiously enough, a direct predecessor of *Hamlet*, *Titus* is technically and literally a "tragedy of blood." ("Blood and revenge are hammering in my ears," says its villain, Aaron; lust is its background, vengeance by means of feigned madness its motive, in a basic son-and-father-and-pathetic-heroine plot.) Nowadays, according to reports from Stratford and London, the piece keeps nurses and ambulances on the ready to take care of swooning audiences. Its full baker's dozen of murders, plus rape and bloody outrage, smack less of tragedy than of butchery. But it has breath-taking action and pathos and compelling rhetoric: "What fool hath added water to the sea/Or brought a fagot to bright-burning Troy?"

The comedies preceding *Romeo and Juliet* are alike in some

respects but as varied as April weather in others. All are irresistibly gay, zestful, light-hearted, but almost all have undertones of occasional seriousness. The very first, for example, the broad Plautine farce of mistaken identity entitled *The Comedy of Errors*, has families broken by shipwreck or near-broken by men's indulgence in the double standard of morality, the dubious sort of seigneurial privilege more maturely considered in later plays. *A Midsummer Night's Dream*, interwoven though it is of gossamer fairy fantasy and broad "Athenian" homespun, dwells on the fact, as does *Romeo and Juliet*, that the course of true love never did run smooth. And, again like *Romeo and Juliet* and *The Tempest* later, it dwells upon the beautiful but fantastic and unsteadfast way of dreams, and the far-ranging, solemn import of the poet's greatest gift, the creative imagination—"strong imagination" as Duke Theseus calls it, but frail: "the best in this kind are but shadows"; "no more yielding but a dream," according to Puck; or, as Mercutio and Prospero put it, "begot of nothing but vain fantasy," "such stuff as dreams are made on."

There is no such stuff, of course, in the earthy half-farce, half-comedy of character, *The Taming of the Shrew*, but this piece, in any case, may have come just after the early comedies. Not so *The Two Gentlemen of Verona* and *Love's Labour's Lost*; these certainly preceded *Romeo and Juliet*. Both glance smilingly at courtly fashions and foibles, each, indebted though they are to Greene and Lyly respectively, in its own fresh, experimental way: *The Two Gentlemen* as Shakespeare's prelude to romantic comedy (to *As You Like It*, for example), and *Love's Labour's Lost* as his best, most high-spirited travesty (if not quite a "satire keen and critical") upon courtly academes, intrigues, and pastimes, fantastic-pedantic learning, "taffeta phrases," and the rest.

Rosalind in *As You Like It* observes that "Men have died . . . and worms have eaten them, but not for love." *The Two Gentlemen*, again, opens with a quizzical suggestion that the story of Young Leander crossing the Hellespont is not the deepest story of great love. Neither is that of young Romeo while he is more in love with love than with Rosaline and happily enjoys his pains—like Chaucer's Sir Thopas fallen in love-longing, or any good conventional Elizabethan sonnet lover. Even so, *Romeo and Juliet* holds the affection of mankind first by virtue of its love story, its poetry, its people; and, next, by its varied, untiring animation, its humor no less than its sadness, and by its idealism. The poetry will speak for itself while a spark of youth and the love of beauty glows on this planet. And the story of the feud-tossed, star-crossed lovers—the one and only story in this remarkably uncomplex, virtually single-stranded piece—will hold its own always with the best loved, most famous love stories young and (shall I say?) old: the tales of Tristan and Iseult, Paolo and Francesca, Dante and his Beatrice, and of Lancelot and Guinevere, Dido and her Aeneas, Abelard and Heloise, Antony and Cleopatra. Woeful lovers, however, do not monopolize our play. Its varied humor deserves better notice than some solemn critics give it. The fun unmistakably starts as the curtain rises upon the big-mouthed, quarreling servants, comfortable "Uncle" Benvolio, young Romeo languishing, and wickedly witty Mercutio, the whole rising to a delightfully animated crescendo of mirth and matter not unlike the first-act finale of a certain charming latterday tragic romance entitled *Cyrano de Bergerac.* Young Romeo at first (he grows with the play), Mercutio in the middle, Juliet's nurse first and last, have comic potential enough to account for at least some of the curious happy-ending inversions recorded in the later stage-history of this tragic romance.

I return to this term because it is the right one. *Romeo and Juliet* is not a tragedy but a tragic romance. There is no tragic guilt in this play except the plague of both the houses; no such complexity as Aristotle held essential to tragedy. This play has pity only, no purgation by pity *and* terror. The unimaginative Prince of Verona at the end says there never was a story of more woe, but this, obviously, is not so. The play ends in death but not in disillusionment or broken faith. Its most nearly tragic development is that the young lovers, in the sadness of parting, forget the truth their love had previously taught them: that love is stronger than death. In this faith Romeo, after the Friar had solemnized the marriage, had defied sorrow, all but denied death: "Come what sorrow can . . . Then love-devouring death do what he dare!" Earlier, young Juliet, suddenly growing into womanhood upon finding her Romeo, had somehow learned Plato's lesson that love is a discerning of the eternal, of the infinite in the finite:

> And yet I wish but for the thing I have.
> My bounty is as boundless as the sea,
> My love as deep; the more I give to thee,
> The more I have, for both are infinite. (II.ii.132–135)[4]

There is an old saying that Shakespeare never repeats. Of course this is nonsense. Every man worth his salt, every good artist, repeats himself, though usually with a difference. So, for example, in *The Merchant of Venice*, Portia repeats in her own way young Juliet's unforgettable experience upon first sensing love's hold upon the infinite. One speech of hers, says Sir Arthur Quiller-Couch,[5] is in some respects more memorable even than her famous speech on the quality of mercy. He is right! It is her speech after Bassanio's happy choice of the casket of *lead*, not altogether without help, perhaps, from the key rhyme of the timely song she had prepared: "Tell me where is fancy *bred*." In her boundless desire to give generously to the man she loves, she, like Juliet, draws upon the infinite. Thus, though she could not have been ignorant of her worth, she mightily underrates herself, counts for nothing her fine mind, her riches, and her better wealth of beauty, tact, and golden charm. Her love, being of the infinite, would infinitely multiply its gifts. Juliet's "the more I give" on Portia's lips becomes something like "the more I *have* the more I'd give to thee." "For you," Portia says,

4 This theme is re-echoed in *Cyrano de Bergerac* and in *Winterset*.
5 *Shakespeare's Workmanship* (New York, 1917), pp. 81–82.

I would be trebled twenty times myself,
A thousand times more fair, ten thousand times more rich,
That, only to stand high in your account,
I might in virtues, beauties, livings, friends,
Exceed account. But the full sum of me
Is sum of nothing, which, to term in gross,
Is an unlesson'd girl, unschool'd, unpractis'd. . . . (III.ii.153–159)

How far from unschooled and unpracticed she is, Shylock learns in the trial scene. So does the good Antonio then and later. For at the trial, and by the "never more" logic of the jolly ring episode later, the profitable verdict Portia had won for Antonio against Shylock, cancels, in effect, Antonio's claims upon Bassanio. Later, Portia redoubles her payment to Antonio with a charming Lady Bountiful gesture which conjures up his lost argosies as the curtain goes down. Thus, she wins love's battle against sentimental friendship personified by Antonio, one of sundry substantial themes in this many-storied, many-faceted comedy. The ending, of course, is not happy for Shylock, and hardly so for Antonio. *The Merchant* is a problem comedy, but a comedy still. Some Elizabethan groundlings thought Shylock no less funny than Launcelot Gobbo, the clown. Times and taste change, but romantic sentiment and the comic spirit still pervade this play. Its opening is charmingly set to true, full-toned poetry. Even the unimportant Salerios and Solanios talk such verse as only Shakespeare could have talked, and only he could have written such prose sentences so well pronounced as those he gave to Nerissa. Bassanio's fair hopes and Antonio's sad anticipatory fears of losing his friend make the opening music, and the comedy chimes out in the moonlit scenes of Portia's homecoming, the laughter and young happiness of married lovers. Meanwhile, there is the comic-romantic struggle of the three casketeers, and between love and friendship (Portia against Antonio), the low-comedy fooling of the Gobbos plus Gratiano's chatterbox nonsense, and the serio-comedy of intrigue, Shylock's pound of flesh story. Stories enough and vital characters enough for half a dozen ordinary plays—unlike this one in power and grace of style, action, thought—for here the whole symphony orchestra soars aloft in splendid, ordered harmony.

Concerning Shylock in particular, one thing is certain. As Kittredge says, Shakespeare in creating Shylock was not attacking the Jewish people any more than he was attacking the Danish people in *Hamlet*. Shylock stands, as do Portia and Antonio and Jessica, in the middle of humanity. All have faults and virtues. Portia, for instance, is no plaster saint. When Morocco, the Moorish prince, comes awooing and asks that she mislike him not for his color, she tells him that to her he looks "as fair" as any of her wooers, yet after he has guessed wrong and gone, she says, "Let all of his complexion choose me so." Lorenzo's "pretty Jessica" unprettily carries off her father's ducats and diamonds and heartlessly throws away her mother's ring, Shylock's turquoise, for a monkey. "I had it of Leah when I was a bachelor," Shylock recalls. He is human, however race-conscious, harsh, and hard-bitten: "Hath not a Jew eyes . . . senses, affections, passions? . . . If you prick us, do we not bleed?" He hates Antonio because he is a Christian and brings down the Venetian rate of usury, but not for this reason only. Bassanio describes Antonio as "the kindest man,/The best-conditioned and unwearied spirit/In doing courtesies," but Antonio, like other good men, is not perfect. He tends to pity himself; he had reviled and spat upon Shylock; and he promises "To spit on thee again, to spurn thee too." Shakespeare seems to have known that neither bad men nor good men are immune to the virus of intolerant hate— still, alas, to be controlled, still to be conquered.

*The Tempest*, one of the latest, certainly the best-loved achievement of Shakespeare's maturest years, deserves more notice than I can possibly give it. There is room only for a brief summary of familiar facts concerning its rationale, quality, and relationships with Shakespeare's other works of its kind and time —the dramatic romances, *Pericles, Cymbeline,* and *The Winter's*

*Tale*. All return again and again to favorite situations, devices,
moods, and thoughts of his earlier times. But all are fresh, "new
and strange," that is to say, sometimes sensationally heightened
for romantic or even melodramatic effect. And all have lovely
poetry, which I must not quote. As regards setting, *As You Like
It* and *A Midsummer Night's Dream* before it had drawn their
audiences into the charmed old recesses of the forest of Arden
and the fairies' magic "Athenian" wood. In the later plays romantic escape moves further back into the long ago and far away:
to ancient Antioch and Tyre and the seaside of Pentapolis in the
play of *Pericles*; to far-off places such as the mountain fastnesses
of *Cymbeline*'s Wales or *The Winter's Tale*'s seacoast of Bo-
hemia; and to even more unpathed waters, undreamed shores—
the unspoiled new countries as yet barely touched by the Elizabethan voyagers: "the still vexed Bermoothes" of *The Tempest*.
There Puck's mischievous spriting and Bottom and his crew are
replaced by Prospero's somber magic, his ministering Ariel of
the winds and the air, and the earth-monster Caliban. Other,
even more earthy-familiar people and scenes are there too. The
brothel scenes in *Pericles* recall the prison scenes of *Measure for
Measure*. The boatswain's lusty cursing early in *The Tempest*,
and Stephano's drunken singing later, with Trinculo in tow, are
not altogether different in kind from the Falstaff scenes of the
Boar's Head tavern and the Gloucestershire orchards. And in
*The Tempest* as in all the dramatic romances and the earlier romantic comedies there are charming young lovers—Perdita and
Florizel of *The Winter's Tale*, Prospero's Miranda and Ferdinand, and Imogen and her Posthumus in *Cymbeline*. I mention
these two last because they are a bit older—though still gloriously
young—and *married* lovers. In these later plays life for young
lovers does not invariably end at the church altar, nor for older
ones in the churchyard. Widowed old Prospero has to live on
(without his magic!) after his daughter marries Ferdinand, and
Ariel has winged off into the blue. Posthumus regains his Imogen, and Leontes his Queen Hermione of *The Winter's Tale*

only after long years of well-deserved suffering for great wrongs done and then expiated. Shakespeare's earlier plays had dramatized great wrongs done—in *As You Like It*, for example, the good duke's forced exile in Arden, like Prospero's from Milan—but not any such expiations. This recurring theme of great wrongs done, of characters shaped, refined, burned clean by suffering and repentance, or, in turn, by the grace of forgiveness, is the special quality of these plays of Shakespeare's wisest, mellowest years. "The power I have on you," says Posthumus to *Cymbeline*'s master-villain, Iachimo, "is to spare you . . . to forgive you": in Prospero's words, "The rarer action is/In virtue than in vengeance."

Though I have had to omit much of the best in this crowded glimpse of Shakespeare's thought and work, it is surely clear that he has rich gifts to give us. In him is God's plenty. He lived life to the full, and loved it all, gratefully. For the gift of life, he says or implies, time and again, "thou owest God a death." He loved, first and last, to tell tales that keep children from play and old men from the chimney corner. He loved children and the old folk ("time's doting chronicles"), music and lovers, laughter and springtime, birds and flowers, mountains and rivers and the infinite sea: life and even the undiscovered country, the mystery of death. That is why he lives today, young as the springtime of his own April four hundred years ago.[6]

6 Some time after I had written this lecture, I came upon J. Minto Robertson's essay, "The Middle of Humanity as Shakespeare Saw It," in *The Hibbert Journal*, XXXIX (1941), 143–155. Mr. Robertson's major objective is quite different from mine. "The non-heroic characters of Shakespeare," he writes, "are what I here aim at studying, the *personae dramatis*, often anonymous, or at most alluded to generically as Citizens, Gentlemen, Soldiers, Lords . . . who occupy the backstage. They are neither the heroes nor the villains [but] the ordinary average men and women in his plays." The reader will observe, however, that I am in entire accord with Mr. Robertson's conclusion. Writing of his "tormented world" of 1940 or thereabouts, he expresses the prophetic hope that "The demoniac dictators will be brought low by 'the middle of humanity.'"

# 2

# Shakespeare and Our World

*This headnote is being written some seven years after the lecture[1] it re-introduces. Meanwhile the immediately impending shadow of the mushroom cloud has mercifully receded. This happy relief— not, alas, release—we owe to brave men moved by faith, not fear. Again and again, however, we have had to face times of trial. New and darker shadows gather over Asia; grave problems multiply on our own continent and in our own country: at home and abroad there remains the peril of great evil in times to come. I have quoted below from our old English poem, "That evil was overcome at last. . . . " So may it be! We must hope and act in the prophetic sense of the sacred text, "It came—to pass."*

THE MORALITY PLAY *Everyman* reminds us that "there is a blind reckoning in time of distress." The old dramatist was saying that dead reckoning, guided by Knowledge and Good Deeds, may find a way to steer through the darkness. So now, as always in times that try men's souls, every man and every nation must marshal its best resources, physical, intellectual, spiritual. We must put on the whole armor of God. When we turn to the great writers—to Shakespeare, for example—what are some of the abiding human questions to which, consciously or unconsciously, we

[1] Delivered at the University of Tennessee on Honors Day, April 30, 1957; revised from *Tennessee Studies in Literature*, II (1957), 105 ff. For quite another (existentialist) "image of Shakespeare . . . for our . . . time" cf. Ian Kott, *Shakespeare Our Contemporary* (New York, 1964).

all seek answers? Not necessarily the accurate, complete answers of mathematics. Instead, the challenging approximations suggested by the other, less exact, but perhaps no less exacting, humanities: by history and archaeology, philosophy and the fine arts, languages and humane letters, and by religion itself, anciently—and still properly—the queen of the humanities. Inevitably, such answers raise further questions. Since they concern man, God's creature and child, they must range from finite into infinite. But such questions may help to bring light into darkness, help to build a working faith. They search inward, unsatisfied with our machine-made tinklings and glimmerings. Of course radio and television have achieved great things. Certainly they have a vast potential for entertainment, for the spread of information, and, under favorable conditions, for the gradual training of eye and ear. But they cannot serve as substitutes for the great books. Too often, they are merely ear-deep, eye-deep. As Portia's song warns Bassanio in *The Merchant of Venice*, they are

> engender'd in the eyes,
> With gazing fed, and fancy dies
> In the cradle where it lies.

In the nature of things, they cannot often provide time for reflective second thoughts. Too often, by sheer necessity, they are —again in Shakespeare's words—"momentary"

> as a sound,
> Swift as a shadow, short as any dream;
> Brief as the lightning in the collied night . . .
> The jaws of darkness do devour [them] up.

Let this be remembered by parents whose children, as one librarian has recently put it, "look and look and look" at television "but are *never* read to." Let it be remembered by all of us who, as the late President Griswold of Yale said, are content to "trade in the mind's eye for the eye's mind."[2] Let us count the cost of the shallow-minded, empty-hearted years ahead.

In truth, the living comfort, the vital strength and sustenance for a working faith, the best near-answers to the unanswerable but inescapable questions that beset the human heart, must continue to come from the great Scriptures of our race. I mean our sacred Scriptures *and* our lay scriptures. For God reveals and fulfills Himself in many ways: in the admonitions of the law and the prophets and the Gospels, but also in the highest aspirations of the human spirit. Prophet, saint, and poet, Isaiah and St. John and St. Paul, the *Book of Job* and the plays and poems of Shakespeare and Milton—what warnings, what comfort, what apocalyptic vision, what light and leading, what meanings may they have for our time? Shakespeare's answers must all but suffice here, but others cannot be left out entirely. If we are to see large issues in focus, we must now and then range afar. "Man," says Emerson, "is explicable by nothing less than all his history"— and, as I have already dared to suggest, by nothing less than all the Scriptures. Why? Partly because, as the man who wrote *Treasure Island* stoutly said, "*all* literature, from Job and Omar Khayyam to Thomas Carlyle and Walt Whitman, is but an attempt to look upon the human state with such largeness of view as shall enable us to rise from the consideration of living to the Definition of life."

No systematic analysis, no "definition" of the complex life of our world can come out of our brief thinking together here. Still, we can hardly avoid looking at one stark reality of these times. The atom bomb has thrown our world out of joint. Hiroshima's carnage and even its early aftermath were frightful. But, in spite of the hydrogen bomb, the cobalt bomb, and the collateral threat of guided missiles and space satellites, the worst damage until recently has been the world-wide harvest of fatalistic material-

[2] Cf. my essay, "In My Mind's Eye, Horatio," in *Shakespeare Quarterly*, VII (1956), 351 ff.

ism, the numbing, craven acceptance of the inevitableness of physical extinction for what we call all the world. True enough, lamentable enough, are the dark Orwellian craters that loom ahead, the black shadows of despair, the poisonous fallout of hate. Like Macbeth, in punishment for our world's fatalistic inertia, our lack of constructive action, all of us, Americans and Russians alike, are gripped by sleepless fears. Perhaps we lack something of Macbeth's murderous resolution; certainly most of us lack his vivid awareness of the world beyond our world:

> We have scotch'd the snake, not kill'd it.
> She'll close, and be herself, whilst our poor malice
> Remains in danger of her former tooth.
> But let the frame of things disjoint, both the worlds suffer
> Ere we will eat our meal in fear, and sleep
> In the affliction of these terrible dreams
> That shake us nightly. Better be with the dead
> Whom we, to gain our peace, have sent to peace,
> Than on the torture of the mind to lie
> In restless ecstasy.

In truth, the most destructive potential of the bomb, like the kingdom of God, is within us. The devil's task is to beget at once foolish complacency and black despair. However near and real and oppressive the menace of our time, we who speak Shakespeare's language should remember the refrain of our Old English poem, *Deor's Lament*, "That evil was overcome at last; this, too, will yield." Let us not forget what all history, all the greatest books and the greatest lives should have taught us: that humanity has before now fought its way through other seemingly hopeless agonies. It has survived terrors unspeakable—invasions of Hun and Tartar and Turk, the unquenchable fires of the Inquisition and the witch hunts of earlier and later centuries, Napoleon's insatiable lust for power, Hitler's fierce hates and demonic ambition—because Man is a spirit and the child of God. If the atom's fiery deluge is let loose upon our earth, we must pray that the Lord will send another ark to ride these fearful waves. Meanwhile, what can *we* do? It has been well said that the task of the humanities is "to create a moral and intellectual atmosphere that will prevent the use of the bomb." Above all, this is the task of religion, which teaches us that no man-made bomb can shatter the spiritual Order, the divine Law, that undershores God's creation. I say these things now, however haltingly, because later in this chapter I mean to illustrate briefly three timely aspects of Shakespeare's thinking which indeed belong to all time: his views on education, on government, and, finally, on religion.

"No one," to adapt a saying of Winston Churchill's, "can understand the experiences of our short lives . . . without continually relating them to the long periods which are constantly mentioned" in "history." And this leads me to add that I hope many of my readers may have seen or read at one time or another John Patrick's delightful play entitled *The Teahouse of the August Moon*. Of course this must sound like a dreadful *non sequitur!* *The Teahouse* is set in Okinawa, whereas we should be looking in the direction of Shakespeare of Stratford to see what he has to say about schoolboys and pedants, about "the burden of lean and wasteful learning" and the bowers of Academe, "the studious universities." Perhaps my *non sequitur* will seem less impossible in the light of two facts. First: all universities are honored by the memorable passage in *The Two Gentlemen of Verona* which describes how young men "sought preferment out" in the time of the Virgin Queen:

> Some to the wars to try their fortunes there;
> Some to discover islands far away;
> Some to the studious universities.

Second: the leading character of the Okinawan *Teahouse*, the mild warrior Captain Fisby, is a former teacher, a humanist—one of that stubborn, ever-hopeful breed of men who flourished at their noblest but never affluent best in the glorious days of the Italian and English Renaissance. Shakespeare was of them, Milton (later!) was for them—and so was Captain Fisby, formerly of "Psychological Warfare," but happily transferred to greener pastures. What had he worked at before the war? He answers his colonel, "I was an associate professor at Muncie." And what did he teach? "The humanities, sir." Thereupon the colonel says the last word: "Captain, you are finally getting a job you are qualified by training to handle—teaching these natives how to act human." "Teaching these natives how to act human!" In the best sense of the word "human"—though the Captain demurs, like a true humanist—what better definition of the humanist's function could one ask? My dictionary, more sedately, defines the humanities as the study of the classics for *humanitas*, "the highest . . . most harmonious culture of all the human faculties and powers." Let us remember also that the Christian humanists of the English Renaissance, Sir Thomas More and Erasmus, Thomas Linacre and John Colet, promoted the study of Greek and Latin not merely to expound the wisdom of the ancients but to further the task of translating the Scriptures for every man—to enable him "to act human" at his best: by learning to approximate the divine commandment, "Be *ye* therefore perfect. . . ."

I am sure that Shakespeare, who knew his Bible and also his captains and colonels and knights at arms, would have been delighted with our American colonel's way of putting the thing: "teaching these natives how to act human." Shakespeare did it himself, in many poems and plays. In *Love's Labour's Lost* particularly, he gave special emphasis to the humanists and their delight in languages and the way of words. That play must wait a while longer, however, while I attempt to draw a rough preliminary sketch-map of the new world of expanding horizons, high achievement in arts and letters, vast promise in science, and mighty historic events which, in sum, made the Renaissance, fostered humanism, produced Michelangelo and Shakespeare, and, in many striking particulars, anticipated the fears and splendors, the marvelous but uneasy glories of our own time and state. "If you look in the maps of the 'orld," says Captain Fluellen, the Welshman in *Henry V*, "you sall find . . . that the situations, look you, is both alike."

The men of the Renaissance, the Tudors in particular, had good reason to keep their eyes on the maps of the world, not the map of England only, as King Lear did when he divided his kingdom and Hotspur did when he plotted his rebellion. Like the jolly conspirators in *Twelfth Night*, they searched and studied especially the "new" maps, "with the augmentation of the Indies," as avidly as they studied the glorious new languages ancient and modern, as whole-heartedly as a lover woos a maid. And no wonder. They were merchant adventurers and world adventurers to boot. "I am no pilot," Romeo tells Juliet,

> yet, wert thou as far
> As that vast shore wash'd with the furthest sea
> I would adventure for such merchandise.

Beckoning in the distance were "unpathed waters, undreamed shores." Many responded: among others Frobisher and Drake, Sir Humphrey Gilbert and Walter Raleigh, while the noble Sidney mourned the Queen's command that he must stay at court. Marlowe says they went "to rip the golden bowels of America." Raleigh, who really knew whereof he writes, says they sought "new worlds for gold, for prayse, for glory." But there were still broader objectives, still greater needs for new maps in that age of crumbling barriers, of ever-expanding horizons on every level. There was the tortured, impassioned striving for self-realization that Michelangelo had known, which is Renaissance individualism. There was, as now with us, the surging sweep of Renaissance nationalism in Italy, in France, in Spain, in England; the hemispheric, global search for new horizons, new routes to the Indies, new Americas; the interplanetary, cosmic reaching out—the work of Copernicus, Tycho Brahe, Kepler, Galileo—into the new world of space, again like our forays into the vastness of the cosmos and the atom. Finally, there was the heady quest of the aspiring mind and spirit of man to command all these pioneer discoveries and unfoldings, the Faustus-like endeavor to compass, as it were, the infinite.

And so my sketch-map of the brave new world is more than half drawn. There is no space for fine lines, for piers, for roads, or perilous seas, or magic ports. Space, indeed, must yield to time. To jog my own memory and others', I shall sketch in, first, a few bold figures—i.e., a few important dates, and then, here and there, some scenes more memorable than most places and most men.

Most dates—mere dates—count for very little, but some few are milestones in history and literature. The Renaissance, or the series of renaissances which some prefer to recognize, has been dated all the way from the fourteenth century or earlier, through the later seventeenth century, from Dante or Chaucer through Milton. For our time-map of the English Renaissance, however, the period may be more sharply drawn: the dates are conveniently round and memorable. The period covers exactly 150 years, from 1492 to 1642, from the voyage of Columbus to the death of Galileo. Within that era, two other dates, 1564, the year of Shakespeare's birth, and 1616, the year of his death, especially deserve remembrance. Let us take these four dates one by one. In 1492, when England's Henry VIII was a babe in arms, Lorenzo the Magnificent died in Florence, and America was born to the western world. In 1564 the Pope ratified and published the decrees of the Council of Trent; John Calvin and Michelangelo died; Rabelais' posthumous giant, the last book of *Pantagruel*, was born—and so were Marlowe and Shakespeare and Galileo. In 1616 Shakespeare and Cervantes died, and William Harvey first publicly lectured on the circulation of the blood. The year 1642, finally, marked the beginning of England's civil war, the closing of the theaters, the end of the golden age of English drama, and brought death to Shakespeare's great contemporary, Galileo, whom young John Milton saw in Italy. In brief, from 1492 to 1642 the world saw 150 years of many-sided achievement. Within that span, from 1564 to 1616, during the all too brief but splendid interlude of Shakespeare's lifetime, there walked upon this earth not only Sidney and Spenser and Bacon, and Marlowe and Jonson and Milton and their fellows, but also, among others, Benvenuto Cellini and Cosimo the Great and Catherine de' Medici, Beatrice Cenci, the philosopher Giordano Bruno, and the poet Tasso. Two or three of these I shall mention again in concluding these marginal notes on certain memorable scenes and personages of the Renaissance. To wit:

1. In 1492, six years before he was tortured, crucified, and burned at the stake, Savonarola prayed at the bedside of the dying Lorenzo the Magnificent. A little earlier Lorenzo and Pico della Mirandola had held their last, whispered discourse on "the sweets of sweet philosophy," while the greatest physicians of Europe vainly prescribed "pastes of precious stones more valuable than any hitherto pulverized." It was more than one long day's dying for the distinguished poet-statesman, patron, and lover of all the arts. From his couch, during the long, slow hours Lorenzo watched all Florence making fiesta according to his own gorgeous designs. Meanwhile, he wrote an affectionate, Polonius-like letter to the hero of the fiesta, his son Giovanni de' Medici, the new Cardinal (later Pope Leo X), who, at the ripe age of seventeen, had just donned the red hat, the dying man's long cherished ambition for his son. (Three years earlier, Lorenzo, while strolling in his gardens, had watched another boy—a sculptor's prentice—of the same age as his own Giovanni. The great man genially observed to the lad that the old faun's head he was carving from the marble had rather too good a set of teeth. Soon after, Lorenzo, returning, was delighted to see that the boy's last touch on the marble had given the faun a

toothless grin. Lorenzo thereupon made a place in his household for the lad, whose name was Michelangelo.)

2. In 1535, Sir Thomas More, having just given his daughter the hairshirt he had habitually worn next his heart, went smiling to the block. Said the author of *Utopia* to the lieutenant of the Tower: "Assist me up, and in coming down I will shift for myself."

3. In 1572, when Shakespeare was eight years old, St. Bartholomew's—the "Massacre at Paris" of Marlowe's play—was instigated by Catherine de' Medici. Thirty thousand Protestants were savagely murdered. Thereupon, Queen Elizabeth, who was not squeamish, wrote to Alençon, her royal French suitor, that he had better not "come to woo me with your sword stained with Protestant blood." Another time she pointed out to another troublesome French emissary "over 300 traitors' heads on pikes on London Bridge," saying, "It is thus we punish traitors in England."

4. When Shakespeare was sixteen, in 1580, Elizabeth, standing on the deck of the *Golden Hind* at Deptford, knighted Sir Francis Drake, just home from his triumphant sweep of the Spanish Main and his circumnavigation of the globe.

5. Six years later, in 1586, Shakespeare, then twenty-two, according to a reasonable tradition may have been a country schoolmaster. Late that year, Sir Philip Sidney fell at Zutphen, his white plume unsmirched, his cup of water given—according to the old story which rings true—to the dying soldier whose need, said Sidney, was greater than his own.

6. Another two years later, in 1588, Queen Elizabeth, mounted and clad in glittering steel, spoke to her army just before the approach of the invincible Armada. (Cervantes had helped to provision it; Lope de Vega was on board; but the Queen was ready for invaders.) As recorded in *The Sayings of Queen Elizabeth*,[3] "I am come amongst you," said she,

---

[3] Ed. Frederick Chamberlin (London, 1923), pp. 14–15.

not for my . . . disport, but being resolved in the midst and heat of the battle, to live or die amongst you all . . . . I know I have the body of a weak, feeble woman, but I have the heart and stomach of a king . . . and think foul scorn that . . . Spain . . . should dare to invade the borders of my realm . . . I myself will be your general, judge, and rewarder . . . . not doubting [that] by your obedience . . . and your valour . . . we shall shortly have a famous victory. . . .

(Winston Churchill remembered this scene.) A little later she said to Lord Howard, her commanding admiral, "I consider you and your officers as persons born for the preservation of your country." Another time she remarked: "I am more afraid of making a fault in my Latin than of the Kings of Spain, France, Scotland . . . and all their confederates." She loved all languages: wrote prayers in English, Italian, French, Greek, and Latin; and relaxed from state affairs by studying Greek with Roger Ascham, as regularly and enthusiastically as great modern statesmen play golf. She harangued ambassadors and academic personages in fluent French or Latin. No wonder she had learned how to write and speak the king's English!

7. In 1592, a young lawyer who at that time was not the Queen's favorite wrote a letter to his uncle, Lord Burghley. In this letter Francis Bacon quietly remarked that he had modest ambitions for office. But, he added, "I have taken all knowledge to be my province."

8. Some dozen years before Shakespeare's death, Sir Walter Raleigh lay imprisoned in the Tower, where, in 1618, he was executed, a victim of James I's greed and of his policy of appeasing Spain. In prison, Raleigh calmly proceeded to write the first volume of his tremendous *History of the World.* He knew, of course, that he could not possibly finish, but he also knew—like Browning's Renaissance Grammarian—that *"now is for dogs and apes, man has forever."*

I hope that some of these flashbacks and forward glances will throw light upon the remainder of our way. So far I have purposely stressed some challenging analogies: between the obsessive nationalism of the Renaissance and our times, the abiding deviltry of savage religious intolerance, our world wars and their far-flung conflicts, and—in spite of Renaissance superficiality, superstition, and quackery—their vast scientific potential and ours. I have touched also upon the pervasive sense of insecurity even in merry England, the inescapable sense, then, as now, that changes more than fill the cup of alteration, that even then, in Shakespeare's time, as now, ever since 1914, the golden age of youth and peace and quiet in the world had gone forever. I might add that they, like ourselves, suffered from inflation. (It is recorded that in 1577 sugar, which had been obtainable not long before for something like eight cents per pound, had gone up to about sixty cents!) Later we shall see certain effects of overexpansion in realms other than the economic—the pangs of intellectual, emotional, spiritual inflation—reflected in the great tragedies. Meanwhile our first concern is with Shakespeare's views on schools and education.

Modern scholarship has shown that his supposedly "small Latin and less Greek," if less systematically cultivated than Queen Elizabeth's, was not negligible. Certainly Queen Elizabeth's Latin and Greek, her delight in dance, music, drama, beauty, her splendid all-around genius, like Lorenzo the Magnificent's rich, many-sided humanism, Leonardo da Vinci's and Michelangelo's marvelously versatile creativity in the arts and sciences, Francis Bacon's rangy powers in the shaping of law and history, philosophy and scientific method, all point in one direction, worlds removed from our expert but narrow specialization. Like his great forerunners and contemporaries, Shakespeare lived in the floodtide of the Renaissance. He was a schoolmaster who was never schoolmasterly. He was humane and wise: a true lover, as Berowne says in *Love's Labour's Lost*, of "that angel, knowledge." Best of all, he was a great artist—actor, playwright, and producer—in the theater, and the greatest poet of all time.

"Ignorance," says Shakespeare once more, "is the curse of God, Knowledge the wing wherewith we fly to heaven." No wonder, therefore, that "the noble word education"—to quote Sir J. M. Barrie—appears frequently in Shakespeare's plays: endlessly indeed, if one counts related terms such as "school," "learning," "teacher," "knowledge." Here I can only sample what seems to me significant in some of these utterances, and, later, in his observations on government and religion. All this on the principle[4] that what is objectively said or done by his characters and sometimes reinforced by the relatively more intimate revelations of the sonnets, is a fair index of the prevailing quality of his own thought.

Orlando in *As You Like It*, "never school'd and yet learned," bitterly resents his wicked brother's failure to provide him the "good education" his father had meant him to have. At the other end, William, son of the not-too-learned Justice Silence (in *2 Henry IV*) is leniently reported to be a "good scholar" ("Indeed, sir, to my cost," says his father) "at Oxford," whence " 'a must" proceed to study law: "to the Inns o' Court shortly . . . Clement's Inn [or] Gray's Inn." In betwixt and between these two, Shakespeare runs the gamut. There are all sorts of pupils, teachers, curricula: "all the learned and authentic fellows," "great scholars," and "learned fools," "great teachers," "false teachers," "parrot teachers," some who "teach young babes," and some who teach the old trivium and quadrivium (see Act I, Scene i of *Taming*); some old, ever-new schoolboys with shining morning faces, creeping, like snail, reluctantly to school, and some who belong to Polonius' studious university (where he acted Julius Caesar), or to Hamlet's Wittenberg or Petruchio's "fair Padua, nursery of arts." All these I must reluctantly pass by, to glance, instead, at Shakespeare's most elaborate dramatic essay on higher education.

[4] Discussed above, pp. 6–8. M. H. Curtis's useful survey of Elizabethan "Education and Apprenticeship," *Shakespeare Survey*, XVII (1964), 53–72, appeared after the present chapter had been completed.

"The court's a learning place," we read in *All's Well*. *Love's Labour's Lost* proves the point. This play was perhaps written, certainly acted, for Queen Elizabeth. She and her courtiers must have delighted in its fantastically high-spirited, timely, and charming extravaganza mirroring the Tudor court's fashionable but genuine love of humanistic learning, especially its delight in languages, the wonder of words, the splendor of verbal pyrotechnics. Tennyson's *Love's Labour's Lost*, *The Princess*, is a timely Victorian fantasy on the higher education of women. Shakespeare's academe, like Tennyson's, is planned, ordained, and supervised by and for royalty and the nobility, to the exclusion of the other sex. Shakespeare's king proclaims that his country, Navarre,

> shall be the wonder of the world:
> Our court shall be a little Academe,
> Still and contemplative in living art.

Resembling somewhat the literary academies of Medicean Florence, it is to be a society of courtly male scholars, minus the endearing elegance of the intellectual female companionship described in Castiglione's famous book of *The Courtier*. *Love's Labour's Lost*'s academe is a super-graduate Institute of Advanced Studies. It offers a three years' feast of reason and a fast of sense, an academic retreat without professors, without a Plato, and with never a fair lady allowed near the premises. By their compact, Navarre and his bookmen "living in philosophy" for three long years, are solemnly pledged to see no woman, to fast one day each week, to eat but one meal on other days, to sleep but three hours nightly, and never wink by day! Berowne, their wisest and best, sees at once that it will not do: "Young blood doth not obey an old decree:/We cannot cross the cause why we were born." And so, of course, it proves. The Princess of France and her three ladies arrive on a diplomatic mission. The four votaries of the higher learning see at once that women's eyes are the true "books, the arts, the academes/That show, contain, and nourish all the world." Forsworn, and put to a hard wooing, they win, at last, the ladies' promises to accept them—after a year's probation. From first to last, however, Navarre and his fellows (and those who see or read their story) have had something to fall back on. For "quick recreation," for "interim" to their "studies" they have the unfailing Elizabethan delight in words and their ways. The fantastic would-be-Spanish grandiloquence, the "high-born words," "fire-new words," and Euphuistic elaborations of the magnificent Armado, the malapropisms of Dull the constable, the execrable puns of the rustic Costard, the airy quibbles of that tiny handful of wit, the page Moth, the sesquipedalian pedantries of the schoolmaster and the curate who have stolen the small scraps of the feast of languages, the niceties of the civil war of wits between the princely and noble young ladies and gentlemen—these are the ingredients of the "sweet smoke of rhetoric" which is *Love's Labour's Lost*. At the last, Berowne promises to turn over a new leaf:

> Taffeta phrases, silken terms precise,
> Three-pil'd hyperboles, spruce affectation,
> Figures pedantical. . . . I do forswear them.

Henceforth, he says, he will speak only "in russet yeas and honest kersey noes." Shakespeare, in fine, smiles at the word-mongers, but he never renounced his own taffeta phrases nor his love of humanistic learning.

Of course this means, among other things, that he was no bookworm. Anticipating Bacon in *The Advancement of Learning* and Emerson in *The American Scholar*, Berowne puts the thing concisely:

> Small have continual plodders ever won
> Save base authority from others' books.

In short, Shakespeare kept his eye upon the whole human scene, including—like Chaucer and Milton—the great world of practical affairs. Because he had the open eye of a keen reporter and a great poet, what he has to say of politics, of history, of government, especially in his English and Roman historical plays, is still memorably relevant. Happily, to be sure, some of his observations are less pertinent now than of yore. "Uneasy lies the head that wears a crown"—even in the kingless democracies, today. But the Western world, at least, no longer suffers from the ancient evil of dynastic wars, from the blood-red rose soiling the white, the ever-threatening "woe to that land that's govern'd by a child," the international perils of royal marriages of convenience. Other, abiding facts of political-governmental life deserve notice here, though I must content myself with summary notes on some few representative items, some foreign, some domestic, somewhat as I did in my earlier sketch-list of Renaissance events and personages.

*On foreign affairs.* When Mussolini's Italy encountered growing domestic difficulties, Il Duce's planned diversion took his armies abroad to Haile Selassie's Abyssinia. Thereupon the American historian Charles A. Beard, remembering his Shakespeare, wrote a book entitled *Giddy Minds and Foreign Quarrels*. He drew, of course, upon the famous principle of statecraft not invented by Shakespeare but consistently practiced by many of his kings. Henry IV, the shrewdest and ablest of them all, made it the basis of his policy from the beginning of his successful usurpation—at the expense of Richard II—to his dying moment, when he urged his son, Prince Hal, to preoccupy noble malcontents, potentially dangerous rivals for power, by busying them in foreign adventures. "Lest rest and lying still might make them" too troublesome,

> Be it thy course to busy giddy minds
> With foreign quarrels.

That is exactly what Prince Hal does immediately upon becoming King Henry V, when he invades France with the glad consent of his bishops, who also need a foreign diversion to protect the church against confiscatory legislation threatened at home. It is written that not long before January, 1862, our Secretary of State, Seward, "had suggested a European war" "as the best means of uniting the North and the South." Lincoln thought otherwise, but the Kremlin still believes in fomenting foreign quarrels as a cover for domestic difficulties. Witness its arms sales to Cuba and Egypt and its Trojan horse distribution of foreign "aid" elsewhere in Africa and Asia. The Soviets and their allies have faith, also, in the converse principle, as set forth in *3 Henry VI*:

> How can tyrants safely govern home
> Unless abroad they purchase great alliance?

This endeavor motivated the inspired travels of Khrushchev and Kosygin, Nasser and Chou En-Lai. Finally, there is the explosive criss-crossing of Chinese-Russian intrigue among Asia's and Africa's emerging nations—a cogent illustration, second only to Hitler's demonstration in his time, of the truth of Shakespeare's collateral observation, in *King John,* that power

> snatch'd with an unruly hand
> Must be as boisterously maintain'd as gain'd;
> And he that stands upon a slipp'ry place
> Makes nice of no vile hold to stay him up.

In the preceding chapter[5] I have mentioned some of Shakespeare's pungent utterances upon war and peace, abroad and at home, but another illustration from *Coriolanus* may be in order here. At Antium, the servingmen in their wisdom hate peace: "a very apoplexy, lethargy . . . sleepy, insensible. . . . Let

[5] Pp. 12–13.

me have war, say I. . . . then we shall have a stirring world again.
. . . The wars for my money!" The proud warrior-patrician Coriolanus agrees, insidiously modern in his cheerful assumption
that war will cure the economic sickness of overproduction and
maldistribution:

> In arms!—
> I am glad on't. Then we shall ha' means to vent
> Our musty superfluity.

Finally, Falconbridge, Hotspur, Antony, and Othello dramatize
the splendid havoc, the romantic glamour of the "royal occupa-
tion," "the pomp and circumstance of glorious war." But war
is also the "son of hell"; its seamy side is realistically exhibited:
the thieving of shady camp followers, the perpetration of
"beastly-shameless" atrocities, "heady murder, spoils, and vil-
lainy."

*Internal affairs.* The Roman plays, as already indicated, are
pertinent because both *Coriolanus* and *Julius Caesar*, like the
English history plays, illustrate trenchantly the evil of domestic
faction, of civil dissension, (the "viperous worm that gnaws the
bowels of the commonwealth,") and of political chicanery, the
manipulation of the fickle and foolish "many" by unscrupulous
leaders. The *Henry VI* trilogy exhibits the most outrageous evil
of all, the bloody tyranny of the mobster-dictator. Hitler's Chief
Justice announced in 1939 that "the Führer's will is the consti-
tution of Nazi Germany," but Shakespeare's Jack Cade had anticipated him: "Burn all the records of the realm! My mouth
shall be the Parliament of England." The king in *Henry VIII*
puts it the other way about: "We must not rend our subjects
from our laws/And stick them in our will." Indeed the basic
premise of democracy is implied in Henry V's midnight talk
with his sturdy common soldiers before Agincourt: "Every subject's duty is the king's *but every subject's soul is his own.*" In
contradistinction to the mobster, the dignity and worth of the

common man is recognized—for example in the words of Feeble, the woman's tailor, who scornfully refuses to contribute to Falstaff's recruiting graft, announces that "no man's too good to serve" his country, and that each one "owes God a death." The commons, "whose love lies in their purses," grumble and growl effectively, in *Richard II* and *Henry VIII*, for example, against the burden of "grievous taxes" unjustly imposed by irresponsible royal exaction. But the significant fact is Shakespeare's insistence that order, degree, and discipline in the state depend upon the maintenance of the "mutual, well-beseeming" rights of king, nobles, and commoners alike. Equally significant, finally, is his awareness of the mounting power of public opinion; witness Henry V's pre-battle consultation with his soldiers, the citizen's protests against tyrannies perpetrated by Henry VI's nobles and by Richard III, and the gardeners' outspoken criticism of Richard II's neglect of his sea-walled garden, England.

Earlier in this chapter, when quoting *Macbeth,* I touched upon what Shakespeare calls "both the worlds," the now and the everlasting. If one reads Shakespeare fairly, one cannot help glancing at both the worlds, because, in his greatest moments Shakespeare recognizes, again and again, that both are indeed One World. I cannot hope to compass the vast range of religious thought and feeling in his work, but within my limits I shall try to sketch something of its impact upon one great and representative play—*Hamlet.*

It opens with the bleak and bitter chill of midnight. The sheeted dead stir, graves yawn, the soldier guard is sick at heart, the ghost appears. Dark clouds brood over the tense action that follows. Young Hamlet shrewdly fights the might of entrenched, unscrupulous power with the cunning of assumed madness. His "mighty opposite," King Claudius, the traitorously gifted brother murderer, first "smiles," then plots fresh crimes of desperation. Polonius and the fair Ophelia are the first victims of this struggle. Later, Hamlet's mother, Queen Gertrude (no longer blindly unaware of the "black . . . spots" upon her soul), and then Ophelia's brother, Laertes, and finally Claudius himself and Hamlet, succumb to the king's poisoned cup and sword. But in this great play all is not darkness. At the very first, a star "burns." It continues to "illume" at least a "part of heaven." Horatio invokes the ghost "by heaven." Hamlet's lips, too, move in prayer ("Angels and ministers of Grace defend us") upon first seeing his father's spirit, and in instinctive assertion of the integrity of his own spirit, the haunting stir of "thoughts beyond the reaches of our souls." Immediately after, he assures Horatio that he does not fear the ghost:

> My soul—what can it do to that,
> Being a thing immortal as itself?

The key to all this lies in a phrase of Hamlet's when he makes his mother see the black wickedness of her breach of the sacramental contract of marriage:

> O such a deed
> As from the body of contraction plucks
> The very soul, and sweet religion makes
> A rhapsody of words.

A more specific affirmation of sweet religion is heard in the play's opening scene, in the exchange between Marcellus and Horatio when the ghost, in accordance with folk belief, had disappeared at cock-crow. Both Marcellus and Horatio know a better gospel than this legend of the cock-crow:

> Some say that ever 'gainst that season comes
> Wherein our Saviour's birth is celebrated,
> The bird of dawning singeth all night long;
> And then, they say, no spirit dare stir abroad,
> No fairy takes nor witch hath power to charm
> So hallow'd and so gracious is the time.

Soon thereafter, Hamlet, in his first soliloquy, laments that "the Everlasting had . . . fix'd/His canon 'gainst self-slaughter." To this theme he returns in the greater soliloquy, "To be or not to be. . . . To die—to sleep." Of course the great problem is "what dreams may come" in that sleep of death:

> the dread of something after death—
> The undiscover'd country from whose bourne
> No traveller returns.

The purlieus of that undiscovered country, however shrouded to sense, are not altogether beyond the vision of the mind's eye, the outer reaches of our souls. They are shadowed forth in Hamlet's vivid sense of the near impinging of hell, his fear, in moments of doubt, that the spirit he has seen may be a devil; in the purgatorial pangs suffered by the ghost, that really "honest" but too perturbed spirit so cruelly cut off unshriven, "Unhous'led, disappointed, unanel'd"; they appear in the grotesque half-revelations of the gravediggers' sardonic jesting and questing about old Yorick's skull and the whereabouts of the living virtue that was in it, the lost quintessence of our dust.

Some few remaining observations especially concern such major personages as Ophelia, King Claudius, Hamlet, and his friend Horatio. Curiously enough, one or two critical utterances concerning certain clergy are heard from or about the fair and ingenuous Ophelia. Worldly cardinals and bishops are realistically portrayed in Shakespeare's historical plays; good and gentle priests minister with loving kindness to their people in such plays as *Much Ado* and *Romeo and Juliet*; but, early in *Hamlet*, Ophelia smilingly warns her brother not to emulate "some ungracious pastors" who prescribe the thorny road to others while they themselves tread the primrose path. Toward the end, though she dies distraught and therefore innocent of sinful self-slaughter, the dead girl is allowed only "maiméd rites" by the "churlish priest"—as her brother calls him—who denies her the "requiem and . . . rest" allowed to "peace-parted souls." (In *Troilus and Cressida*, Shakespeare may have had in mind a not altogether dissimilar clergyman when he observed that " 'Tis mad idolatry/To make the service greater than the god.")

King Claudius, in his abortive prayer for divine mercy (without repentance) achieves one of the greatest moments in *Hamlet*:

> My words fly up, my thoughts remain below;
> Words without thoughts never to heaven go.

I must add that prayer, the word and the thing, is deeply woven, many times over, into the texture of the plays. Witness, for example, the bootless prayer of Angelo, the false judge, in the powerful play entitled, from the apostles' phrase, *Measure for Measure*, and the memorable passage in *Antony and Cleopatra*:

> We, ignorant of ourselves
> Beg often our own harms, which the wise powers
> Deny us for our good. So find we profit
> By losing of our prayers.

Hamlet himself, though he tells Ophelia that he has more chargeable "offences than thoughts to put them in," is no lost soul like the guilty Claudius. His somber awareness of the world's burden of evil is tempered by resigned acceptance of divine Providence: "There's a special providence in the fall of a sparrow." "There's a divinity that shapes our ends,/Rough-hew them how we will." Therefore all is not bleak and hopeless. At the last, Hamlet persuades Horatio to stay in this harsh world to tell his story, but only to absent himself from felicity *awhile*. And Horatio, in bidding his friend good night, calls upon flights of angels to sing him to his rest.

There are those who see only casual slaughter, only frustrated negation in the endings of all the great tragedies.[6] They fail to

---

6 See above, pp. 8–11.

see, for example, that Lear, in his stormy agony, has learned the truth of his servant Kent's great saying that "nothing, almost, sees miracles/But misery"; that the raging tempest has taught him to cast off his false gods, and, in prison with his child Cordelia, to take upon them the mystery of things, as if they were the true God's spies.[7] Others see in the ending of *Macbeth* only a tale told by an idiot, signifying nothing. They forget that this is God's judgment; that life has become an idiot's tale for Macbeth in punishment for his mortal sin; that in the last of this tragedy, young Siward, who dies in the field and in the faith, face fronted, standing up, dies only to become "God's soldier." Shakespeare knew, as Cleopatra says, that "some innocents scape not the thunderbolt." He has no solution for the ancient mysteries—death, evil, suffering. But to read him discerningly may help us toward the right way. He knew that men must sometimes walk in darkness. But he reminds us to listen for the bird of dawning and to face the light.

7 Cf. "The Gods and God in *King Lear*," my article in *Renaissance Papers* (South Carolina and Duke Universities, 1955), pp. 32–39.

# 3

# The Man Who Wrote Shakespeare[1]

A FEW YEARS AGO we all saw by the papers, as Mr. Dooley used to say, that the man who wrote Shakespeare was about to be discovered in documents to be dug out of the tomb of Sir Thomas Walsingham, in Chislehurst, England. Mr. Calvin Hoffman, a one-time "drama critic from Long Island" who had a flair for the dramatic, was the prophet of this new revelation. He had previously publicized his discovery that Christopher Marlowe was the true author of Shakespeare's works. Hoffman's first trumpet blasts were recorded in such magazines as *Esquire* and *Coronet*; then came his full-blown book, *The Murder of the Man Who Was Shakespeare*, published in May, 1955. When first writing about these matters, early in 1956, I observed that in fairness one ought to wait and see what came out of the tomb in Chislehurst. The answer came on May 1, 1956, when the tomb was opened but yielded nothing. Even so, that year was peculiarly timely for a backward glance. Somewhere on this planet two hundred and fifty years earlier, prophetic lightning had flashed across the sky when Benjamin Franklin was born. Two hundred years earlier the angels above had made celestial music when Mozart was born in Salzburg. One hundred years earlier The Greatest of Literary Problems—who wrote Shakespeare?—was born. For in that year 1856 our American Delia Bacon, then in

1 Revised from *Tennessee Studies in Literature*, I (1956), 1 ff., with additions.

England, finished her book, *The Philosophy of the Plays of Shakespeare Unfolded.* Our consul in Liverpool, Nathaniel Hawthorne—all honor to him!—helped her to get the book published, subsidized it out of his own pocket, and generously praised it in his Preface, even though he clearly disclaimed editorial responsibility and doctrinal faith except in the book's right to a hearing. The wheel is come full circle! A round century ago, Delia Bacon (and W. H. Smith, her immediate British rival) claimed that Francis Bacon was the man who wrote Shakespeare—or at least headed a secret coterie who did, with Sir Walter Raleigh and Edmund Spenser among the contributors. For Mr. Hoffman, Marlowe was the man. Perhaps! Whoever he is, everyone now agrees that he, "of all modern, and perhaps ancient, poets had the largest and most comprehensive soul." Therefore the question who he really was and is, is worth asking again, now that the waters of more than a hundred years have run over the dams of the world. In this brief survey I cannot attempt to discuss all the answers of these hundred years. I shall emphasize those of the beginning and the end, moving from Bacon to Marlowe as the crow flies, sketching in-betweens as best I can, summarizing the pros and cons of the main arguments for the chief contestants, and concluding with a word as to the significance of the whole curious business.

First, then, a quick roll call of the candidates and a listing of some of the notables often proudly claimed by the anti-Stratfordians for their side. The list of would-be Shakespeares is formidable. From the first, some theorists seem to have guessed that among the secret conclave of poet-philosophers and men of affairs headed by Bacon, Raleigh, and Spenser, some practicing dramatists might have been included. Facetiously in Sir J. M. Barrie's *Greenwood Hat* fantasy, "The Truth About W. S.," and seriously in Alden Brooks' 700-page tome, *Will Shakespeare and the Dyer's Hand* (New York, 1943), not only Christopher Marlowe but also Lyly and Peele, Nashe and Lodge, Kyd and

Samuel Daniel, and even Ben Jonson are mentioned in passing. More serious claims, some supported by many books, are those of other great Elizabethan noblemen, including some true poets in their own right and rivals of Raleigh at court: the Earl of Rutland, Sir Philip Sidney (though he died altogether too early, in 1586), and his friend, another of Elizabeth's early favorites, Sir Edward Dyer. Then come Shakespeare's patrons, the Earls of Southampton and Pembroke, great literary patrons both, but neither one a notable writer. Among more recent favorites are William Stanley the 6th Earl of Derby, and Edward de Vere the 17th Earl of Oxford. Finally, to round off the score and more of candidates, there are Sir Anthony Shirley, the Persian traveler, and, on the distaff side, two noble ladies. One of them is none other than Lady Bacon herself—not to be confused with Miss Delia Bacon! (Says Barrie, tongue in cheek: "It was really Lady Bacon who wrote all the plays." Will Kemp, the player, told him so, in the Elysian Fields.) The other great lady, in all seriousness, is none other than the minor poet and famous patron of poets, "Sidney's sister, Pembroke's mother," the Countess of Pembroke.

With due respect to these fair and great ladies, their Shakespearean claims are not sufficiently substantial to detain us, and the same must regrettably be said for most of the distinguished men on our list. The best of them, the Prince of Poets Edmund Spenser and the noble Sidney, were no dramatists and died too early. Again, premature death or other obvious facts of life virtually exclude all the dramatists named—Greene, Lyly, Kyd, Jonson, and the rest—with the possible (?) exception of Christopher Marlowe—of whom more later. Sidney's friend Dyer wrote one fine lyric, "My Mind to Me a Kingdom Is," and Shakespeare, in Sonnet 111, says that his "nature is subdu'd / To what it works in, like the dyer's hand." But these two facts do not make a case for Dyer's authorship of the plays, even though *Shakespeare and the Dyer's Hand* has much curious collateral information, plus vast ranges of conjecture, spiced with sharp abuse of Shakespeare, the player. Derby and Oxford perhaps deserve closer notice, but, in the main, the claims made for each of these two cancel the other's. Their devoted proponents insist, in effect, that each of the two men must have written all of Shakespeare's sonnets and tragedies because each man was made miserably unhappy by his wife's infidelity. Further, the argument runs, the plays exhibit such intimate knowledge of courtly lore, foreign places, foreign languages, etc., as could have been derived *only* from the career of Derby—or of Oxford, respectively.

The same sort of reasoning, of course, had led the Baconians —and Mark Twain—to hail Sir Francis as the author, because nobody else knew enough law to have written the plays. By the same reasoning, Henry Pemberton's book, *Shakespeare and Sir Walter Raleigh*, emphasizing "the poet's remarkable familiarity . . . with all things maritime," fixes upon Sir Walter as the true author. By the same blissful disregard of time, general probability, and the fact that even great men whose public careers are fully recorded cannot normally do more than one full lifetime's work in a lifetime, we had better be prepared for future claims that the diplomats Sir Henry Wotton and Lord Herbert of Cherbury, and the beloved physician Sir Thomas Browne must each have been the sole author, since nobody else knew enough diplomacy and medicine, respectively. The theorists reject the unsensational likelihood that the plays were the work of the actor Shakespeare of Stratford, though this is the unanimous report of his contemporaries and friends: the actors Hemings and Condell (named in his will, and compilers of the great First Folio edition of his works), fellow-playwrights such as Jonson and Thomas Heywood and Drayton and Webster, critics and poets—great and little, early and late—such as Francis Meres (1598) and John Weever (1599), and, later, Ben Jonson and John Milton. These contemporaries were all misinformed or else guilty of conspiratorial falsehood. The plays and sonnets, say the Oxfordians, cannot be the work of that "illiterate," "clumsy," "litigious" onetime "butcher's prentice" of Stratford: Delia Bacon long ago had "proved" that "the Earl of Leicester's stable-boy" was not the man. For at that time, as Mr. Calvin Hoffman observes, "compulsory education was . . . unknown," and Shakespeare "never received a formal education." He will not do. The idea would seem to be that the great Giver of all life and genius could not possibly have smiled upon Shakespeare, who, like Bunyan and Blake and Burns and John Keats and Bernard Shaw and Benjamin Franklin and Abraham Lincoln and Mark Twain, had no formal education: he never went to college! Nor does it matter that scholarship during the last century or so has developed certain fresh data. For example, the fact that Shakespeare's Stratford had an excellent grammar school, which taught considerably more Latin and Greek than most of our universities. And the fact that during part of Shakespeare's boyhood, his father, then the prosperous and probably not illiterate mayor of Stratford, had means to pay for his son's schooling. But no records whatsoever of the Stratford school's registrar's office survive. Therefore, say the Oxfordians and Mr. Hoffman, only "wishful thinking" could make Shakespeare anything other than unlettered and unschooled. The son of Shakespeare's fellow-actor, Christopher Beeston, reported in his day that "Shakespeare understood Latin pretty well, for he had been in his younger days a schoolmaster in the country." This plausible report our theorists reject or ignore. Yet it is a fact that such schoolmasterly preparation, and such schooling as the theater itself provides, have produced many a fine storyteller and dramatist; witness, in our time, James Hilton's Mr. Chips, and Thornton Wilder and Maxwell Anderson, and many a successful actor-playwright before and after; for example, Molière and Pinero and Noel Coward.

Perhaps we have been getting a bit ahead of our orderly exposition. On the credit side, I think we have disposed, at least temporarily, of most of our noble and miscellaneous claimants for the honor of writing Shakespeare. Thus, our process of elimination entitles us to mix a metaphor. Presently, we may sink our teeth in the remainder biscuit: pay our respects to Miss Delia and Sir Francis Bacon and to the Baconians, and then to Mr. Hoffman's plea for Christopher Marlowe. First, however, a word more about Mark Twain and some of the other great converts claimed by the anti-Stratfordians. Hoffman, apparently borrowing ammunition from the late Professor Lefranc, the distinguished supporter of the Earl of Derby, lists among those who hold "that Shakespeare just cannot be accepted as the author ... such men as Nathaniel Hawthorne, Lord Palmerston, Walt Whitman ... Mark Twain, Prince Bismarck, Oliver Wendell Holmes, Sigmund Freud ... John Bright, Henry James, Ralph Waldo Emerson . . . Charles Dickens." Mark Twain himself says he "wishes" he "knew who" wrote the plays. Actually his book, *Is Shakespeare Dead?* (New York, 1909), combines delightful spoofing—pilot-cub memories of Mark Twain's argufying against his anti-Baconian master pilot—with his life-long, chivalric inclination to support the underdog even in literary problematic issues. Henry James, too, seems to have had more or less playfully serious moments of doubt; and Dickens is reported to have seen elements of "fine mystery" in Shakespeare's life—as what sensitive reader does not? For the rest, some items of Mr. Hoffman's list, like other parts of his case, can be accepted only with substantial reservations. Even if Freud and Bismarck and other powers and potentates were won over wholeheartedly, trained literary historians are missing here and, with the solitary exception of the distinguished French scholar, Lefranc, from all the rolls of the anti-Shakespeareans. Most of the poets and men of letters claimed by Hoffman were really not in his camp. Even Walt Whitman, though strongly influenced by his Baconian friend William O'Connor, was always open-minded. His poem on the Shakespeare-Bacon cipher says, "I doubt it not . . . In every object, mountain, tree, and star . . . a mystic cipher waits." But he also said "I do not admit Bacon," and he denied, in spite of O'Connor, that Ignatius Donnelly's *Great Cryptogram* "settled" anything. Oliver Wendell Holmes was a stout Shakespearean in spite of Mr. Hoffman, who confuses the Autocrat of the Breakfast Table with Judge Nathaniel Holmes of Missouri. Emerson also, as a recent biographer[2] observes, was "no Baconian," though he, too, befriended Delia Bacon, thought her a "genius but mad," and gave her a letter to Carlyle—who soon came to share Emerson's view of her, and Hawthorne's. For Hawthorne too, as I have already indicated, was not one of the faithful. In his "Recollections of a Gifted Woman" (a chapter from *Our Old Home*), he says that Delia Bacon was unquestionably a "monomaniac," that he maintained a "sturdy unbelief," that her "ideas," however nobly conceived, were "erroneous."

Yet Hawthorne adds something that bears repetition a century after Delia Bacon died, entirely broken in mind and thus mercifully oblivious to the "brutal vituperation" which greeted her book. "We Americans," Hawthorne wrote, "cannot afford to forget her high and conscientious exercise of noble faculties. . . . Her labor," though "outwardly irreverent to the name of Shakespeare," really entitled her "to the distinction of being that one of his worshippers who sought, though she knew it not, to place the richest and stateliest diadem upon his brow." A diadem? Or—a brickbat, for "the peasant of Stratford," as she called him? Hawthorne was right, even so. To oversimplify, we may say that, for Delia Bacon, Shakespeare idolatry took three main lines. (1) The Stratford actor could not possibly have known enough to write the great plays and poems. Moreover, the portraits, busts, and memorial inscriptions at Stratford do not fit the noble poet of the plays and may be modern frauds. (2) The "diadem" of which Hawthorne speaks: Only a mighty philosopher such as Bacon—aided by the noblest of his circle— could have planned the great plays' schematic and purposive exposition of the "science" of human life, or executed their grand design: to dramatize deep social, economic, and political

[2] Ralph L. Rusk, *Life of Ralph Waldo Emerson* (New York, 1949), pp. 387, 393.

lesson-stories intended to free "the oppressed and suffering masses" from the shackles of fear, ignorance, and tyrannical absolutism. (3) This high endeavor was so dangerous that it had to be made secretly. "It was a time," Miss Bacon writes, when "*ciphers* and puzzles were not for child's play merely, when they had need to be close" lest their "secrets . . . open . . . into the Tower . . . the scaffold and the block."

Space is not available here for an adequate revaluation of Miss Bacon's book. Most of it is impossibly misty, rhapsodic, long-winded; but its best pages—say one in ten—have sensitive insights and shrewd judgments which, as Hawthorne recognized, "quite take the color and pungency out of other people's critical remarks." But this book and all subsequent Baconiana have some very blind spots. The noblest of these lies close to the fantastically idealistic concept—temporarily borrowed from Delia Bacon by Walt Whitman[3] through O'Connor—that, in Shakespeare's historical plays in particular, "the essentially controlling plan and purpose" was to "sap" and "undermine" the established order of political absolutism. Less creditable is the Baconians' failure to see that the supposed likenesses, the "parallels" between Shakespeare and Bacon's known work are merely Elizabethan commonplaces; that Bacon's crowded public career left no room for a lifetime's making of plays; that—to borrow, in part, Charles Lamb's quip—even if Bacon had had a mind to write them, he had not the heart, the imagination. Witness his chilly essay "Of Love," and then Shakespeare's *Romeo and Juliet* and the sonnet "Let me not to the marriage of true minds/ Admit impediments."

Long ago, Delia Bacon's book was damned but not quite dead. For half a century and more its progeny spawned like the dragon's teeth. It brought forth scores of gnarled champions, hundreds of portentous volumes: *The Great Cryptogram, The Bi-Lateral Cipher, The Greatest of Literary Problems,* and all

[3] For discussion, see "Shakespeare and Walt Whitman" in my *Shakespeare and Democracy* (Knoxville, 1941), pp. 58–60.

the aftermath of legalists, cryptographers, Derbyites, Oxfordians, and others already mentioned, all using, if not the same ciphers, virtually the same old arguments and "parallels," and many afflicted with the same old blind spots, plus some new ones. We must see how these affect the claims for Marlowe—after another word about ciphers. Not long after Mr. Hoffman's enterprise, *Life* magazine's story about the cipher "Hunt for a *Hamlet* Treasure at Hamlet's Elsinore" proved that this profitable element of the Baconian technique dies hard. Sensational success has also rewarded two other modern variations of the Baconian technique. One, a revival of the Baconian attack on the Stratford busts, the portraits, etc., was exemplified in Mr. Hoffman's widely publicized and picturized argument that Marlowe must have written Shakespeare because a supposed Marlowe portrait looks like a supposed Shakespeare portrait. The reasoning here is identical with that behind the Oxfordians' blast of January, 1940, when the *Scientific American* published a front-cover picture supposedly of Oxford, and a story arguing that Oxford wrote the plays because the picture had previously been mistaken for a true picture of Shakespeare. Of course the headlines do not say that doubtful pictures do not necessarily make doubtful originals! At any rate, history repeats itself! In the late 1930's there was considerable excitement in Williamsburg, Virginia, because of a reputed Shakespeare-Bacon cipher buried in Bruton Church Yard. Some twenty years later came Mr. Hoffman's well-advertised tomb-digging at Chislehurst, exactly one hundred years after Delia Bacon's thwarted plan (*vide* Hawthorne) to dig into Shakespeare's grave in Stratford Church. To have done with ciphers: unfortunately they prove either too little or too much. For example: that Bacon's cipher gives him not only *Hamlet* but also, let us say, *The Ring and the Book* or *The Waste Land*, or, as the great cryptographer Ignatius Donnelly actually suggested, Burton's *Anatomy of Melancholy* and Montaigne's *Essays*. Or, according to another view, to Shakespeare himself would be left only the authorship of the 46th Psalm, wherein "the 46th word from the beginning is 'shake' and the 46th word from the end is 'spear.' " This pointed suggestion comes from a pleasantly un-Baconian book entitled *Let Candles Be Brought In*,[4] the autobiography of Sir Geoffrey Shakespeare, a distant cousin.

And so we come to Shakespeare and Marlowe. Ben Jonson, who knew both, differentiated sharply between them. He praised Marlowe's "mighty line," deprecated the players' praise of Shakespeare for "never blotting out a line," but delighted in his "excellent phantasy, brave notions . . . gentle expressions," and "loved the man" and "honor[ed] his memory, on this side idolatry, as much as any." Almost all of this he wrote into his posthumously published *Timber or Discoveries*. Shortly before Shakespeare's death in 1616, however, Jonson had recorded his friend Shakespeare's name among the actors who had appeared in Jonson's own play, *Every Man in His Humour*, in 1598. In the commendatory verses prefixed to the great First Folio edition of Shakespeare, 1623, Jonson—closely echoed nine years later by young John Milton—spoke out most fully concerning Shakespeare. He identifies not Marlowe of Canterbury and Chislehurst but Shakespeare, the actor and playwright of Stratford, the "sweet swan of Avon" so highly esteemed not only by the great nobles—the Earls of Pembroke and Montgomery—named in this First Folio's dedication, but also by the ruling monarchs. The man of Stratford was the

> Soul of the age!
> The applause, delight, the wonder of our stage!
> My Shakespeare, rise: I will not lodge thee by
> Chaucer or Spenser, or bid Beaumont lie
> A little further, to make thee a room:
> Thou art a monument without a tombe.

4 London, 1949, p. 350.

Though, by the learned Jonson's standard, Shakespeare had "small Latin and less Greek," Aeschylus, Euripides, and Sophocles would have been delighted to "hear" his "buskin tread," and he excelled by "far" his immediate contemporaries:

> how far thou didst our Lyly outshine,
> Or sporting Kyd, or Marlowe's mighty line!

Would he might reappear upon the banks of Thames,

> Sweet Swan of Avon . . .
> That so did take Eliza and our James!

Besides Jonson, three other eulogists in the same First Folio unmistakably identify the poet of *Romeo and Juliet* with the actor of Stratford: his "stage," his "tiring room," his "actor's art," and his "Stratford Monument." Among other critics, players and poets who did as much before or after, I shall mention three, because they also differentiated clearly between Shakespeare and Marlowe. Thus, Francis Meres, in 1598, hailed "honey-tongued Shakespeare" as "the most excellent . . . among the English . . . in both kinds for the stage . . . Comedy and Tragedy," while at the same time listing among "our best for Tragedy" only: "Marlowe . . . Kyd . . . Shakespeare, Jonson." Thirty-seven years later, Thomas Heywood the poet-dramatist to whom actors and the theater had long been "a world" to love, still remembered clearly who was who among his fellows, including "famous Kyd," "excellent Beaumont," "Learned . . . Jonson," and, among others, both "Kit . . . Marlowe" and "mellifluous . . . Will . . . Shakespeare." Similarly, four years after Jonson's tribute, Shakespeare's friend Michael Drayton differentiated between "neat" Marlowe's "brave translunary things/That the first poets had" and "Shakespeare['s] strong . . . clear . . . conception" and "smooth . . . comic vein."

But these straightforward contemporary reports did not impress Mr. Calvin Hoffman. Marlowe wrote Shakespeare. As regards Ben Jonson's testimony in particular, unlike Delia Bacon, who virtually ignores it, and others who speciously try to argue it out of court, Mr. Hoffman denounces it as a falsehood. "Jonson's feelings" in the First Folio eulogy "were feigned." "Throughout" his "long lifetime he jeered and damned all . . . Shakespeare's plays." "He was, of course, ignorant of Marlowe's authorship" and of the whole "tremendous imposture," but, even so, "his hypocrisy was truly odious. . . . He would have written anything for money"; he was "the 'glamor boy'. . . regularly hired to write eulogies." Therefore it was "logical . . . for the First Folio publishers" to employ his "hired and complimentary pen." In charity, it must simply be said that Mr. Hoffman does not know his Ben Jonson.

The remainder of his case for Marlowe rests substantially upon the familiar objections to the Stratfordian already sufficiently reviewed here: his lack of "formal education" and the supposed lack of credible biographical and professional information about him; and, at the other end, first upon many parallels Mr. Hoffman finds between Marlowe's acknowledged writings and Shakespeare's, and, second, upon Hoffman's sensational interpretation of the undeniably puzzling circumstances of Marlowe's death in 1593. Forty years ago, Leslie Hotson discovered the official record of the coroner's inquest which resulted in Marlowe's killer being pardoned by the Queen on the plea of self-defense. Soon afterwards this man was re-employed by the Walsinghams, whom Marlowe, as a secret service agent, had also served previously, at home and abroad. Since Marlowe was then under serious indictment for atheism, Hoffman conjectures that the Walsinghams had another man killed and buried in his stead, and that, during the next twenty-odd years, hidden on their estate, Marlowe wrote all of Shakespeare's plays. Believe it or not? Certainly the burden of proof—though Mr. Hoffman and all his ilk angrily deny this fact—rests upon the proponents of far-fetched theories of this sort. Far likelier, to put it mildly, would seem the possibility that

Marlowe's murder was planned and condoned because he, a secret agent, may have known too much for the safety of someone higher up. Indeed, as one of Mr. Hoffman's competing theorists puts it, "If Marlowe had escaped death by some fortunate occasion, he certainly would not have continued living about— or near—London . . . courting identification by writing plays as before." How could "he have hid himself year after year from the many who knew him?" How, I might add, could he have hid from his friend George Chapman? From Chapman, who, in his laborious continuation of Marlowe's unfinished masterpiece, *Hero and Leander,* invoked his friend's "deathless memory" and, recalling that "free soul['s] . . . late desires," promised to keep his own "pledge" not to leave "half this Musaean story" unfinished? Mozart, born some two hundred years ago, also died early, tragically. Not one of his friends was with him at the last; not one could so much as certify that it was his body that was thrown into a pauper's grave. Then, during the next twenty-odd years, as after Marlowe's death, another great master's work won the public ear. His name was Beethoven. Some of his early work was markedly like Mozart. The reason? It must be, of course, that Mozart, not Beethoven, wrote all the nine symphonies and the great concertos! With modest allowance for time differences, this theory makes almost as much sense as the other.

What, then, of the likenesses, the parallels between the thought and words of Marlowe and Shakespeare? A considerable portion of them are Elizabethan commonplaces, the fact being that the Elizabethan poets, as one critic has put it, "habitually quoted each other—without giving credit—to an extent . . . unbelievable to-day." Others are not "parallels" but actually complimentary quotations by Shakespeare, *with* credit to Marlowe. Thus, in *As You Like It,* Shakespeare after gently touching on Marlowe's death ("Dead shepherd, now I find thy saw of might") quotes a line from *Hero and Leander* ("Who ever lov'd, that lov'd not at first sight?"). Mr. Hoffman carefully lists this last line among his "parallels" but omits there Shakespeare's own previous line, the allusion to Marlowe as the dead shepherd. It is true, of course, that many passages in Shakespeare owe much to Marlowe. This proves that young Shakespeare was strongly influenced by Marlowe, as young Beethoven was influenced by Mozart. The "parallels" between Shakespeare and young Milton, that is to say, the Puritan poet's reminiscent borrowings from Shakespeare,[5] are at least as substantial as Shakespeare's borrowings from Marlowe. Yet Shakespeare did not write Milton, as he should have done, according to Mr. Hoffman's reasoning. Marlowe's known work is that of a true and great poet. There is a glow, an aspiration, a fierce splendor in him, but almost no human kindness, little humor, no compassion. He did *not* write Shakespeare.

And now, having heard "doctor and saint . . . great argument about it and about"—what follows? Why all this laborious hundred years' quest for the man who wrote Shakespeare? To what end? Three or four answers occur to me. In the first place, the Shakespeare Industry—as one book-title goes—*pays* if vigorously spiced and publicized: witness the *Scientific American*, *Esquire*, *Coronet*, and *Life*, not to mention the work of more learned historians. This is so because, as Sir Thomas Browne suggested long ago, we all love to lose ourselves in a good mystery, even if it be only a who-done-it. Next, anti-Stratfordianism was a belated reaction from the first fine careless rapture of Romanticism in general and of Shakespeare idolatry in particular. It was akin to late eighteenth-century and early nineteenth-century anti-Ossianism and to Wolf's anti-Homerism. As one critic has suggested, it was a kind of "secularized higher criticism." On its positive side Baconianism at its best is a part of our cultural history. Among those who were willing to give it a hearing, such men as Hawthorne, Emerson, Carlyle, and even Mark Twain and Walt Whitman, paid tribute at once to the mighty poet and

[5] See below, pp. 139 ff.

to the wisdom of the great philosopher-scientist. And the best of the later enthusiasts—such as M. Lefranc—have not labored altogether in vain. They have uncovered much substantial data on historic and literary background, for *Love's Labour's Lost*, for example, and other plays. They have stimulated research into the "lost years" of Shakespeare's youth and reminded scholars and all the world that many puzzling questions still await answers. In one sense, even Mr. Hoffman is on the side of the angels. It is excellent for all the world to be vigorously reminded of Shakespeare and of Marlowe. In the end, indeed, though nothing more concrete has come out of Chislehurst, an element of mystery remains—the miracle of genius. Chaucer, it has been well said, specialized in omniscience, but we cannot be sure that he ever went to college. We know that Benjamin Franklin did not, yet he knew and was known by all the world. Franklin was no poet, but the myriad-minded man from Stratford was like the many-sided Franklin in at least one respect. Like him, the wise and gentle Shakespeare out-tops mere knowledge and lives in the hearts of men.

SOME RELATIVELY RECENT BOOKS AND ARTICLES
CONCERNING THE SUBJECT OF THIS CHAPTER

Reginald C. Churchill, *Shakespeare and his Betters* (London, 1958).

Giles E. Dawson, "The Anti-Shakespeare Theories," *Encyclopedia Britannica*, XX (1960), 457–458.

William F. and Elizabeth S. Friedman, *The Shakespearean Ciphers Examined* (Cambridge, England, 1957).

H. N. Gibson, *The Shakespeare Claimants* (New York, 1962).

Alfred Harbage, "Shakespeare as Culture Hero," *Huntington Library Quarterly*, XXVII (1964), 211–227.

Abel Lefranc, *A la découverte de Shakespeare* (Paris, 1945–1950).

James G. McManaway, *The Authorship of Shakespeare* (Washington, D. C., 1962).

George L. McMichael and Edgar M. Glenn, *Shakespeare and his Rivals* (New York, 1962).

Milward W. Martin, *Was Shakespeare Shakespeare?* (New York, 1965).

*Shakespeare Cross Examination* (Chicago, 1961).

A. W. Titherly, *Shakespeare's Identity* (Winchester, England, 1952).

Harry Trosman, "Freud and the Controversy over Shakespearean Authorship," *Journal of the American Psychoanalytic Association,* XIII (1965), 475–498.

Frank W. Wadsworth, *The Poacher from Stratford* (Berkeley, Calif., 1958), and "The Authorship Question," *The Shakespeare Newsletter,* XIV (April-May, 1964), 46.

Louis B. Wright, "The Anti-Shakespeare Industry," *Virginia Quarterly Review,* XXV (1959), 289–303.

See also *Baconiana* and *Shakespearean Authorship Review,* and Gordon Ross Smith, *Classified Shakespeare Bibliography, 1936–1958* (University Park, Penna., 1963), pp. 573–585.

# 4

## *"With All Deliberate Speed"*

### Byron, Shakespeare, *et al.*[1]

ALL GOOD WRITERS, all good poets, have a way with words. As children love candy, many writers love "taffeta phrases, silken terms precise." Some prefer tougher texture, sterner stuff, but very few can resist a splendid phrase, a winged word that really soars. "Good phrases," says Justice Shallow, "are surely, and ever were, very commendable." A small footnote on the history of our time can be found in the background of the challenging phrase in which our Supreme Court on May 17, 1954, ordered "racially nondiscriminatory" integration of the public schools "with all deliberate speed." In 1960 I published some evidence which supports the conjecture that in using this striking phrase our judges may have re-echoed not only the thunder of English law but also the paradoxical cadence of English verse and prose,[2] perhaps including Shakespeare's. Then, as late as 1964–1965, having meanwhile kept in mind certain questions raised by distinguished jurists who were interested in my attempt to trace the origin of the phrase, I came upon some new material now presented in Part II, below.

[1] Revised from *Tennessee Studies in Literature*, V (1960), 111–118, with additions.

[2] For helpful suggestions or information, the writer is indebted to Professors Paul A. Freund of the Harvard Law School and Kenneth Curry, Walter E. Stiefel, and Martin Feerick of the University of Tennessee, and to Mr. Anthony Lewis of the New York *Times*.

# I

A word, first, as to the immediate and local realities behind and before our phrase. In 1960, six years had passed since the Supreme Court's decision was issued. It was altogether arguable then, however, that to effect a fundamental social change, even with all deliberate speed, six years are too few. Thus, when in the city of Knoxville on August 11, 1959, immediate integration was publicly urged upon the school board, its chairman replied, according to the Knoxville *News-Sentinel* of that date, "As far as I know, the Board intends to carry out the decision of the Supreme Court. I understand that we intend to implement integration of the System with all deliberate speed. But the Board has not decided when would be the ideal or proper time for integration to be carried out." The wisest comment I know, and still the most pertinent to the point at issue, is Abraham Lincoln's remark when he was urged, in September, 1861, to proceed with immediate emancipation of the slaves. "It will do no good," Lincoln said, "to go ahead any faster than the country will follow. . . . You know the old Latin motto, *festina lente. . . .*"[3] (Now, in 1965, the right way is to accept and follow the legislated law of the land.) It must be remembered, however, that in 1959, on the very day of the Knoxville school board session, the day before the reopening of schools in Little Rock, Governor Faubus was quoted on the radio as speaking in diverse tones, as follows: (1) he invited citizens to join in a great public rally to protest integration; (2) he professed to deprecate riotous opposition to Little Rock's token integration; (3) he asserted once more that integration could be achieved only by force of federal bayonets.

[3] Carl Sandburg, *Abraham Lincoln*, one-volume ed. (New York, 1954), p. 267. "*Festina lente*, Make haste slowly. A frequent saying of Augustus Caesar. Cp. *Eile mit Weile*" (*New Standard Dictionary*, 1914). Cf. also Shakespeare, *Romeo and Juliet*, II.iii.94: "Wisely and slow; they stumble that run fast."

Previously, the Supreme Court itself had issued on May 31, 1955, a supplementary decree to define "with all deliberate speed." It stated that "full implementation" of the "constitutional principles" involved may require solution of varied local problems. "While giving weight to these public and private considerations, the Court will require that the defendants make a prompt and reasonable start toward full compliance."[4]

A comment by a legal authority seems pertinent at this point. According to Mr. Robert B. McKay, writing in the *Virginia Law Review* (XLIII, 1205–1245) for December, 1957:

> By the choice of this suggestive phrase, "with all deliberate speed," the Court has made what appears to be *a significant addition* [my italics] to the tradition of flexibility in constitutional jurisprudence. "Deliberate speed" as a measure of the reasonableness of compliance . . . seems a worthy companion to such other artfully indefinite phrases in the Constitution itself as "due process," "equal protection of the laws," and "commerce among the several states." (P. 1206)

However significant its application to the case in point, the earlier history of our phrase may justify a layman's query whether its use here really constitutes an addition—i.e., I take it, a *new* addition—to juristic tradition or practice.

To underscore my query and to introduce my notes concerning possible literary associations of "with all deliberate speed," I quote from another distinguished authority on constitutional law, Professor Paul A. Freund of the Harvard Law School. In a paper entitled "Understanding the School Decision"[5] Mr. Freund states that:

> The phrase "deliberate speed" is a term of legal art deriving from 18th century chancery practice, and not, as certain litterateurs surmised, from the

---

[4] "With All Deliberate Speed," *New York University Law Review*, XXXI (June, 1956), 999–1000.

[5] Reprinted in *Desegregation and the Supreme Court*, ed. B. M. Ziegler, Problems in American Civilization Series (Boston, 1958), p. 85.

haunting refrain in Francis Thompson's religious poem, "The Hound of Heaven": "Deliberate speed, majestic instancy."[6]

Two items require notice here. (1) Mr. Freund's derivation of our phrase from eighteenth-century chancery practice would seem to invalidate the suggestion that it constitutes a recent addition to judicial practice. (2) To Mr. Freund's statement concerning the priority of the Court of Chancery's phrase over Francis Thompson's, I shall add some details for which I am, in part, indebted to a recent letter from Mr. Freund. I had written him that I found the whole phrase "with all deliberate speed" in a letter written by another famous English poet in 1819, about seventy-five years before Thompson published "The Hound of Heaven" in 1893. In generous response to my request, Mr. Freund supplied further information as to the facts underlying his published statement, as follows:

When I said that the phrase is taken from English chancery practice, I was . . . repeating . . . a remark of Justice Holmes which turns out to be very difficult indeed to verify. . . . No one seems actually to have discovered an instance of the usage in English chancery practice, although a number of scholars have recently made an effort. [Mr. Freund adds, however, that] Mr. Justice Frankfurter, drawing on Justice Holmes, used the phrase in at least one opinion[7] prior to the segregation cases.

---

6 The first stanza closes as follows:

> But with unhurrying chase,
> And unperturbed pace,
> Deliberate speed, majestic instancy,
> They beat—and a Voice beat
> More instant than the Feet—
> "All things betray thee, who betrayest Me."

*Works of Francis Thompson* (London, 1913), I, 107. (Cf. below, p. 66, on Mr. Doyle Hennessy's letter of September 1, 1958, in the New York *Herald Tribune*.)

7 Later, Professor Freund and Mr. Anthony Lewis, of the New York *Times* Washington Bureau, kindly sent me the following references covering, in all, five such prior uses of the phrase by Mr. Justice Frankfurter: (1) *Radio Station WOW* vs. *Johnson*, 326 U. S. 120, 132; (2) *Addison* vs. *Holly Hill*, 322 U. S. 607, 619; (3) *Chrysler* vs. *U. S.*, 316 U. S. 556, 568 (dissent); (4) *First Iowa Hydroelectric* vs.

Recently I have found an instance, noted in the second part of this chapter, of the specific use of our phrase in connection with eighteenth-century law courts. At the present point of our inquiry it should be said that, however difficult the verification of Justice Holmes's remark as to the origin of the phrase, Justice Frankfurter had no doubt that Justice Holmes was right. Almost certainly, moreover, Justice Frankfurter was right too; witness my later notes on Chancery and a certain poet. Justice Frankfurter himself states the case in a letter published in the New York *Herald Tribune*, September 26, 1958, in answer to a letter of September 1 (in the same paper) by Mr. Doyle Hennessy, who had stated that the "origin" of the phrase, "whether consciously chosen or not, is Francis Thompson's 'The Hound of Heaven.' " Justice Frankfurter's reply is essential here:

The phrase has a legal lineage older than Thompson's poetic use of it. In a letter dated March 7, 1909, Mr. Justice Holmes wrote his friend Sir Frederick Pollock [in a lynching case] "we had to take steps to deal with the contempt of our authority . . . which we have done in your Chancery's delightful phrase, with all deliberate speed."[8]. . . Again, in his opinion in *Virginia* vs. *West Virginia* 222 U. S. 17, 20, he stated "in the language of the English Chancery, with all deliberate speed."

I, too, am an admirer of Francis Thompson, and therefore wonder whether his use of an old Chancery phrase is one of those strangely coincidental things that happen[9] or whether, perchance, he saw the phrase somewhere and stored it away for the superb use that he made of it, just as Coleridge utilized materials derived otherwise than from his own mind to produce the magical result of Kubla Khan.

Cordially yours,<br>
Felix Frankfurter.

*Federal Power Commission*, 328 U. S. 152, 188 (dissent); (5) *Sutton* vs. *Leib*, 342 U. S. 402, 411 (dissent). Cf. Mr. Lewis' note in the New York *Times*, September 1, 1958, "Random Notes," p. 27.

[8] *Holmes-Pollock Letters*, ed. M. DeW. Howe (Cambridge, Mass., 1941), I, 151–152.

[9] Thompson's fondness for studied paradox—witness, in the same poem, his phrases, "traitorous trueness . . . loyal deceit" (*Works*, I, 108), might possibly point toward coincidence. So far as I know, he had no particular contacts with law or lawyers.

However this may be, it is time now to turn to the earlier English poet who had familiarly used this striking phrase long before Francis Thompson. And it should be noted at once that this earlier poet, George Gordon, Lord Byron, had lifelong and bitter associations with the Court of Chancery.

In 1806, then eighteen years old, Byron wrote an angry letter to his lawyer, who had apparently threatened action to curb his extravagance and his mounting debts. "The Court of Chancery," he wrote, "may perhaps put in Force your Threat." Then follows a passage which curiously anticipates Dickens' strictures in *Bleak House.* Said Byron:

I had always understood [Chancery] formed a Sanction for legal plunderers to protract the Decision of Justice from year to year, till weary of spoil it at length condescended to give Sentence, but I never yet understood even its unhallowed hands preyed upon the Orphan it was bound to protect.[10]

Thirteen years later, in 1819, John Murray published for Byron the first three cantos of *Don Juan*, and thereby hangs a tale. In the first canto, stanza xxxvii, Chancery once more receives honorable mention. Byron's hero,

> Juan, was sole heir
> To a Chancery suit, and messuages, and lands.

Before Murray could publish to a waiting world the verses about Don Juan's Chancery suit, he received one of Byron's characteristic letters. Dated April 6, 1819, it informed Murray that Byron had finished Canto ii, and that he would "have none of your

---

10 *Byron, Letters and Journals*, ed. R. E. Prothero (New York, 1904), hereafter cited as *Byron, Letters*, I, 98–99; for further outbursts against the law's delays, cf. IV, 162–163, *et passim*. See also *Bleak House*:
"The Lord Chancellor leaned back in his very easy chair . . . all seemed perfectly at their ease, by no means in a hurry . . . while the sickness of hope deferred was raging in so many hearts . . . as if nobody had ever heard that all over England the name in which they were assembled was a bitter jest . . . was held in universal horror, contempt, and indignation. . . . Keep out of Chancery, whatever [you do]." (Chapters XXIV, V)

damned cutting and slashing." Then comes our Supreme Court phrase. Not long since, Byron adds, he had been

> in a state of great exhaustion, attended by such debility of stomach that nothing remained upon it; and I was obliged to reform my "way of life" which was conducting me from the "yellow leaf" to the ground *with all deliberate speed*.[11]

I have quoted above Mr. Freund's statement that Justice Holmes's derivation of this phrase from Chancery practice has been very difficult to verify. In his letter Mr. Freund adds that "meanwhile the search for English [Chancery] instances goes on, and your discovery in Byron is a curiously tantalizing lead . . . [which] deserves to be explored, if possible, into the form of the decree in his Chancery suit." Here Mr. Freund refers to a fact to which I had also called his attention, that in 1813 "a Chancery suit had been started"[12] by Byron's attorneys against the defaulting would-be purchaser of Byron's estate, Newstead Abbey. This suit, however, as I have since learned, was settled out of court, and Byron later sold Newstead to an old schoolmate.[13] I must add what I did not until recently realize: that Byron, even so, was constantly, indeed incessantly, "in Chancery"—from boyhood to the end of his life. A few additional illustrations must suffice.

There was, to be sure, one relatively bright interval, in 1805, when Byron, at seventeen, was at college as a ward in Chancery and actually very much pleased with "the very handsome allowance" of five hundred pounds a year "made from my fortune by the Chancellor." Twelve years later, in 1817, when Byron was in self-imposed exile, he commanded his lawyer to fight what he bitterly described as "the last piece of treachery." This was Lady Byron's ultimately successful endeavor to have their child, Ada (*Childe Harold*'s "Ada, sole daughter of my house and heart"),

---

[11] *Byron, Letters*, IV, 283, 285.
[12] L. A. Marchand, *Byron* (New York, 1957), I, 399.
[13] *Byron, Letters*, II, 162.

made a ward in Chancery—like Ada Clare of *Bleak House*, and the children of Byron's friend, Percy Bysshe Shelley.[14] A couple of years later, in 1819, Byron wrote his publisher that he expected Eldon, the Lord Chancellor, to rule against him in Chancery litigation against infringements upon *Don Juan*—on the ground of its immorality, as the court had ruled against Shelley on the ground of atheism in *Queen Mab*.[15] Again, in 1822, two years before Byron's death, he wrote that he "greatly doubt[ed] the present Chancellor" would "hear . . . fairly any case of mine." Next year, on August 8, 1823, Chancery threw out a suit brought for Byron to suppress a pirated edition of *Don Juan*.[16]

Let us turn, finally, to a collateral question—and to Shakespeare. Though "with all deliberate speed," curiously enough, has not been found in any of the legal phrase books nor in any specific Chancery record, Byron's use of the phrase and his endless philippics against Chancery furnish collateral support to Justice Holmes's derivation. Assuming that the phrase came from Chancery, one may still wonder, however, from the Chancery practice *of what date*? Since Chancery was an established court by the end of the sixteenth century, I, for one, have wondered specifically whether by any chance Shakespeare might have anticipated Byron in using "with all deliberate speed"—the point being that Shakespeare, too, in his own person and as a member of his dramatic company, had had many a rub with old father antic, the law. Did Shakespeare ever write "with all deliberate speed"? The answer is no, and yet perhaps not altogether No. Shakespeare has everything but "with all *deliberate* speed." He speaks—as indeed, according to Ben Jonson, he wrote—of proceeding "with *all speed*,"[17] "*with speed*,"[18] "*with all swift*

---

[14] *Ibid.*, IV, 75–76, 6, 67–68, 259.
[15] *Ibid.*, IV, 380.
[16] *Ibid.*, IV, 147, and *The Law Journal* (London, 1823), I, 239–240.
[17] *I Henry IV* IV.iii.48.
[18] *Hamlet* III.i.177.

*speed,"*[19] *"with all good speed."*[20] Of course "deliberate" is the
important word. Still, perhaps not altogether impertinent to our
inquiry is another Shakespearean passage—clearly a legal passage—in *The Merchant of Venice* (*ca.* 1596). In III.iv.54–56,
just before Portia's man Balthasar goes off to consult for her,
before Shylock's trial, the learned lawyer Dr. Bellario, she urges
her messenger to

> Waste no time in words
> But get thee gone. I shall be there before thee.
>
> *Balthazar.* Madam, I go with all *convenient* speed.

This brings me to a leading question. May not "with all *deliberate* speed" be simply a paradoxical but readily recognizable,
and perhaps fairly early, variant of the older and very familiar
Chancery phrase "with all *convenient* speed"? At any rate, note
the following curious coincidence: (1) this "convenient" phrase,
sometimes with slight variations, recurs in English prose and
verse all the way from Shakespeare and Izaac Walton and Swift
and Pope[21] to Robert Browning ("To that then, with convenient
speed . . . with all speed," *The Ring and the Book* V.116; II.698);
(2) the phrase is also heard, over and over again, on the legal
side of the fence: in the legal phrase books, in a humorous letter
written April 1, 1838 ("with all convenient dispatch") by Abraham Lincoln, and in the recorded decisions of Chancery courts
in England and the United States.[22]

---

19 *Richard II* V.i.54.

20 *Ibid.* I.ii.66. See also below, p. 27 and n. 26.

21 On Walton, see text, immediately below. See also Swift, *Tale of a Tub*
(1704), "it is my earnest Request that" the study of his work "may be entered upon
. . . with all convenient speed"; ed. A. C. Guthkelch and D. Nichol Smith (Oxford,
1958), p. 185. In *The Memoirs of Martinus Scriblerus* (*ca.* 1742, by Swift, Pope,
and others), ed. C. Kerby-Miller (New Haven, 1950), p. 172, see the "Advertise-
ment" at the end of Book 1: "There will be publish'd with all convenient speed,
the Second Book of these Memoirs, Being the Travels of M. Scriblerus." (This second book did not appear.)

22 Professor Freund writes: " 'With all convenient speed' was quite familiar and

Just possibly the thing is not mere coincidence, for I have happened to find one late contemporary of Shakespeare, the Complete Angler, Izaac Walton (1593-1683), who comes tantalizingly close to using both phrases in one and the same document, not many pages apart. In his *Life of Dr. Donne* (1639) Walton observes that when Donne at last made up his mind to take holy orders, the Bishop of London ordained him deacon "with all convenient speed."[23] So also in Walton's *Life of Sir Henry Wotton*: when that distinguished diplomat was appointed Provost of Eton College, he was "made Deacon with all convenient speed."[24] But the interesting thing is that earlier in his *Life of Dr. Donne* Walton had used what sounds almost like a nicely calculated paraphrase of "with all deliberate speed." At the age of twenty, Donne had undertaken a "serious" and reverent "search" into "the body of divinity as then controverted betwixt the reformed and the Roman Church. The cause was weighty, and wilful delays had been inexcusable . . .: he therefore proceeded in this search *with all moderate haste*."[25] If "with all moderate haste" and "with all deliberate speed" are indeed sisters under the skin, then Shakespeare deserves double notice in this brief chronicle of our phrase. For Walton's "with all moderate haste" repeats two familiar passages from *King Lear* and *Hamlet*: (1) Lear's demand that he be told "with all modest haste" why his messenger, Kent, has been put into the stocks, and (2) Horatio's reply to Hamlet's question as to how long the ghost had stayed in the opening scene; i.e., "while one with moderate

---

is still used in Chancery practice in both England and America." He cites Mr. Justice Jackson's decision of 1944 in *Herb* vs. *Pitcairn*, 324 U. S. 117, 128: "These cases are continued for such period as will enable counsel . . . with all convenient speed to apply to the Supreme Court of Illinois. . . ." Two other instances which I have noted date from 1892. See West's *Words and Phrases* (St. Paul, Minn., 1940), XLV, 365, *Olsen* vs. *Hunter-Benn* and *Gill & Fisher* vs. *Browne*. For Lincoln's letter, see Sandburg, *Lincoln*, p. 59.

[23] *Izaac Walton's Lives*, Nelson's Classics (London, n.d.), p. 40. (Cf. n. 25.)
[24] *Ibid.*, p. 116.
[25] *Ibid.*, p. 19 (Cf. n. 23.) My italics.

haste might tell a hundred."[26] (Curiously enough, this phrase reappears in the masterpiece of another world poet who was a special lover of *Hamlet*. In the first Prologue to Goethe's *Faust*, the director of the theater has the last word. A good theater man, he perhaps recalls Shakespeare's observation that the poet's eye glances from heaven to earth, from earth to heaven. At any rate, he invites the player and the poet to

> Let the narrow stage encompass
> the whole vast round of creation
> Range o'er the world *with moderate haste*[27]
> from heaven to hell.)

It is certain that Shakespeare knew the virtue of "convenient," "modest," "moderate," and "sober speed" (*2 Henry IV* IV.iii. 86). "Deliberate," as I have said, is not his adjective here, but he comes very close to it when he makes King John summon his dissentious nobles "with all expedient haste" (*King John* IV. ii.268): expeditiously but not unwisely so; therefore almost necessarily with deliberate haste.

Of course, coincidence has long arms. Even so, not only Shakespeare but also Izaac Walton deserves another word here. His reiteration of the familiar Chancery phrase "with all convenient speed" within a few pages of "with all moderate haste," sounds as though Walton—who seems to have been not altogether remote from the law[28]—might have been thinking first and last

---

[26] *Hamlet* I.ii.238; *King Lear* II.iv.25.

[27] Perhaps I should have translated, instead, "with all deliberate speed"? (Later: I find that Bayard Taylor had translated, "And move . . . *deliberately* . . . from Heaven . . . to Hell.") Goethe's original runs as follows:
> So schreitet in dem engen Bretterhaus
> Den ganzen Kreis der Schoepfung aus
> Und wandelt *mit bedaecht'ger Schnelle*
> Vom Himmel durch die Welt zur Hoelle.

*Goethes Faust*, ed. Erich Trunz (Hamburg, Germany, 1949), p. 15.

[28] Certainly his friend Donne was deeply versed therein.

of one and the same legal commonplace and its antithetical or
paradoxical corollary. Though Walton tried his hand at versify-
ing now and then, he was certainly neither a Lord Byron nor a
lawyer. Little is known of his education. But it is known, or
knowable, that in his will, written by himself in 1683, he speaks
of "the extreme crewelty of the law of this nation," and that in
at least three places in *The Complete Angler* he pays somewhat
left-handed compliments to the gentlemen of the bar. He mentions, for example, a man of "plentiful estate" whose "many
law-suits . . . damped his mirth"; another "poor rich" man whose
"purse-proud law-suit lasted during the life of" him; and, finally,
those "harmless" men, "the primitive Christians," who were "as
most Anglers are, quiet men and followers of peace; men that
were so simply wise as not to sell their consciences to buy riches
. . . such simple men as lived in those times when there were
fewer lawyers."[29]

## II

Earlier in this book[30] I have touched upon some of the causes
and effects of the grave troubles which continued to afflict our
country in connection with, if not solely in consequence of, the
decision to integrate the public schools with all deliberate speed.
The present supplement to my earlier findings concerning the
background of the phrase has grown out of two continuing in-
quiries: (1) to see what, if any, further source of the phrase
might be traced back to Shakespeare's lifetime, and, (2) to look
for evidence of its literal recurrence earlier than the Byron passage and, as legal scholars have hoped, for a specific link with
the actual parlance of eighteenth-century courts of law. My new
findings especially concern (1) Sir Edward Coke (1552–1634),

[29] *The Complete Angler*, Everyman edition, pp. xx, and (The Fourth Day) 176,
(The Fifth Day) 207, (The First Day) 13.
[30] Chapter I, pp. 11–13.

Queen Elizabeth's famous attorney-general, Francis Bacon's life-long rival, and James I's chief justice; (2) a great admirer[31] of Lord Coke, also a lawyer, clerk of an important Scottish court, and master of the king's English: Sir Walter Scott (1771–1832).

Sir Edward Coke, in the English preface to Part 8 of his *Reports*, written and published in "the 6oth Year of my Age"[32] (1611), sets forth with unmistakable clarity the principle if not the exact wording of our Supreme Court phrase—the essential balance between *deliberation* (to assure ripeness of judgment) and *speed* (to avoid the injustice of what Hamlet calls "the law's delays"). "With all deliberate speed" is implicit in Lord Coke's dictum: "Many Times in *Deliberations* Judgments grow to ripeness, but in *over-hasty* Process never." This qualifies his immediately preceding sentence, in which he insists upon reasonable *speed*: "We that are Judges of the Realm have resolv'd to *cut off all* superfluous and *unjust Delays*."[33] (My italics.)

The exact phrase "with all deliberate speed" I am now able to trace back a few years before Byron, and, by its context, to the eighteenth-century courts of law to which Professor Freund held it belonged, though at last report he had not heard of an actual instance of its use in the pertinent documents of the time. I have found the phrase in Sir Walter Scott's *Rob Roy* (1817),[34] but its *eighteenth*-century pertinence is clear. The facts are that Scott was admitted to the bar in 1792, became deputy sheriff of Selkirkshire before the end of the century, and was less active as a legal practitioner after the turn of the century as his literary activities multiplied, and that in *Rob Roy* he specifically applies the phrase to legal practices current, as he says,

31 See Scott's *Rob Roy*, *The Waverley Novels* (Edinburgh, 1860), VII, 225, Chapter 8: "Sir Edward Coke wisely saith," etc.

32 I quote from the Savoy edition (London, 1738), of the *Reports*, Part 8, p. xxxiii. The date of the Harvard Law School copy of the first edition is 1611.

33 *Ibid.*, p. xxix (Signature A III recto in Harvard's first edition).

34 For a lead in this connection, I am indebted to a former graduate student and colleague of mine, Mrs. Kathleen S. Feerick.

at the time of "the great rebellion which agitated Britain in the year 1715."[35] At this point of the story, the narrator, Francis Osbaldistone, had recovered most of the valuable papers stolen by the villain, his cousin. Here is the passage:

the most valuable part of the papers . . . had been recovered. For that portion which . . . had [been] converted into cash and expended . . . on political intrigues, there was no mode of recovering it but by a suit at law, which was forthwith commenced and proceeded, as our law-agents assured us, *with all deliberate speed.*[36]

*Rob Roy*, incidentally, has no little to say of magistrates and law clerks, including some sharpsters masquerading as law clerks who make plentiful use of law-phrases in and out of book.[37]

Coincidence has long arms, but poets have long memories. All good writers—journalists, novelists, judges,[38] poets—cherish winged words, memorable phrases. That is one reason why

[35] *Rob Roy, Waverley Novels*, VIII, 340, Chapter 37. Rob Roy himself died in 1738.

[36] *Ibid.*, VIII, 337, Chapter 36.

[37] *Ibid.*, VII, 214, 222, 225, 231, Chapters 7 and 8.

[38] While these pages were being revised for the press, this country was saddened by news of the death of Justice Felix Frankfurter. In its page-long tribute, the New York *Times* of February 23, 1965, discussed the part the distinguished judge played in the 1954 decision, as follows:

"There is reason to believe that the court could not have reached that decision unanimously—and perhaps not at all—if the justices had thought the result had to be immediate, total desegregation. The decisive formula was the one permitting implementation of the decision 'with all deliberate speed' and in that formula the hand of Justice Frankfurter was evident. *The very phrase was his*—used in at least five opinions before the school case." Editorially, on February 24, the *Times* added: "Nor was it an accident that he contributed the phrase 'with all deliberate speed'—with its nicely balanced double imperative—to the Supreme Court's desegregation decision."

As regards the phrase I have italicized, we have seen that Justice Frankfurter inherited it from Justice Holmes and a long line of distinguished forebears in law and letters. Even so, Justice Frankfurter certainly cherished the phrase. As proof, as a possible indication that some of his colleagues may have been interested, and

poets, as Shelley says, are the unacknowledged legislators of mankind. They pick up great phrases as small boys pick up marbles and birds' eggs. But they keep the great phrases alive, the phrases which sometimes, in the utterance, shake the world.

---

as a generous document of the man himself, I print a letter sent me by Justice Frankfurter. Its envelope, above the inscription "Supreme Court of the United States," is marked " F. F."

Supreme Court of the United States<br>Washington, D. C.

CHAMBERS OF
JUSTICE FELIX FRANKFURTER

December 13, 1960

My dear Professor Thaler:

Unlike Disraeli, I have the bad habit of not acknowledging publications that come to me until I have had a chance to read them, and I have only now got around to your piece on "with all deliberate speed." It is a fascinating essay and a real contribution to the history of the phrase. I deem it so illuminating that I should like to share it, without sending it around from man to man, with a half dozen of my friends. I wonder if you can spare me that number of off-prints.

With appreciation,

Sincerely yours,

[Signed]    Felix Frankfurter

# PART TWO

# Behind the Scenes
## Dramatic Technique, Old and New

# 5

## Behind the Scenes

### Shakespeare's Off-Stage Characters and "Mutes"

I

IN THE 1963 STRATFORD, Ontario, Shakespeare Festival's production of *The Comedy of Errors*, the director gave to Nell, the earthily rotund kitchen wench, a tremendously effective one-word speech which Shakespeare himself had neglected to write. By mistaken identity, though poor Dromio of Syracuse does not realize this until later, she "claims" him: she "haunts me . . . *will* have me" (III.ii.82–145), says Dromio. On stage the Ontario director made her signalize her claim by a reverberating "D - R - R - O - M - I - O!" shouted from the housetop and ringing through the theater. A good conductor does not misinterpret his score. This director did no violence to the poet, even though in his script poor "wondrous fat" Nell is, strictly speaking, a mute. Shakespeare gives her not a word. Is she, however, strictly an off-stage character?[1]

Before answering, let us note that Shakespeare employs mutes and/or off-stage characters in every one of his plays. Criticism has scarcely noticed this,[2] nor the more important fact that he

---

[1] As R. A. Foakes puts it: "Nell, the unseen 'kitchen wench' . . . never appears on stage." New Arden *Comedy of Errors* (Cambridge, Mass., 1962), pp. xxv, 56.

[2] Scattered notes and suggestions touching on the subject appear in Sir A. Quiller-Couch's *Shakespeare's Workmanship* (New York, 1917), pp. 96, 101, 104; W. J. Lawrence, *Shakespeare's Workshop* (Boston, 1928), pp. 39 ff.; H. Dugdale Sykes, *Sidelights on Elizabethan Drama* (London, 1924), p. 10; E. H. Wright, *The*

usually employs these characters for more or less definitely recognizable dramatic purposes. Most of the occasional exceptions, intrusive or redundant mutes or off-stagers, are surplusage which the poet took no time or pains to remove. The many-sorted others serve useful purposes as varied as rainbow colors or April weather. Some are solidly mute on stage, some equally so off stage, but by no means all off-stage characters are mute. Some, indeed, are fluent, loquacious, eloquent, not only while their lamp still glows but at the very moment of death. One of these is Antony's first wife, "shrill-tongu'd Fulvia" ("There's a great spirit gone . . . *Can* Fulvia die?") who, according to Cleopatra, "scolds" (off stage) to her last breath (I.i.32, ii.122–126, iii.58). Another is Falstaff in *Henry V*, who dies off stage with the thrice-invoked name of God on his lips. Similarly, in the other histories and in the Roman plays, many a personage originally important on stage, by a sort of memorial reconstruction becomes an off-stager. Examples are dead Brutus and Cassius in *Antony and Cleopatra*, Hotspur in *2 Henry IV*, and Richard II ("that sweet, lovely rose") in *1 Henry IV*. Occasionally the procedure is reversed: Prince Hal's very first appearance is that of an off-stager in *Richard II* (V.iii). Most unforgettable and most eloquent of them all, of course, is Falstaff's final exit, but we shall hear later of others speaking with almost equal eloquence though long since dead. One or two instances must suffice for the moment.

First of all, in *All's Well That Ends Well*, the king's affectionate remembrance of Bertram's father:

> your good father. . . .
> Would I were with him! He would always say—
> Methinks I hear him now; his plausive words
> He scatter'd not in ears, but grafted them

---

*Authorship of Timon of Athens* (New York, 1910), pp. 2, 33, n. 2; Alfred Harbage, "Shakespeare and the Myth of Perfection," *Shakespeare Quarterly*, XV (1964), 4–5; and in my *Shakspere's Silences* (Cambridge, 1929), especially p. 36, which cites St. John Ervine concerning Romeo's Rosaline.

> To grow there and to bear— "Let me not live"—
> Thus his good melancholy oft began,
> On the catastrophe and heel of pastime
> When it was out— "Let me not live," quoth he,
> "After my flame lacks oil, to be the snuff
> Of younger spirits, whose apprehensive senses
> All but new things disdain . . ." (I.ii.31, 52–61)

Another memorable off-stager—this one very much alive—is angrily quoted by Hotspur, who reports to King Henry IV "the bald, unjointed chat" of the perfumed courtier who nonchalantly demanded Hotspur's prisoners on the battlefield of Shrewsbury:

> And as the soldiers bore dead bodies by
> He call'd them untaught knaves, unmannerly,
> To bring a slovenly unhandsome corse
> Betwixt the wind and his nobility.
> With many holiday and lady terms
> He question'd me. . . .
>        and but for these vile guns
> He would himself have been a soldier.
>           (*1 Henry IV*, I.iii.42–47, 63–64)

Small wonder that Hotspur answered "neglectingly"!

To return to Dromio's Nell: is she not only a mute but also an off-stager? Observe once more that not all mutes are equally mute, nor are all off-stagers equally off stage. Some belong unmistakably and entirely to both categories. For example, both that "honest man," Dame Quickly's husband in *1 Henry IV* (III.iii.108, 65) and the monk who poisons King John (*King John* V.vi.23) are altogether mute and off stage. Dighton and Forrest smother, off stage at Richard III's behest, the little princes in the Tower, but these two murderers, far from mute, are eloquently and literally quoted at their abominable task:

> "Lo, thus," quoth Dighton, "lay the gentle babes."
> "Thus, thus," quoth Forrest, "girdling one another
> Within their alabaster innocent arms. . . ." (*Richard III* IV.iii.9–11)

And some near-mutes not unimportant in their respective plays are probably more or less audible after all. Shakespeare gives no specific utterance[3] to Launce's sour-natured but irresistible dog Crab in *The Two Gentlemen of Verona* (II.iii; IV.iv), but dogs can bark; and no speech to the little Princess Elizabeth at her baptism in *King Henry VIII* (V.v), but babes can cry! Nor are off-stagers all of a kind. No one can fail to recognize the contribution to the opening action of *Macbeth* of such off-stage persons as the Thane of Cawdor and King Sweno of Norway and the merciless Macdonald, nor that of the monk-poisoner mentioned above to the catastrophe of *King John*. More important, however, in that play's unlisted *dramatis personae* is the real presence of King John's brother, Queen Eleanor's son, the father of Faulconbridge, in whose face and tongue and form the other two at once find "perfect Richard" (I.i.90), that is to say, Richard "Coeur-de-lion," "The very spirit of Plantagenet" (I.i.85, 167).

Did Shakespeare, then, cast Dromio's Nell as an off-stager? I think he meant her to be, like a good child, seen if not heard. What good showman could fail to let such a one be seen at full length and breadth? Seen if not heard also may be a quite differently proportioned but not necessarily altogether off-stage character in *A Midsummer Night's Dream*—the "lovely boy stolen from an Indian king" whom jealous Oberon finally filched from poor Titania. Or, if this young charmer is not actually seen on stage, we may safely guess that another is much in evidence. I mean old Capulet's fair niece in *Romeo and Juliet*, that "pale, hard-hearted wench, that Rosaline" (II.iv.4), who, having smilingly rebuffed young Romeo's amorous posturing, is expressly invited to the Capulet's feast and is all but certain to shine there among other "earth-treading stars," the most "admired beauties of Verona" (I.ii.25, 88). Romeo's Rosaline[4] and Banquo's ghost,

---

[3] But plenty of it, by way of burlesque, to stolid creatures such as Wall and Moonshine in *A Midsummer Night's Dream*!

[4] Cf. the last citation in note 2, above.

among others, are notable Shakespearean mutes who do not qualify as off-stagers. It is with those who do so qualify, and with the many parts they play, that I am chiefly concerned.

They are of many sorts. Thus, they include not only those off-stage persons who are, relatively speaking, nearby—almost, as it were, in the wings. Such, for example, are Lady Macduff's murdered children (*Macbeth* IV.iii.216; ii). Macduff asks, "*All my pretty ones? Did you say all?*"— that is to say, all off stage but one small boy, who was not mercifully hidden there from the murderers. Less moving than this off-stage glimpse of Macduff's pretty ones, but not altogether unlike it, is that of Cleopatra's children, "Caesarion . . . Together with my brave Egyptians all" (III.xiii.162, 164), that is to say, "all the unlawful issue" (III.vi.7) of Cleopatra and her Antony. One of these little ones she remembers poignantly at the last, when she applies the asp to her breast:

> Peace, peace!
> Dost thou not see my baby at my breast
> That sucks the nurse asleep? (V.ii.311–313)

Relatively nearby, again, is the off-stage friar whose untimely quarantine kept Friar Laurence's message from reaching Romeo exiled in Mantua. (This intended companion to Friar John in his mission to Mantua is barely mentioned in the play [V.ii.4] but he is certainly not unimportant as an agent in the plot. Under-standably, therefore, a good movie version of the play recently showed both priests quarantined *on* stage.)

Included also among our off-stagers are some far away and long ago. Some are mere shadows but well-beloved, like Euriphile, dead foster-mother of the stolen princes in *Cymbeline*. Others like her are Hamlet's father as Hamlet sees him in his mind's eye, and Portia's father, who had planned the casket lottery of *The Merchant of Venice*, and Viola's, who had, in her hearing, spoken well of the noble duke, Orsino. In *Twelfth Night* also, we hear of Olivia's too-dearly mourned brother; and, in *Measure for Measure*, of Frederick, the great soldier lost at sea, well-beloved brother of Mariana of the moated grange (III. ii.215–232). Still others drop out of the shadows, if only for a great moment, by virtue of a long-remembered but almost forgotten name (Coriolanus, battle-weary—in I.ix.81–90—forgetting the name of his "poor host" whom he wants to save); or because of an unforgotten face or a memorable phrase (Hamlet's "Alas, poor Yorick"—poor Yorick whom young Hamlet loved and the Gravedigger did not); or because of the haunting cadence of an old song—such as poor Barbara, maid to Desdemona's mother, had sung before her death:

> She was in love [Desdemona recalls] and he she lov'd prov'd mad
> And did forsake her. She had a song of "Willow."
> An old thing 'twas; but it express'd her fortune
> And she died singing it.                     (*Othello*, IV.iii.27–30)

Others again are eloquently silent, but no less eloquently alive for purposes of the drama. Notable among these silent offstagers are Lady Macbeth's dead father (had Duncan "not resembled/My father as he slept, I had done't") and the babe she had loved, who had taught her that it is sweet to be a mother (II.ii.13; I.vii.55). Back to the living also comes Shylock's dead wife, Leah, whose ring Jessica callously threw away for a monkey. It was his turquoise: "I had it of Leah when I was a bachelor." My later summary will show that the true touchstone for all these off-stage persons or effects, the common denominator of their purpose, is their contribution, however brief, to characterization, or plot, or to the tone-color and setting of the play.

Meanwhile, I shall not labor the point that their very brevity is indeed the soul of their artistry. By virtue of their remarkable dramatic economy much is said in little, if not in silence.[5] For

---

[5] The subject is discussed in my study mentioned in note 2.

example, by the stroke of genius already noted, Shakespeare spot-
lights one small boy in the scene with his mother, Lady Macduff.
No Pied Piper caravan of little children clutters this scene, yet
all Macduff's "pretty ones" are given—if not restored to—essential life by his anguished outcry. It exemplifies Marlowe's
principle, "Infinite riches in a little room," and Lessing's, that
a dramatist may sometimes be "greater in what he does not say
than in what he says."[6]

## II

After so many words of mine, hereafter in this chapter I shall,
as a rule, trust Shakespeare's mutes to speak for themselves. All-
inclusive enumeration, not to say discussion, of them is imprac-
ticable and unnecessary. Instead, I shall attempt a somewhat
closer analysis of the nature and dramatic functions of Shakespeare's off-stagers as such, but representative rather than

[6] Cited by Koester, *Shakespeare Jahrbuch*, I, 146; cf. Furness, Variorum *Macbeth*, p. 79. Professor A. C. Sprague's recent article, "A *Macbeth* of Few Words"
(*All These To Teach*, Essays in honor of C. A. Robertson, Gainesville, Florida,
1965, pp. 80–101), is delightfully pertinent here. It reprints a rare "Shakespearean
acting version amusing in itself and typical of its time" (p. 82). On August 31,
1809, "*Macbeth*, a Ballet of Music and Action," i.e., "a *burletta*," was presented
in London, at the Royal Circus (the Surrey), under Elliston's management. I
quote from "Act II, Scene vi" of this version, set in "a room in Macduff's castle."

"Enter Lady Macduff and *her two children* [my italics] . . . Rosse enters
. . . announces Macduff's flight. . . .
*The Murderers enter*
*L. Macd.* O, save me from these fierce and cruel men,
Unless that by their looks my tender babes are slain.
The Murderers each of them savagely seize one of the children, when Lady
Macduff gets between them. . . .
*L. Macd.* Save them. . . .
[*The Murderers refuse her.*]
Each of the murderers seize a child and run off with them, Lady Macduff
following.
[*They are supposed to be murdered, but very properly
off the stage.*]"

broadly inclusive examples must suffice. As specific bases for my analysis I shall summarize outstanding off-stage persons and/ or their doings in four plays approximately representative of Shakespeare's early, middle, later, and last work, *Romeo and Juliet*, *The Merchant of Venice*, *Othello*, and *The Tempest*.

1. *Romeo and Juliet.*—Rosaline, obviously a tantalizingly silent but charming person—on stage *and* off—in her own right, though soon eclipsed by Juliet, serves the double purpose of starting the love story and helping to characterize Romeo before he grows up. With her at the Capulets' feast appear many mute but colorful stage-fillers: kinfolk and friends named in the invitation read by Romeo, plus masquers, musicians, and servants galore, including some off-stagers known to us only by their appropriate names, Susan Grindstone, Potpan, Anthony, and the rest (I.v.11). Quite different in kind but not without matching inadvertence elsewhere in the plays are certain—or, rather, many *un*certainly pluralized—off-stage figures hastily introduced and soon forgotten. Capulet's dead children, mentioned by him to Juliet's wooer, Paris—"The earth hath swallow'd all my hopes but she" (I.ii.14)—are swallowed up, rather, in a limbo of half-begotten characters; witness Capulet's later remark, "Wife, we scarce thought us blest/That God had lent us but this only child" (III.v.165–166). Far from any such limbo, however, are a couple of other off-stage characters whose memories are near and dear to Juliet's Nurse. One is her dead daughter, Susan. Juliet (says the Nurse)

> and she (God rest all Christian souls!)
> Were of an age. Well, Susan is with God;
> She was too good for me.

Nearer still to mother earth and to the Nurse, and as racy as herself, was her jolly husband: "my husband (God be with his soul! 'A was a merry man)." He was the merry soul who had picked up little three-year-old Juliet when she tumbled down and jested thrice over about her falls to come (I.iii.18–57).

2. *The Merchant of Venice.*—I have previously mentioned two off-stage persons in this play who measurably contribute to plot and characterization, respectively: Portia's father, whose good inspiration at his death led him to devise the casket lottery happily won by Bassanio; and Shylock's Leah, who gave her betrothed the ring with which her Jessica absconded. Here also are the usual background figures: musicians, servants, some mutes or near-mutes, some on stage and some off—including, among the latter, some half-dozen of Portia's early suitors (the Neapolitan, the County Palatine, the Frenchman, young Falconbridge of England, and the rest) who gave up the quest for the golden fleece (I.ii.42–115). Off-stagers of minor importance supply a comic touch or two to the role of Launcelot Gobbo: the Negro woman, "The Moor" who "is with child by" him, and Margery—"Margery, indeed"—wife to his true-begotten father, sand-blind old Gobbo (II.ii.37, 96). More important is Portia's off-stage cousin, the learned Dr. Bellario, whose "notes and garments" and legal advice sent to her from Padua help her to win her case against Shylock. Curiously enough, the last scene of the play introduces a superfluous off-stage person. "Who comes with" Portia back to Belmont? Lorenzo asks. The Messenger replies, "None but a holy hermit and her maid" (line 32), but of this holy hermit, as Dr. Johnson and Sir Arthur Quiller-Couch[7] have noted, "nothing is seen or heard afterwards."

3. *Othello.*—Above, I have mentioned the dying song of poor Barbara, the Willow song which Desdemona sings with some

---

[7] Quiller-Couch, p. 96, quotes Dr. Johnson: "The Poet had first planned the fable some other way; and inadvertently, when he changed his scheme, retained something of the original design." But perhaps this shadowy hermit harks back to Portia's original "vow"—explained to Lorenzo in III.iv.28—"to live in prayer and meditation" in a nearby monastery until her husband's return? Another "old religious man" turns up off stage in the last scene of *As You Like It* (line 166) but he is useful. Upon meeting him in Arden, Duke Frederick is "converted" (cf. Quiller-Couch, p. 101).

foreboding ("Mine eyes do itch. Doth that bode weeping?") that it may be her own swan song. Earlier in this play there appear several more off-stagers who doubtless belong with others of their ilk who are theatrical excess baggage, people of whom Shakespeare may have intended to make something when he started a play, only to drop them or perhaps to forget them, without removing the *corpora delictorum*. In spite of much small print in the Variorum, this is the best explanation of Iago's venomous opening allusion to Cassio's—as one gathers later—non-existent wife: "a fellow almost damn'd in a fair wife" (I.i.21). Surplus persons also mentioned early in the play are two others not heard from again: one "Signior Angelo" who sends the Duke an erroneous message about a supposed Turkish expedition against Rhodes (I.iii.16), and another who seems momentarily in urgent demand—one never learns why—when Cyprus, a trouble spot then as now, proves to be the real Turkish objective:

> *Duke.* 'Tis certain then for Cyprus.
> Marcus Luccicos, is not he in town?
> *1 Sen.* He's now in Florence.
> *Duke.* Write from us to him; post-post-haste
>     dispatch. (I.iii.43–46)

Not surplus are two other off-stagers, though they come in for but passing notice: Othello's mother and father and their handkerchief. "That handkerchief," Othello first tells his wife, "Did an Egyptian to my mother give," as a talisman to hold her husband's love, whereas "To lose't or give't away were . . . perdition." And this, "she, dying, gave" her son for his wife (III.iv.55–68). Later, Othello gives a different account, almost the converse of Shylock's remark about Leah's ring: that "pledge of love" which he and his father "so lov'd"

> I saw . . . in [Cassio's] hand.
> It was a handkerchief, an antique token
> My father gave my mother. (V.ii.49, 214–217)

Whoever the first giver, the handkerchief ironically becomes the token of the unbroken mutual love of Othello's parents.

4. *The Tempest.*—Early in this play, as in *Othello*, another surplus off-stager is mentioned, this time in Ferdinand's report to Miranda.

> Myself am Naples,
> Who with mine eyes . . . beheld
> The King my father wrack'd.
> *Mira.*                    Alack, for mercy!
> *Fer.* Yes, faith, and all his lords, the Duke of Milan
> *And his brave son* being twain. (I.ii.434–438)

But this son of the usurping duke, as the commentators have observed, is given no other notice whatsoever. This is not true of another princely off-stager, the King of Naples' daughter Claribel, whose marriage to the King of Tunis brought all the noble voyagers to their Tempest. Still another royal personage is hidden in the early shadows of the play. One would have been glad to see or hear more of her, but the passing mention is grateful and affectionate. It occurs in Prospero's opening talk to Miranda, about their past and present. When he tells her that her father was Duke of Milan, she asks, "Sir, are not you my father?" He replies,

> Thy mother was a piece of virtue, and
> She said thou wast my daughter,

his "only heir" (I.ii.55–57). Of Miranda's mother, as of Cordelia's (*Lear*, IV.iii.36) we hear too little, presumably because Shakespeare chose to give the center of the stage to Lear and to Prospero. After all, however, perhaps the most notable off-stage character in *The Tempest* is still another mother. She is, of course, Caliban's mother, the foul witch Sycorax, she who had pegged Ariel, Fradubio-like, into a cloven pine for a dozen years. She is well remembered in her son's curses ("As wicked dew as e'er my mother brush'd/With raven's feather . . . Drop on you both"), in his half-allegiance to her god, Setebos, and in the bitter resentment occasioned by the loss of his island, her bequest (I.ii.258–373).

## III

By way of summing up the major functions of Shakespeare's off-stagers, in plot-making and characterization, I shall supplement the materials above by some notable illustrations from other plays. First, however, a concluding note on his mutes, and then another on those curious nondescripts, his "surplus" characters.

As already noted, some of the off-stage mutes, such as Euriphile in *Cymbeline*, are shadowy creatures. Others—for example, illegitimate Edmund's mother in *King Lear* ("yet was his mother fair, there was good sport at his making")—come startlingly alive in themselves or in relation to those who belong to them. "The whoreson must be acknowledged," says his father, the Earl of Gloucester, who learns, later, that the just gods scourge mortals for their "pleasant vices" (I.i.23; V.iii.170). Perhaps more obviously or directly useful are the on-stage mutes. Individually, these achieve varied effects: fat Nell's broad humor, Rosaline's smiling comic sophistication, the terror of Banquo's silent ghost at Macbeth's banquet. Groups of mutes or near-mutes often serve as dynamic or pictorial or spectacular stage-fillers. Witness the numerous and lively comic servants "Maud, Bridget, Marian, Cisley, Gillian, Ginn" in *The Comedy of Errors* (III.i.31); Petruchio's "loggerheaded grooms" in *The Taming of the Shrew* (IV.i.128–140): all ragged but "Adam, Ralph and Gregory," with Gabriel's "pumps unpink'd," "Peter's hat" faded, "Walter's dagger" missing; and their fellows in *Romeo and Juliet*. Or, for more martial-chivalric effects, there are suggestions of more or less off-stage but picturesque groupings of Lear's hundred knights returning from the chase

(I.iv), and, in *Henry V* (III.v.40; IV.viii.97), the long roster of great French noblemen before and after Agincourt. Also mute and more or less off stage are the revels of two other groups, the unnamed fellows of Peaseblossom and Mustardseed in *A Midsummer Night's Dream*, and of Ariel's fellows, Prospero's meaner ministers in *The Tempest*. These help to bring fairy lands and magic wonder to the stage. (Not unrelated to these effects are the dark revels of the witches in *Macbeth*. Of course the three weird sisters, however fantastical, are "inhabitants of the earth" on stage. "Pale Hecate" herself, however, is twice alluded to by Shakespeare—in II.i.52 and III.ii.41—only as an off-stage figure whose "offerings . . . Witchcraft celebrates" and whose "summons/The shard-borne beetle" answers. It is generally agreed that the portions of the two scenes of the surviving text in which she appears on stage—III.v and IV.i.39–43—are not the work of Shakespeare but of Middleton.)

The limbo of the half-begotten in which dwell Capulet's surplus children in *Romeo and Juliet*, Cassio's wife in *Othello*, and Milan's brave son in *The Tempest*, has a not inconsiderable population. For readily understandable reasons, loose ends are not infrequent in Shakespeare's plays, and surplus off-stagers occasionally crowd the beginning or the middle. I shall cite half a dozen supplementary examples.

1. An early play, *The Two Gentlemen of Verona*, has two Sir Eglamours. One is Silvia's squire of dames, who rather awkwardly runs out of the play when the outlaws beset her in the forest (V.iii.7); the other, quite unnecessarily of the same name,[8] is "the fair Sir Eglamour . . . a knight well-spoken" of by Julia's waiting woman in her early account of her lady's suitors (I.ii.9).

---

[8] There are other instances in the plays of careless duplication of names: two Jaqueses in *As You Like It*, two Balthasars in *The Merchant of Venice* (III.iv.45; IV.i.154), and a quite expendable Clauidio side by side with King Claudius in *Hamlet* (IV.vii.38–40).

In the first act, also, Julia's "father stays" dinner for her (ii.131), only to be forgotten by the end of the second act, when Julia, pursuing false fleeting Proteus, leaves "all that is mine . . . My goods, my lands, my reputation" to her maid's "dispose" (vii.86–87) instead of to her father.

2. Petruchio, arriving home for his shrewish-wife taming, at once introduces a surplus character or two—one canine and one cousin—never again mentioned:

> Where's my spaniel Troilus? Sirrah, get you hence
> And bid my cousin Ferdinand come hither. [*Exit Servant*]
> One, Kate, that you must kiss and be acquainted with.
> (IV.i.153–155)

3. In *2 Henry IV* (I.ii.269) there is an intrusive—or at least misnamed[9]—off-stager: "old Mistress *Ursula*," whom Falstaff has "weekly sworn to marry." She can hardly be any other than the same candidate for this honor who turns up in the next act as the hostess he "did . . . swear . . . to marry" (II.i.92–112)—the authentic Mrs. Quickly of all the Falstaff plays: "*Nell* Quickly," later wife to Ancient Pistol (*Henry V* II.i.20).

4. *Much Ado About Nothing* has at least three characters in excess. The first is Hero's mother, "Innogen his [Leonato's] wife" of the Folios' opening stage direction. Next comes Claudio's "uncle here in Messina" who is reported to have broken "out into tears" of joy for his nephew's success but then becomes another first-act-first-scene casualty (lines 18–29). Finally, at the very beginning of the first act's second scene, Antonio's son, according to his father, is busy providing music off stage, but this young man is utterly lost, or at least disinherited, by the last act, when Hero is described as the only "heir to both" her father and Antonio (V.i.299).

5. *All's Well That Ends Well*, like *Much Ado*, has one char-

---

[9] See note 8, but cf. M. A. Shaaber, New Variorum edition, *2 Henry IV*, pp. 85–86.

acter who appears in a stage direction but says and does nothing in the play: one Violenta in III.v.[10] Unlike her and her kind, Lafeu's daughter, "fair Maudlin" (V.iii.68)—though she too is not only silent but never appears on the stage—is expressly invented for plot purposes to test once more Bertram's willingness to marry at the king's behest. When Helena thereupon turns up alive, nothing more is heard or said of fair Maudlin.[11]

6. *Measure for Measure*, like *Hamlet*, has a useful off-stage pirate. We shall meet him again shortly. But this play gives almost the whole of a short scene, upon the return of the fantastical Duke, to five friends of his (Flavius, Valentinus, Rowland, Crassus, and Varrius), not one of whom says or does anything, and only the last of whom is so much as seen for a moment (IV.v). These are not indispensable men![12]

Why these extras, this surplusage? First, because Shakespeare obviously worked with almost unbelievable speed: because his mind worked that way (like Hamlet's: "Ere I could make a prologue to my brains, They had begun the play"), and because of the Elizabethans' insatiable appetite for new plays, at advanced prices of admission. In his *Newes From Hell*, 1607, Thomas Dekker had observed that "it was a Comedy to see what a crowding, as if it had been at a new Play, there was vpon the *Acherontique* Strond." Dekker does not say whether the Acherontic crowd had to pay double the usual price of admission, but the patrons of the Globe and those of the Henslowe theaters almost certainly had to when a new play was on for a first per-

<hr>

10 Cf. W. A. Neilson and Charles J. Hill, New Cambridge edition, *Shakespeare, Complete Plays* (Boston, 1942), p. 354, and W. J. Lawrence, pp. 40–45. Lawrence categorically—but erroneously, I think—dismisses Violenta (and, with her, Petruchio's cousin Ferdinand, and Hero's mother, and Milan's son in *The Tempest*) as "an ugly oversight" not of Shakespeare's but of some "remorseless . . . play-patcher" or "reviser."

11 Cf. *Shakspere's Silences*, pp. 32, 56, 85.

12 Similarly, the off-stage Countess of Richmond, in *Richard III* (I.iii.20–29), might well have been left out of the play.

formance.[13] At any rate, Shakespeare the actor-producer-play-wright wrote an average of almost two memorable plays a year (possibly, for example, such nearby masterpieces as *A Midsummer Night's Dream* and *Romeo and Juliet*, or *The Merchant of Venice* and *Henry V*) during his actively productive period of about twenty years (*ca.* 1592–1612). Understandably, therefore, he might not bother to iron out minor inconsistencies which would not matter anyhow until long after his time, when the technique of the well-made play was invented. Shakespeare's greatest gift was his glorious balance of powers: his sure instinct, as noted above, for artistic economy, *and* his boundless fertility. What wonder that some seed fell on stony ground?

As for Ragozine, *Measure for Measure*'s off-stage pirate, he, unlike *Hamlet*'s pirates, is dead; but, like them, he is useful for the plot. The point is that Shakespeare's off-stage characters serve as plot helpers in all sorts of useful ways and in all the strategic places: in the beginning, the middle, and the end. Thus, the Princess Claribel's marriage starts Prospero's enemies upon their tempestuous voyage; the treacherous Thane of Cawdor, aided and abetted off stage by Macdonald and by Sweno of Norway, starts the gracious Duncan's fall; and old Norway's weakness, early in *Hamlet*, allows Fortinbras to trouble the mind's eye of uneasy Denmark. Again, the King of France, off stage, starts the action against matchless Navarre and his bookmen in *Love's Labour's Lost* by sending his daughter to press a claim not unlike that of Fortinbras, and Portia's father's casket scheme sets up Bassanio's problem at Belmont. The off-stage King of France, just mentioned, conveniently dies just in time to delay for at least a year what might have been the happy ending of *Love's Labour's Lost*; the friars' belated quarantine in *Romeo and Juliet* hastens Romeo's tragic end; and the notorious pirate

[13] Cf. Thaler, *Shakspere to Sheridan* (Cambridge, 1922), pp. 233–234, and Grosart's *Dekker* (London, 1885), II, 118.

Ragozine lives and dies off stage toward the end of *Measure for Measure* (IV.iii.75) in time to let his head substitute for Claudio's. Toward the end also, Portia's cleverness and Dr. Bellario's off-stage counsel defeat Shylock, and in *The Merry Wives of Windsor* the Garter host and an off-stage vicar—not to mention sundry off-stage horse-thieves in the background—manage to achieve the happy ending[14] whereby sweet Anne Page is married to Fenton. As in the beginning and end, so in the middle. Petruchio and his Kate are uproariously married, off stage, in the middle of *The Taming of the Shrew* (III.ii.30–184), by a priest who is irreverently cuffed (off stage, save the mark!) for his pains. And, again and again, off-stage murderers do their bloody work, or try to, in the middle of the action in play after play—such as *Titus Andronicus* (IV.ii.167), *Richard III* (IV. iii), *Macbeth* (IV.iii.4–8), and *Pericles* (IV.i.1).

A good many of Shakespeare's off-stage characters, finally, are like Falstaff, albeit with a difference. They are not only virtuous in themselves but the cause of virtue in others—that is, of life abundant. Mischievously charming or gracious or impudently repellent as one or another may be, such off-stagers as Rosaline and Bertram's father and Hotspur's battlefield courtier are vibrantly alive, each in his own person. In addition, each one also significantly *brings out* someone else: Romeo the would-be lover, Bertram's brash immaturity, Hotspur's virile impatience. Though these off-stage people are of many sorts, they repeatedly shadow forth or, at times, outline more or less sharply, certain naturally recurring persons or relationships: mothers and fathers, husbands and wives, brothers and sisters, friends or lovers. To start with the last of these—not the least amusing though perhaps least important—one thinks, for example, of Touchstone "in love" with his off-stage Jane Smile (*As You Like It* II.iv.45), of Launce's anonymous off-stage milkmaid in *The*

---

[14] Cf. note 7 on the ending of *As You Like It*.

*Two Gentlemen* (III.i.268), and Slender's off-stage Alice Short-
cake in *The Merry Wives* (I.i.211). Minor also but not negligible
bits of character sketches, intrinsic and extrinsic, are those which
touch upon the bonds between off-stage fathers and their daughters, such as the two Portias (Cato's daughter, wife to Brutus,
and Bassanio's Portia), Helena's father, the famous physician of
*All's Well* (whom Bertram had all but pushed out of her remembrance), and Viola's father, and Justice Silence and his
daughter Ellen, that "fairest . . . black ousel," and his son William at Oxford who was so burdensome to his father's purse (2
*Henry IV* III.ii.6–12). Again, on the distaff side, there are Miranda's mother and Imogen's—whose diamond ring was Imogen's
treasured parting gift to Posthumus—not to mention, once more,
Othello's mother and father and their handkerchief, or Caliban's
witch-mother Sycorax, or the sainted parents of the somewhat
lily-white Malcolm of *Macbeth* (IV.iii.108–110), or the off-stage
brothers of Olivia and Mariana.

More important, in conclusion, are those incidental strokes
of characterization achieved, as we have seen, by off-stage persons
who bring out what might otherwise have been hidden in some
of the major figures of the plays: Juliet's Nurse as she happily
dramatizes her memory of her daughter and her merry husband;
Lear's Gloucester blissfully unaware of the just gods' coming
judgment while he indulges in unblushing plain talk with Kent
concerning the fair mother of his handsome son, illegitimate
Edmund; Lady Macbeth recalling her dead father and the babe
at her breast; and Shylock remembering his Leah.

# 6

## *Poetic Scene Painting in Shakespeare*

FOREVER YOUNG, like the figures on the Grecian Urn, the theater and dramatic art at their best have also the mellowing grace of ancient wisdom and beauty. Because tradition is a living power in the theater, any valid study of dramatic technique must often look before and after. Take, for example, the opening and the unfolding atmosphere of *The Second Shepherds' Play*, of *Hamlet*, and of *Winterset*. The Wakefield master, Shakespeare, and Maxwell Anderson paint the scene, in verse or prose, as only poets can. "Lord," says the first shepherd, "What these weders ar cold!" and the second and third shepherds agree: what with storms and tempest and hideous "frostys," "rude . . . floodys," and "wyndys and ranys"—"Wo is hym has neuer rest!"[1] *Hamlet*, of course, makes this point in few and memorable opening words. The midnight bell tolls Francisco's welcome relief from guard duty: "For this relief much thanks. 'Tis bitter cold,/ And I am sick at heart." Here, as in *Winterset*, foul deeds of old "rise" swiftly, inexorably, because they are woven into the very texture of the action and the tension of atmosphere. Captive good—heart-sick, unsure, but with growing clarity and force—struggles against captain ill. Rottenness rules in Hamlet's Denmark; "sleep and rot" pervade Manhattan's typhus-loaded river-

[1] J. Q. Adams, *Chief Pre-Shakespearean Dramas*, hereafter cited as JQA (Boston, 1924), pp. 145–147, lines 1, 8, 57–58, 127–128. All quotations from pre-Elizabethan plays are from JQA.

bank bridgehead of misery, crime, and injustice, the "roost of punks and gulls" and gangsters, according to *Winterset*'s opening stage direction and dialogue.[2] Once more, the climate is right: "God, it's cold here" in Act I (last speech); "cold as the tomb of Christ" in the middle of Act II; "fine sleet begins to fall" in I.iii, and "rain still falls" as the last act opens. Indeed, "tough weather" and "icy" cold pierce through to the very end. There the poetic scene painting and the symbolic theme of the play are climaxed in Mio's apostrophe to the "silent powers that make the sleet and dark": "On this longest night, when the winter sets his foot on the threshold . . . to spring . . . let fall some mercy with the rain."[3]

In this chapter I shall have further occasion to touch on the practice of some of Shakespeare's predecessors, fellows, and followers in the art of poetic scene painting, and on some of the critics' observations on the subject. My main concern, however, is to bring together a necessarily limited but sufficiently representative sampling of his own practice to make possible an adequate analysis of the major characteristics—variations, kinds, forms, and purposes—of this element of his dramatic technique. To define my terms by way of brief preliminary illustration, I cite first a few examples of *variations* (of mood, manner, and form) in poetic scene painting. All is "merry" in Shallow's orchard when "the sweet o' th' night" comes in.[4] So, in another quick flash of broad humor, in one lean line of verse, Falstaff "lards the lean earth as he walks along."[5] Again, in the most famous instance of sustained serio-comic poetic scene painting, this same Falstaff dying (in prose!) "babbled of green fields."[6]

---

[2] Maxwell Anderson, *Eleven Verse Plays* (New York, 1939), p. 3.

[3] *Ibid.*, p. 129; cf. pp. 42, 113.

[4] *2 Henry IV* V.iii.52–53.

[5] *1 Henry IV* II.ii.116.

[6] *Henry V* II.iii.9–28. (Less triumphant a scene is his descent "glowing hot," "into the Thames" of *Merry Wives* III.v.122.)

Death scenes such as Falstaff's, and, in other moods, Ophelia's, Lear's, and Desdemona's, and the pseudo-death scenes of Juliet and Imogen, are among the favorite *kinds* or subjects of poetic scene painting, as are also sunrises, sunsets, and storms. One *purpose* of this technique is to challenge the imaginative response of the audience: to enable it to see quickly, clearly, in the mind's eye, an off-stage scene. Another purpose is to picture vividly, for spectators not near the stage, what might otherwise remain hidden or distantly obscure: what they might otherwise fail to hear or see or feel.

In recent times outstanding Shakespearean producers—for example, Granville-Barker,[7] Margaret Webster,[8] and Tyrone Guthrie[9]—have dealt significantly, as we shall see, with sundry aspects of our subject. Illuminating critical comment had appeared, meanwhile, in Bradley's observations[10]—for example, upon *Macbeth*'s blood and darkness—and, with varying degrees of eloquence and clarity, in the explications of the host of imagists and symbolists succeeding Miss Spurgeon and G. Wilson Knight. Most of these critics, however, have been too preoccupied with other matters to look closely at the technique of poetic scene painting, for example, at such considerations as the following.

Poetic sunrise scenery is as ancient and honorable as Homer, Euripides, Virgil, Ovid, and Sir Philip Sidney,[11] and as modern as the avant-garde. It is not surprising, therefore, to find a bit of sober sunrise scenery in the old Wakefield *Noah* play: "The son [sun] shynes in the eest. Lo . . . yond?"[12] Less obvious, perhaps, is the fact that this sort of scene painting can be and is still being

---

[7] *Prefaces to Shakespeare, Fourth Series* (London, 1947).

[8] *Shakespeare Without Tears* (New York, 1957).

[9] *A Life in the Theatre* (New York, 1959).

[10] *Shakespearean Tragedy* (London, 1929), pp. 333–338.

[11] Homer, *Iliad* XI.1; Euripides, *Ion*, Ion's first speech; Virgil, *Aeneid* III.521; Ovid, *Metamorphoses* VII.112; Sidney, *Astrophel and Stella* XCIX.10.

[12] JQA, p. 108, line 453.

varied, on occasion, to supply a pleasant comic touch—as, for example, in *Cyrano de Bergerac*'s sunrise, in Ragueneau's bake-shop ("Over the coppers of my kitchen flows /The frosted-silver dawn"),[13] and in Dylan Thomas's *Under Milk Wood*: "Stand on . . . Llareggub Hill, old as the hills, high, cool and green. . . . you can see all the town below you, sleeping in the first of the dawn" (dreaming luscious dreams)![14] More important is the fact that Shakespeare not infrequently makes his sunrises high-light subtle variations not only in mood or atmosphere but in characterization. This is familiar enough so far as the achieving of mood or atmosphere is concerned. One instance is the appro-priately grey dawning of a memorably bleak day, the day of Julius Caesar's assassination: "Here lies the east. . . . /and yon grey lines/That fret the clouds are messengers of day" (*Julius Caesar* II.i.101, 103–104). Another, in *Troilus and Cressida*, is the mention of the ribald crows ("the busy day/Wak'd by the lark hath rous'd the ribald crows") on the "cold" morning of the lovers' forced parting, when false fleeting Cressid starts on her progress toward the merry Greeks (IV.ii.8–9; iv.58). Still another is the differentiation between Friar Laurence's somberly "grey-ey'd morn" overcoming "the frowning night" and Romeo and Juliet's radiant though cloud-fretted farewell as the lark ushers in the dawn (II.iii.1; III.v.1–36; see below, p. 118). But the sun-rise here, as in *Hamlet*, also shadows forth something of the in-wardness of the persons concerned: the gently homiletic friar in his early morning moralizing, the troubled rapture of the lovers, and, in *Hamlet*, Horatio, walking like "the morn in russet man-tle clad," clear-eyed, upward-looking, not blind to the heavenly vision. Unlike him, the elder Hamlet's ghost uneasily "scent[s] the morning air" as the glowworm's light grows paler. And, para-doxically enough, that "adulterous beast," the elder Hamlet's brother, King Claudius, even while about to send Hamlet to die

13 Brian Hooker translation, opening of Act II.
14 P. 25, New Directions (New York, 1954).

in England, has still a touch of his earlier "traitorous" grace, if only of speech: "The sun no sooner shall the mountains touch / But we will ship him hence."[15]

The general import of our subject, naturally, has often been noticed,[16] as, for example, in an article by Mary C. Hyde, which states that "Shakespeare wrote scenery into *As You Like It* as he did into all [his plays] because the theatre of his day demanded it."[17] For good and obvious reasons, this is the point of view also of many of our ablest and best-informed Shakespearean producers. Granville-Barker, for instance, notes that in *Othello* "Shakespeare prescriptively makes his storm out of poetry . . . 'A fuller blast ne'er shook our battlements' " and that "the scene painting ends" with the arrival of Othello's own "tall ship."[18] So also Margaret Webster—no Globolator, and not blind to the values of settings, costumes, design, and "modern taste" in the theater: "Language," she writes, is Shakespeare's "supreme and enduring glory," and must remain the producer's and the player's supreme technical instrument. "Such scene painting" as that

15 IV.i.29–30; I.v.42–90. In strong contrast to these three sunrise scenes in *Hamlet* is the mystic glow of that hallowed season when "The bird of dawning singeth all night long" (I.i.160).

16 E. g., in Walter Borman's "Shakespeares scenische Technic," *Shakespeare Jahrbuch*, XXXVII (1901), 181–208, and in Barbara Ward's "The Play Is Still the Thing," *New York Times Magazine*, October 10, 1954, pp. 19 ff. See also Ronald Watkins, *On Producing Shakespeare* (London, 1950), pp. 168–169, *passim*. The title essay of D. W. Rannie's *Scenery in Shakespeare's Plays* (Oxford, 1931), deals not with "stage scenery" but with "extra-theatrical . . . background . . . similes, metaphors or other figures of speech taken from phenomena of landscape" which he "somehow contrived to put . . . into his plays" (p. 127). More pertinent is Professor Rudolf Stamm's paper (which came to my notice after I had completed this study) on "Shakespeare's Word-Scenery" in *Veröffentlichungen der Handels Hochschule St. Gallen* (Zürich, 1954), X, 1–34. This is, however, devoted primarily to "an analysis of the opening scenes of *Macbeth*." Stamm differentiates between four "types of word-scenery": (1) scenes "simply *named*"; (2) scenes "visualized . . . decorative[ly]"; (3) scenes "*identified*. . . . perfectly harmonized . . . with the inner life of the play"; (4) scenes intermediate between the effects of (2) and (3).

17 "Katherine Hepburn's *As You Like It*," *Shakespeare Quarterly*, I (1950), 55.

18 *Prefaces to Shakespeare, Fourth Series*, pp. 16–20.

of Macbeth's bird-haunted castle, "does not appeal primarily" to the audience's "eyes but to their hearts."[19] Realistic (physical) scenery, as Robert Speaight, another actor-critic, puts it, can indeed "destroy . . . the poetic realism which was the secret of the Elizabethan achievement."[20] Sir Tyrone Guthrie, more recently, also holds that Shakespeare's "dramatic construction . . . does not permit" realistic scenery. Thus, Lorenzo and Jessica's duet as the last act of *The Merchant of Venice* opens ("How sweet the moonlight sleeps upon this bank!") "paints the scene, lights it and furnishes it—with genius. If these lines are to be spoken, does it seem a good idea to reinforce them with . . . sequins and a structure of chicken wire covered with grass matting?"[21]

Some producers, actors, and critics answer Guthrie's question in the affirmative. Take for example my citations above from Maxwell Anderson, a good Shakespearean—the opening stage direction (describing the physical scenery) *and* the poetic scene painting of the dialogue in *Winterset*. These suggest that poetry and realistic scenery need not be mutually exclusive; may, indeed, in spite of the tremendous scenic overplus of nineteenth-century staging, properly reinforce one another in the staging of Shakespeare. One well-known supporter of this view is J. C. Adams, who states flatly that "the Elizabethan drama from beginning to end tended to support stage illusion by scenic realism."[22] W. M. Merchant, in his recent book on *Shakespeare and the Artist*, quotes this remark and agrees unqualifiedly. While recognizing the fantastic extravagance of nineteenth-century décor, he attacks the other extreme: "We have been so anxious to sweep away the actor-managers and their lumber that we have repeated to the point of hypnosis 'it's all in the words.' . . .

---

[19] *Shakespeare Without Tears*, pp. 226, 54.

[20] *William Poel and the Elizabethan Revival* (London, 1954), p. 79, quoted by Margaret Webster, p. 55.

[21] *A Life in the Theatre*, p. 205.

[22] *Joseph Quincy Adams Memorial Studies* (Washington, 1948), p. 238.

*The contrary is clearly the truth.*"[23] While thus de-emphasizing
the word, and perhaps over-emphasizing the importance of
"architectural facade" and "theatre structure," Mr. Merchant
recognizes clearly the importance of "long established tradi-
tions" in the theater (p. 5). In this connection, I think it may
be in order here, before turning more directly to Shakespeare's
own practice, to look a little closer at some of the surviving
scenes painted in medieval drama.

*The Second Shepherds' Play* is, of course, by no means the only
case in point. As one might expect, most of the Nativity plays
have their own bitter weather—the York *Birth of Jesus*, for example, with "thes beestis mylde" in their stalls and Joseph
speaking:

> Lorde, what the wedir is colde!
> The fellest freese that euere I felyd!
> I pray God helpe tham that is alde,
> And namely tham that is vnwelde [infirm].
> (JQA, p. 143, lines 71-74)

This play, too, has the wondrous "light/That . . . shynes" about
the infant Saviour, the "swete thyng" (lines 87–93) on the
Virgin's knee—"this ilke light . . . from Gods Sonne almight"
which surrounds Him as it breaks through the shadows of the
Chester *Harrowing of Hell* (JQA, p. 187, lines 25–26), and,
once more, the wondrous "grett Lythtys . . . so shene," so "fere-
full to see" in *The Conversion of St. Paul* (JQA, p. 217, lines
250–255). *The Birth of Jesus*, like many another medieval and
later play, also has its "feyre, bryght star" (JQA, p. 143, line 78;
p. 160, line 562) burning in the firmament. The Magi hail it,
"Behold the star . . . brightly shining (JQA, p. 29), and it is the
*Shepherds'* guiding light: "Yone brightness wil vs bring/vnto

---

23 Oxford, 1959, pp. 13–14, 7n., 4 (my italics). As regards "the other extreme,"
cf. Bradley, *Shakespearean Tragedy*, p. 49; "In Shakespeare's theatre . . . there
was no scenery."

that blisful" bower.[24] (In passing, one recalls the beautiful line
which shines out of the gloomy prison in *Measure for Measure*
IV.ii.219: "Look, th' unfolding star calls up the shepherd.")
Elsewhere, sun and moon and stars are eclipsed ("clerkys the
clyppys it call"), the light of the world goes out, and the sheeted
dead arise when the Lord is "done to dede [death]" in the Wakefield *Resurrection*:

> The son [sun] for wo it waxed all wan;
> The moyn and starnes of shynyng blan;
> And erth it tremlyd . . .
> And dede men rose vp bodely, both greatt and small."
>                               (JQA, p. 192, lines 116–124)

So, in *The Conversion of St. Paul*, Saul rose up from blindness
after the Holy Spirit "appear[ed] above him." The scale, says
St. Paul, "ys fallen from my eyes twayne /Where I was blynyd
and cowd nott see" (p. 218, lines 291–299). (This suggests another note in passing. The poetic virtue of most of the little
scenes here noticed is obviously derivative: scriptural-liturgical,
but in its modest way it is virtue still. In another key, Cleopatra's
barge, as most of us know it, is no less Shakespeare's because it
was previously Sir Thomas North's. Splendid prose can, on occasion, evoke poetry. Long ago, the clerics in charge of the Easter
tropes had written something resembling gorgeous stage directions which might have pleased Sir Thomas North. Witness this
excerpt from the *Elevatio Crucis* of the grand old Abbey Church
of Durham:

[the] procession [moved] from the High Altar to the south Quire dore,
where . . . four antient Gentlemen [held] upp a most rich Cannopye of
purple velvett, tached round about with redd silke and golde fringe . . .
the whole quire waitinge uppon [the "marvelous beautifull IMAGE OF
OUR SAVIOUR. . . . with the Holy Sacrament"] with goodly torches and

---

24 *The Shepherds* of the "Non-Cycle" group, not the Wakefield *Second Shepherds'*. See JQA, pp. 77 ff.

great store of other lights, all singinge, rejoyceinge, and praising God. . .)
(JQA, pp. 4-5)

Quick enumeration must suffice to indicate something of the
considerable variety of other objects of more or less poetic scene
painting in medieval drama and in a few of Shakespeare's immediate predecessors and contemporaries. They range from "the
seven starnes . . . on the firmament" (p. 107, lines 422–423) seen
by Noah's wife—not to mention the dove ("byrd full blist" with
her branch "of an olif tre") and the Ark, resting on "the hyllys
of Armonye" (Armenia, pp. 107–109, lines 422–511), or the
green leaves of Moses' burning bush, and all the plagues of
Egypt (the locusts, toads and frogs): "the waters . . . turnyd into
reede bloyde" and the Egyptians shouting "Help! . . . we drowne"
(pp. 129, 131, lines 274–277, 414)—to the women singing lullaby
("lully, lulla. . . . be styll, my lyttul chylde!") in *The Slaughter
of the Innocents* (pp. 164–65, lines 829–835). "Oyle waxyth
redde as blood" in a boiling "cawdron" in *The Play of the Sacrament* (p. 255, lines 592–594), and other pieces feature rudimen-
tary scene painting of sunrises, sunsets, "cittie, castell and riuer"
and "fayre . . . /Valleyes, woodes . . . and /Halls."[25] Among these,
it might be noted, there would seem to be two or three slight
and casual but curiously interesting anticipations of great moments in Shakespeare. Compare, for example, Joseph's prayer
(quoted above)[26] for the aged and infirm, as he takes shelter in
the manger, with Lear's compassionate thought-taking, as he
enters the hovel, for the poor naked wretches biding the pitiless
storm (III.iv.28–36; cf. IV.i.67–72). "This blasted heath" upon
which Banquo and Macbeth (I.iii.77) encounter the witches is
a coincidental but striking variation upon "thys fayer hetth,"
the scene of Abraham's proposed sacrifice of his son in the Brome

25 See *Noah*, JQA, p. 108, line 453; *Tres Clerici*, JQA, p. 59; *Prophets*, JQA, pp.
135–136, lines 219, 265–267.
26 P. 103.

*Isaac* (JQA, p. 123, line 407). And the closing scenes of *Everyman* and *Hamlet* have a common undertone: flights of angels sing Everyman to his rest long before Horatio bids good night to his sweet prince: "Methynketh that I here aungelles synge . . . /Where Euerymannes soule receyued shall be."[27]

To illustrate some of the kinds and variations of poetic scene painting by Shakespeare's immediate predecessors and fellows, a fairly close look at one famous play must serve our purpose. Marlowe's *Tamburlaine*, familiar though it is, is our best document.

Obviously, this play abounds in grandiose scenic effects. These, as I have suggested above, would reach and thrill even the most far-off and toughest groundling. He could not fail to hear and see Tamburlaine's vast trampling hordes in their black and red and gold. Nor could he fail to see, flashing before his mind's eye, off-stage[28] scenes or off-time scenes, great events of far away and long ago. Barbaric splendor of historic-geographic background[29] is the end sought. The means, often fused, are many. Thus, sound[30] effects crash and reverberate through the play— ". . . the clang /Of Scythian trumpets! . . . the basilisks /That, roaring, shake Damascus' turrets down!" (IV.i.1–3). The famous line, "And ride in triumph through Persepolis" (II.v.49–54), is repeated and reiterated. And color effects are equally notable. The weakling king, Mycetes, "long[s] to see" Theridamas' "milk-

---

[27] JQA, p. 302, lines 891–893; *Hamlet* V.ii.370–371.

[28] E. g., Tamburlaine's order to his soldiers to "show" the virgins of Damascus "my servant, Death, /Sitting in scarlet on their armed spears" (V.ii.54–55). My text for this group of plays is Tucker Brooke and N. B. Paradise, *English Drama 1580–1642* (Boston, 1933).

[29] "East India and the late-discovered isles; /. . . the wide vast Euxine sea, /And . . . the ever raging Caspian lake" (I.i.166–168).

[30] The facts do not bear out Professor A. L. Rowse's assertion that "Almost the only sense he [Marlowe, in *Tamburlaine*] appeals to is the visual"—*Marlowe* (London, 1964), p. 64.

white steeds" return "Besmear'd with blood, that makes a dainty show" (I.i.74–80). The spectacular terror of Tamburlaine's tents and accoutrements begins with "milk-white. . . . mildness"! Then follow "red as scarlet" wrath, and dead "coal-black" to "menace death and hell" to all (III.iii.161; V.i.9; IV.i.50–63). Earlier came Tamburlaine's order to "lay out our golden wedges to the view" of the Persians, who also have their "camels laden all with gold" (I.ii.139; II.ii.62). Finally and most characteristically Marlovian is the tumultuous, dynamic-heroic sweep of his scene painting. "Millions infinite of men" ride in triumph, not only through Persepolis: " . . . with our sunbright armour as we march,/We'll chase the stars from Heaven and dim their eyes" (III.iii.33; II.iii.22–23). Most notable in the second part of *Tamburlaine* are the tremendous heroics of Zenocrate's death scene, when Tamburlaine, "raving . . . desperate and mad" burns "the cursed town" nearby (II.iv). Then comes the long drawn out agony and defiant posturing of his own final bout with "the ugly monster Death" (V.iii).

Of course this tempestuous and sensational scene painting is the special quality of Marlowe and more particularly of *Tamburlaine*. Yet some of its objectives and some of its qualities appear also, with varying degrees of emphasis and shades of sophistication, in the work of his fellows, from Peele and Greene and Kyd to Webster and Beaumont and Fletcher. Like Tamburlaine's men, Kyd's victorious Spanish army also rides "in triumph" round "about the . . . walls" of its capital. And old Hieronimo, plucked from his bed by murderous night cries, finds his "sweet son['s]. . . . bloody corpse dishonoured . . . amidst these dark and deathful shades" (*The Spanish Tragedy*, II.v.1–22). In short, Marlowe's recurrent scene painting of blood and terror, "midnight" evil, and self-torturing misery, in such plays as *Tamburlaine* and *Edward II*, is matched by the scenic background of Hieronimo's experiences and his family's in *The Spanish Tragedy*, by Aspatia's ("Sorrow's monument") in *The Maid's Trag-*

*edy*, and, with an added touch reminiscent of Lady Macbeth, by the heroine's agonies in Webster's *Duchess of Malfi*: "Sure I did hear a woman shriek: list ha! . . . /It may be 'twas the melancholy bird . . . /The owl, that scream'd so."[31] Again, not unlike the ingenuous sensuousness of Marlowe's milk-white tents and golden wedges are Peele's scene painting of the golden world (Juno's "Tree of Gold" in *The Arraignment of Paris*)[32] and Greene's pleasant pictures of merry Fressingfield—England's own "groves" and "sweetest bowers" and "silver streams"—in *Friar Bacon and Friar Bungay* (X.58; I.6) not to mention, in the same play, the charming Marlovian-Keatsian banquet of sense (". . . for thy cates, rich Alexandria drugs [and] Persia['s] spicery") (IX.260–277) arranged by the good Friar for the delectation of the Emperor, and of the audience. Occasionally, however, a bit of scene painting subtler than anything in *Tamburlaine* stands out in these plays. Then one thinks not of Marlowe but of Shakespeare—for example, of King Lear, seeking to persuade himself and the audience that he still hears the well-remembered voice, ever soft, gentle, and low, of his child, Cordelia, and that he (and the audience) can still see the stir of her breath: "Look on her! look! her lips!" Such is that glimpse, magically vivid, though the audience can catch it only at a distance, of the dead Duchess of Malfi when she is "discovered" by the guilty duke, her brother: "Cover her face; mine eyes dazzle: she died young."[33]

What has gone before indicates that Shakespeare's practice in this kind was in the great tradition, and what follows should clinch the point. Of course I cannot marshal all the available

---

31 II.iii.1–9. (Cf. *Macbeth* II.ii.3: "It was the owl that shriek'd.")

32 "the root of gold . . . the bark of gold . . . the leaves of burnish'd gold" (II.ii.40–43).

33 IV.ii.274. (Cf. "Dazzle mine eyes . . . ?" *3 Henry VI* II.i.25.) Anti-climactic, later, are the scenes of the "ancient [reverend] ruins" wherein the Duchess' grave is set, and of the "foul storm . . . the devil['s] own" just before her husband's murder (V.iii.2–15; iv.20–23).

evidence. Once more a representative sampling must suffice, and my illustrations must needs come, even at the risk of stressing the obvious, chiefly from major plays. To avoid repetitious elaboration, my notes are, as a rule, limited to summary analysis of scene painting play by play, seven in all (about one-fifth of the canon)—some early, some late, some of each sort: "tragedy, comedy, history, pastoral." For what they may yield in a comparative view, I have arranged these summaries in three groups: (1) *Titus Andronicus* (*ca.* 1592) and *Antony and Cleopatra* (*ca.* 1607), Shakespeare's earliest essay in tragedy and one of his latest masterpieces; (2) *Richard III* (*ca.* 1593), his sensational early success in the "tragical-historical," and *Macbeth* (1606), to represent the great four in tragedy; (3) *A Midsummer Night's Dream* (1594–1595), *Romeo and Juliet* (1594–1595), and *As You Like It* (1599 or 1600), three early and later achievements in romantic drama: romantic fairy-fantasy, tragic romance, and pastoral-romantic comedy, respectively.

## I

*Titus Andronicus.* W. M. Merchant draws primarily on this play—especially on its original stage directions, as in the "Sound drums and trumpets" and the processional entry at I.i.69—to exemplify those scenes which, he thinks, "depend *not on the dialogue*" (my italics) "but on the grouping, the situation which must be seen . . . the actual structure of the theatre."[34] A fair reading of the play, however, indicates that its effectiveness depends at least as much upon the dialogue, including the poetic scene painting, as upon the processionizing[35] and the physical horror. Witness, for example, Titus' speech immediately after the stage direction just quoted, "Lo, as the bark that hath dis-

[34] *Shakespeare and the Artist*, p. 13.
[35] This is also true of other plays which make much use of processional spectacle or humorous or romantic stage business; e. g., *Henry VIII, Antony and Cleopatra, Taming, Cymbeline, Winter's Tale, Pericles, Tempest.*

charg'd her fraught . . . /Cometh Andronicus, bound with laurel boughs, /To resalute his country with his tears." Throughout the play, the word, however rhetorical, not only suits but illuminates the action. I list some outstanding examples.

1. Titus Buries His Sons.—"In peace and honor rest you here, my sons; . . . /Here lurks no treason, here no envy swells. . . . /In peace and honor rest you here, my sons" (I.i.150–156).

2. Lurid Setting: the Rape of Lavinia, Murder of Bassianus. —"The forest walks. . . . /Fitted by kind for rape and villany. . . . The woods are ruthless . . . deaf and dull. . . . Here never shines the sun . . ." (II.i.114–128; II.iii.96).[36]

3. A Contrasting Hunt's-up.—"The hunt is up, the morn is bright and grey," after which follows more amorous scene painting by Tamora in the "sweet shade" for her "lovely Aaron" (II.ii.1; iii.10–30).

4. Lavinia Bleeds (in words no remote spectator could fail to hear and see).—"Speak, gentle niece. What . . . hand/Hath . . . hew'd . . . thy body . . . ?/Alas, a crimson river of warm blood . . ./Doth rise and fall between thy rosed lips" (II.iv.16–24).

5. Titus Weeps (in vain).—"O earth,[37] I will befriend thee with more rain . . . /Than youthful April shall with all his show'rs. . . . /So thou refuse to drink my dear sons' blood" (III.i.16–22).

6. Aaron's Child Found (off stage).—"I heard a child cry underneath a wall" and Aaron, hushing it " 'Peace, tawny slave, half me and half thy dam. . . . /Peace, villain, peace!' " (V.i.24–33).

*Antony and Cleopatra.* The massive range, the vastness of geographic-historic space in this play, owes much to its splendid group spectacle—the world-sharers and their captains confer-

---

36 Cf. ". . . the melancholy vale,/The Place of death and sorry execution," *Comedy of Errors* V.i.120–121.

37 Anticipating *Richard II*'s "Dear earth, I do salute thee" (III.ii.6).

ring and carousing afloat, armies marching, whole navies in flight—but also to imposing individuals indelibly pictured in the lightning flash of desire, beauty, death. The following list begins with group effects.

1. On Pompey's Galley.—The triumvirs and their generals "dance . . . the Egyptian Bacchanals," "batter" their ears "with the loud music"—"Till that the conquering wine hath steep'd their sense" (II.vii.109–114).

2. Ventidius Rides in Triumph.—"Now, darting Parthia, art thou stroke. . . . Bear the King's son's body /Before our army" (III.i.1–4).

3. Battle Scenes.—"Strike not by land. . . ." "Set we our squadrons on yond side o' th' hill /In eye of Caesar's battle. . . ." "The Egyptian admiral, /With all their sixty, fly and turn the rudder." "This foul Egyptian hath betrayed me! /My fleet hath yielded to the foe" (III.viii.3, x.3; IV.xii.10–11).

4. Octavia's Farewell.—"The April's in her eyes. It is love's spring, /And these the showers to bring it on" (III.ii.43–44).

5. Antony, In the Field.—Kisses and sends "this orient pearl" to Cleopatra; promises "kingdoms" more, and "So he nodded, /And soberly did mount an arm-gaunt steed" (I.v.41–48). (*At sea*) "The noble ruin of her magic, Antony . . . (like a doting mallard) . . . flies after her" and despairs: "I . . . have instructed cowards /To run. . . . indeed I have lost command" (III.x.19–21; xi.7–23). (*Rebounds*) "You that will fight, /Follow me close. . . . — /He goes forth gallantly. That he and Caesar might /Determine this great war in single fight!" (IV.iv.33–37) (*Dies*) "Carry me now, good friends. . . . I am dying, Egypt, dying. . . . —Noblest of men, woo't die? . . . O, wither'd is the garland of the war!" (IV.xiv.139; xv.41, 59–64).

6. Cleopatra's First (off-stage) Meeting with Antony.—"The barge she sat in, like a burnish'd throne /Burn'd on the water. . . . /Age cannot wither her nor custom stale . . ." (II.ii.196–210, 240–245). (*Her lamp dims*) "Hast thou the pretty worm of Nilus

there /That kills and pains not?" (*and goes out, gloriously*)
"Show me, my women, like a queen. . . . Give me my robe, put
on my crown. I have /Immortal longings in me. . . . Peace,
peace! /Dost thou not see my baby at my breast . . . ?—She looks
like sleep, /As she would catch another Antony /In her strong
toil of grace" (V.ii.228, 242–247, 283–284, 312–313, 349–351).

These two plays have splendid or terrible pictures, unforgettable tableaux (the tomb of the Andronici, Lavinia lost, Cleopatra's barge), and grand processionizing (Titus' opening entry,
Ventidius' triumph). But the scene painting of *Titus*, in keep-
ing with almost everything in this piece, is hectic and melodramatic: all bloody tears and agony too lurid to be humanly
credible. *Antony and Cleopatra*'s poetic scenery has its own
"loud music" but also sober restraint, psychological depth. Its
partings—for example, Antony's from Cleopatra and from Octavia—and its death scenes—Antony's, Cleopatra's—give authentic life and grandeur to the principals of the play. On the whole,
the difference between the scene painting of the two plays is the
difference between vivid rhetoric and compelling poetry.

## II

*Richard III.* The play opens not with scene painting but
mood painting and a pun: Richard gloats over the waning winter of his faction's discontent, "made glorious summer by this
sun of York"—the sun badge of dead York's son, King Edward
IV. Soon after comes an unusual and powerful bit of scene
painting—the sea-bottom of Clarence's dream, "a thousand fearful wracks; /A thousand men that fishes gnaw'd upon. . . . /In-
estimable stones, unvalued jewels" (I.iv.24–63). Other notable
scenes:

1. Richard "Praying."—"On his knees . . . /Not dallying with
a brace of courtesans . . . /But praying to enrich his watchful
soul. . . . /See where his Grace stands, 'tween two clergymen . . .
a book of prayer in his hand" (III.vii.73–77, 95–98).

2. Prison Scenes.—"O Pomfret, Pomfret! O thou bloody prison, /Fatal and ominous to noble peers! . . . Richard the Second here was hacked to death. . . ."[38] (*The Princes in the Tower*)[39] "I do not like the Tower, of any place. . . . —Pity, you ancient stones, those tender babes . . . /Rough cradle for such little pretty ones! /Rude ragged nurse, old sullen playfellow /For tender princes. . . . —The tyrannous and bloody act is done. . . . 'Lo, thus . . . the gentle babes. . . . We smothered . . .'" (III.i.68; IV.i.99–103; iii.1–17).

3. Bosworth Field.—For Richard, ominous weather and foreboding dreams: "Here will I lie to-night; /But where to-morrow? . . . —Into my tent; the dew is raw and cold. . . . —Have mercy, Jesu! Soft! I did but dream. . . . /The lights burn blue. It is now dead midnight. /Cold fearful drops stand on my trembling flesh" (V.iii.7–8, 46, 179–182). On the eve and morn of battle, "the sky doth frown and low'r upon our army" but not, in spite of Richard's assertion, upon Richmond's. To him, on the contrary, the sun's "golden set" on the eve of battle "Gives token of a goodly day to-morrow. . . . —The silent hours steal on /And flaky darkness breaks within the east. . . . —The sweetest sleep, and fairest-boding dreams" cheer him "on [to] 'Victory' " (V.iii.284–288, 19–20, 86–87, 228–232).

*Macbeth.* The scenic-poetic effects in this play are numerous, varied, and memorable. Notable is their continuous impact upon the action, and, as in *Hamlet*, their compelling start. The inversion of the world's physical and moral order is noisily thrust forward by the opening hurlyburly of war and treason and battle lost and won. The consequent "fair is foul, and foul is fair," by virtue of Macbeth's unconscious but significantly prompt echo (I.i.10; iii.38), becomes a prophetic utterance, no mere witches' atmosphere of fog and filthy air. Yet this is precisely the right atmosphere for the "blasted heath" upon which they first meet Banquo and Macbeth, for the ominous sights and

---

38 III.iii.8–11: cf. *Richard II* V.v.
39 Cf. *Richard II* V.i.1–4.

sounds which anticipate and accompany Duncan's royal progress toward death, and for the evils that follow. Among other famous scenic passages, I list the following:

1. Macbeth's Castle.—The "lov'd mansionry," the sweet and gentle air of this "pleasant seat," as seen by Duncan and Banquo, does not deceive the audience. Immediately before, it had heard, in ominously contrasting anticipation, Lady Macbeth's—and the raven's—welcome: "The raven himself is hoarse /That croaks the fatal entrance of Duncan /Under my battlements" (I.vi.1–6; v.39–41).

2. Duncan's Murder.—(*Banquo's "heavy" apprehension*) "The moon is down. . . ."[40] There's husbandry in heaven; /Their candles are all out." (*Macbeth abuses the curtained sleep*) "Now . . . /Nature seems dead. . . . Now witchcraft celebrates . . . and wither'd murther . . . towards his design /Moves like a ghost" (II.i.2–5, 49–56). (*Lady Macbeth listens*) "It was the owl that shriek'd, the fatal bellman. . . . I heard the owl scream and the crickets cry" (II.ii.3, 16). (*Other reports*) "Lamentings heard i' th' air, strange screams of death. . . . 'Twas a rough night. . . . And yet dark night[41] strangles the travelling lamp. . . . 'Tis unnatural, /Even like the deed that's done." [42]

3. The Knocking at the Gate.—"Here's a knocking indeed!"—a score of knocks, to the nicely fitting staccato accompaniment of twenty-odd lines of devil-portering jests (II.iii).[43]

4. Banquo's Murder: Sunset and Rain.—"The west yet glimmers with some streaks of day. /Now spurs the lated traveller apace. . . ." (*Fleance's torch*) "A light, a light! . . . It will be rain to-night.—Let it come down!" (III.iii.5–16).

[40] II.i.2–7. Cf. *The Two Noble Kinsmen*, "The moon is down. . . . all the stars are out too" (III.ii.35; iv.1).

[41] Cf. *Troilus and Cressida* V.viii.17: "The dragon wing of night o'erspreads the earth."

[42] II.iii.61–66; iv.7–11. Cf. *Julius Caesar* I.iii.

[43] Similar accompaniment, minus the gallows humor, sets off the knocking at the gate in *Romeo and Juliet* (III.iii.70–79), *Othello* (V.ii.84–101), and *Troilus and Cressida* (IV.ii.35–45).

5. At the Banquet.—"Banquo's safe? . . . —Safe in a ditch he bides, /With twenty trenched gashes in his head. . . . —The table's full. . . . /Thou canst not say I did it. Never shake /Thy gory locks at me" (III.iv.25–27, 46–51).

6. The Witches' Cauldron.—"In the poison'd entrails throw. . . . /Scale of dragon, tooth of wolf . . ." (IV.i.4–38).

7. The Sleep-walking.—"How came she by that light? . . . Look how she rubs her hands. . . . Hark, she speaks! . . . /Here's the smell of the blood still . . ." (V.i.25–56).

8. Birnam Wood.—"I . . . doubt th' equivocation of the fiend, . . . 'Fear not, till Birnam wood /Do come to Dunsinane!' and now a wood /Comes toward Dunsinane. . . . —Now near enough. Your leavy screens throw down" (V.v.43–46; vi.1).

9. Macbeth at Bay.—"They have tied me to a stake. I cannot fly, /But bear-like I must fight the course" (V.vii.1–2).

Two interim conclusions would seem to follow. (1) The means and ends of poetic scene painting in tragedy and historical drama—witness also *Antony and Cleopatra*—seem essentially similar if not identical. (2) There is no absolute correlation between maturing craftsmanship and the attainment of excellence in this technique. Scene painting in the early *Richard III* is not all rhetoric, nor is all the scenery in the later *Macbeth* great poetry, though most of it certainly is. Sensational effects, though less strident than in *Titus Andronicus*, dominate *Richard III*. The lights burn blue, discovering tender babes smothered, and cursing or weeping women calamitously full of words. But words become poetry in the painting of Clarence's dream, in the ragged gray stones of the Tower, and in Richard's midnight agony before Bosworth Field. Still, as Lincoln said, "nothing equals *Macbeth*." Its power lies partly in its subtly varied scenic poetry, from the opening hurlyburly to the contrasts between the temple-haunting martlet and the shrieking owl, the knocking at the gate, the sleepwalking, and the coming of Birnam Wood to Dunsinane.

### III

*A Midsummer Night's Dream*. Poetic scene painting belongs
to the springtime magic of this play as bees belong to flowers,
because the major subjects painted—moonlight, the lovers' enchanted wood, the night of the dream, and the sunrise—naturally belong to poetry. To wit:

1 and 2. Moonlight and the Enchanted Wood.—"Four happy
days. . . . /And then the moon, like to a silver bow" shines upon
the royal wedding. Lysander's Hermia promises to meet him
"when Phoebe doth behold /Her silver visage in the wat'ry
glass," in the same "wood, a league without the town" where
Helen and Hermia—resting "upon faint primrose beds"!—were
wont to exchange maidenly counsel. And thither Quince the
Carpenter calls his actors, to "the palace wood . . . by moonlight.
There will we rehearse" (I.i.2–11, 165, 209–215; ii.104–105). In
this wood, meanwhile, Puck encounters the garden-club fairy
("dew[ing] her orbs upon the green,"—"wander[ing] /Swifter
than the moonës sphere"), and there "Ill met by moonlight,
proud Titania" blames Oberon for his jealous "dissension."
"Therefore. . . . /The seasons alter. Hoary-headed frosts /Fall
in the fresh lap of the crimson rose"; but he will not yield nor
join their "dance . . . /And . . . moonlight revels." Here, too,
Demetrius and Helena, both more or less "wood within this
wood" run their wild goose chase after the other pair; Titania
rests by night on her "bank where the wild thyme blows";[44]
Peter Quince, at rehearsal, comments upon the difficulties of
physical scene painting—how "hard . . . that is, to bring moonlight into a chamber"; and Puck explains how he crowned Bottom when that "shallowest thickskin . . . /Forsook his scene and
ent'red in a brake" (II.i.6–9, 60–61, 88–117, 140–141, 192, 249;
III.i.48–50, ii.13–15).

---

[44] Cf. *Love's Labour's Lost* V.ii.89–90: "Under the cool shade of a sycamore /I
thought to close mine eyes. . . ."

3 and 4. Dark Night, Sunrise, and Hunt's-up.—"The heavy gait of night. . . ."[45]—How chance Moonshine is gone . . . ?—O grim-look'd night . . . with hue so black . . . which ever art when day is not!" (V.i.375, 318, 171–172) "I can no further crawl. . . . Here will I rest me. . . . —Come, thou gentle day! . . . once . . . show me thy grey light. . . . —Night's swift dragons cut the clouds full fast, /And yonder shines Aurora's harbinger. . . . —I do hear the morning lark. . . . —Now . . . since we have the vaward of the day, /My love shall hear the music of my hounds. . . . match'd in mouth like bells" (III.ii.444–446, 418–419, 379–380; IV.i.97, 107–126).

*Romeo and Juliet.* "In fair Verona, where we lay our scene," from the very beginning to the end, this play's scene painting runs the gamut from broad humor to tragic-romantic ecstasy. After the Capulet-Montague servants' opening squabble ("Do you bite your thumb at us . . . ?") come Potpan's failings at the Capulets' feast ("He shift a trencher! he scrape a trencher!"), and old Capulet's warm hospitality ("More light, you knaves! and turn the tables up, /And quench the fire, the room is grown too hot")[46] (Prol.2; I.i.51–55; v.2–30). Meanwhile the Nurse remembers her merry husband's oft-repeated jest at the (off-stage) scene of little Juliet's weaning and the great fall thereof (I.iii.24–48); Mercutio airily sketches the scene of the Nurse's entry, like a stately ship, with her man Peter in tow ("A sail, a sail!—Two, two! A shirt and a smock . . .); and Capulet, a "mouse-hunt" of old, stirs up the pots in his kitchen ("Look to the bak'd meats, good Angelica") to prepare for Juliet's wedding (II.iv.108–110; IV.iv.5–13). Earlier, Romeo's first glimpse of Juliet at the ball —"O, she doth teach the torches to burn bright" (I.v.46)—highlights the scene in poetry. Rapt lyricism, the special grace of this

---

45 Cf. *2 Henry VI* IV.i.4: "The tragic melancholy night," and, among other conventional variations, "The day begins to break and night is fled, /Whose pitchy mantle overveil'd the earth" (*1 Henry VI* II.ii.1–2).

46 "The day is hot, the Capulets abroad" (III.i.2).

play, progressively dominates most of the later scene painting. Familiar though they are, some of these passages must be included in this record.

1. The Balcony Scene.—"But soft! What light through yonder window breaks?" "How cam'st thou hither . . . ? /The orchard walls are high and hard to climb. . . ." ". . . stony limits cannot hold love out. . . ." "How silver-sweet sound lovers' tongues by night . . . !" (II.ii.1–168).

2. Juliet's Epithalamion.—"Gallop apace, you fiery-footed steeds. . . . /And bring in cloudy night immediately" (III.ii.1–4).

3. Sunrise Farewell.—"It was the nightingale, and not the lark . . ." (III.v.2; see above, p. 100).

4. Juliet's Fears.—"Or shut me nightly in a charnel house, /O'ercover'd quite with dead men's rattling bones . . ."—". . . a vault . . . /Where bloody Tybalt . . . /Lies fest'ring in his shroud" (IV.i.81–82; iii.40–44).

5. Romeo's Apothecary.—[47] ". . . in his needy shop a tortoise hung, /An alligator stuff'd . . . /Green earthen pots, bladders, and musty seeds" (V.i.37–57).

6. Juliet, Supposed Dead.—"Death lies on her like an untimely frost /Upon the sweetest flower of all the field."—". . . here lies Juliet, and her beauty makes /This vault a feasting presence full of light. . . . Shall I believe /That unsubstantial Death is amorous . . . ?" (IV.v.28–29; V.iii.85–108).

*As You Like It.* The central scene here is the forest of Arden. The good duke best paints its pastoral peace and quiet,[48] having discovered its most precious jewel, "Sweet are the uses of adversity." But even Duke Frederick's murderous wrestler knows Arden's old-Robin-Hood-of-England charm: how the "young gentlemen flock" there "and fleet the time carelessly as they did in the golden world" (I.i.122–125). Details of the scene are painted by various hands in sundry colors. Jaques is first dis-

---

[47] Cf. *King John* IV.ii.193: "I saw a smith stand with his hammer, thus. . . ."
[48] Cf. the "shadowy desert, unfrequented woods" of *The Two Gentlemen* V.iv.2; also *Love's Labour's Lost* V.ii.89.

covered lying under an ancient "oak . . . /Upon the brook that
brawls along this wood"; later, he discovers the deluge preceding the happy ending: "There is, sure, another flood toward,
and these couples are coming to the ark" (II.i.31–32; V.iv.35–
36). Touchstone, newly arrived, decides that "When I was at
home, I was in a better place" (II.iv.17). Celia and Rosalind, un-
deterred by this same "desert" place (so "inaccessible, under the
shade of melancholy boughs") buy their sheepcote, "fenc'd
about with olive trees. . . . in the neighbor bottom. . . . by the
murmuring stream" (II.vii.110–111; IV.iii.78–80). The hunters
kill the deer, and Amiens and others sing under or of the greenwood tree, the winter wind, and a lover and his lass. Orlando,
having carried old Adam into this paradise of gentle hearts,
green-gilded snakes, and ramping lionesses, woos his Rosalind
with tongues—his bad verses—hung in every tree. Rosalind, for
her part, orchestrates her quartet of lovers "like the howling of
Irish wolves against the moon" (V.ii.118–119), and the formerly
more or less wicked Oliver and Duke Frederick and Jaques
abide in Arden—converted, to matrimony, or religion, or harmless meditation (V.ii.5–14; iv.160–191).

The charm and the lyric grace of these three plays, their commingling of wonder, fun, pity, beauty, ecstasy, owes much to
their poetic scene painting. The objectives and qualities thereof, as my summaries indicate, do not differ essentially as between the several dramatic species. It is also clear, once more,
that while many of the greatest achievements in this technique
belong to the later plays, others, hardly less remarkable, came
early *and* late.

In conclusion, my illustrations at large will answer some questions concerning what I have called the variations, kinds, forms,
and purposes of Shakespeare's scenic poetry. Its range of mood
and manner, in prose and verse, is surely as wide as Polonius
himself could have wished: tragical-comical-historical-pastoral—
and lyrical-romantic to boot! Witness, once more, the Falstaff

scenes and those of Juliet's nurse, not to mention Juliet's own, and Imogen's and Perdita's and Miranda's. In the narrower sense also, the kinds or subjects of poetic scene painting are tremendously varied and numerous. There are scenes upon scenes of death and birth (as in *Titus* and *Cymbeline, Othello* and *The Winter's Tale* and *Henry VIII*), of storm and cold and rain and sunset and dawn, of enchanted gardens such as Juliet's (and other gardens in which recognizable apricots or pippins grow), of hunt's-up music and prison gloom, of ocean depths and mountain tops, Dover Cliff and the fastnesses of Wales, the sedgy Severn and the silver Trent, and of more generalized or idealized settings: unpathed waters, undreamed shores, the great globe itself, and all the glimpses of the moon. Indeed, moonlight and starlight shine through play after play; their scenes know the soft stillness of the night and its grim terror, the marching months and the changing seasons. Homely, more or less humble, familiar subjects fill out the scenes: Richard II's roan Barbary proudly carrying the usurper Bolingbroke, and that "happy" arm-gaunt steed which bore the weight of Antony; and Lear's dogs (not to mention Launce's Crab and *The Two Gentlemen's* other "squirrel"!); and birds—lark and nightingale, martin and cuckoo and wren—singing, nesting, or on the wing; and flowers without end, daffodils, violets, pansies, rosemary, and rue. The magic of poetry so transmutes these creatures that what might have been neutral scenery becomes vibrant life.

As regards more specific variations in "form," Shakespeare's scene painting also runs the gamut. At one end stands what he himself calls "Description . . . suit[ing] itself"—at some length— "in words /To demonstrate the life"[49] of such a vivid scene, for example, as that of Hotspur's elegant courtier, sniffing perfume at Holmedon battlefield;[50] or, in another famous description, to strew melodious but somewhat formal garlands upon

[49] *Henry V* IV.ii.53–54.
[50] *1 Henry IV* I.iii.33–64; cf. above, p. 81.

the fair Ophelia, sunk in muddy death. At the other extreme stand many brief lines or briefer phrases, including some of the greatest in Shakespeare, which paint unforgettable scenes in lightning flashes: "this blasted heath," "Fair is foul and foul is fair," " 'Tis the time's plague when madmen lead the blind," "Out, damned spot," "Keep up your bright swords, for the dew will rust them," and "Nothing almost sees miracles / But misery."

Among the functions of poetic scene painting, I call attention, once more, to its recurring use for purposes of dramatic contrast, as in the varied sunrise scenes observed by the several protagonists of *Hamlet, Romeo and Juliet,* and *Richard III.* Allied to this purpose, of course, is the establishing of fundamentals of tone color, as in the opening of *Macbeth* and *Hamlet,* and to a greater or lesser degree, realistic or symbolic, in the storm scenes of *Lear, Othello,* and *The Tempest.* Still another purpose, also repeatedly marked above, is to paint off-stage scenes such as Titania's wild-thyme bank, Ophelia's death, and Cleopatra's barge, and to do this economically, with such power as to make the hearers' imaginary forces work. Often, too, this scene painting helps the audience to see and feel what, no matter how strategically near the stage, it could otherwise hardly manage to see—as for example, the ingredients of the witches' cauldron in *Macbeth* or the hoped-for mist on the mirror, and the feather, as Lear, dying, thinks that Cordelia lives. In short, as Sir Philip Sidney says, the poet's purpose is to *move,* not merely to show the playgoer's eyes but to stir his heart. These findings, finally, do not run counter to Mr. Merchant's contention that "the plays make their full theatric impact by a union of word, music, grouping and setting."[51] True, with but one qualification: in the beginning was the word, and also in the end.

51 *Shakespeare and the Artist,* p. 14. (Cf. above, pp. 102–103.)

# 7

## Delayed Exposition in Shakespeare[1]

> What? Michael Cassio,
> That came a-wooing with you, and so many a time
> When I have spoke of you dispraisingly,
> Hath ta'en your part—to have so much to do
> To bring him in? OTHELLO
> III.iii.70–74

DESDEMONA'S PRETTY PLEA to Othello for Cassio's reinstate-
ment has been much discussed. Critical attention has centered
upon the seeming discrepancy between Desdemona's remarks
and Cassio's question to Iago very soon after Othello's wedding,
when Cassio apparently professed ignorance of the circumstances:

> Cas. Ancient, what makes he here? . . .
> Iago.　　　　　　　　He's married.
> Cas.　　　　　　　　　　　　To who? (I.ii.49–52)

My chief purpose here is to emphasize a point which most of the
commentators have ignored. Whatever inconsistency there may
be between Cassio's early query and Desdemona's charming recollection later on, from the point of view of dramatic technique
the importance of Desdemona's remark lies in the fact that it is

1 This chapter revises and supplements the article by the same title in *Shake-speare Quarterly*, I (1950), 140 ff.

a significant illustration of Shakespeare's use of delayed exposition—a device familiar in modern drama but scarcely recognized in Shakespearean criticism. I hope to show that Shakespeare was thoroughly familiar with this technique—witness the fact that he, and some of his contemporaries, used it more or less effectively in many plays. To make the evidence speak fairly for itself, I must define my terms, the implications of "delayed exposition." And for this purpose I must notice, first, the commentators' difficulties in reconciling the two passages just quoted.

The Furness Variorum *Othello* (p. 37) records many a queasy question growing out of the early exchange ("He's married.—To who?") between Iago and Cassio. "Surely," Theobald observed, "this is a terrible forgetfulness in our author. How came Cassio such a stranger to this affair, when it afterward appears he went a-wooing with Othello and took his part in the suit?" To which Singer replied, reasonably enough: "It was probably a mere oversight of the poet." Another explanation, however, has seemed equally reasonable to other critics. "Cassio's seeming ignorance," Blackstone suggested, "might only be affected, in order to keep his friend's secret till it became publicly known." In effect, one or the other or a partial combination of these views has been adopted by many later critics. According to A. C. Bradley, for example, "It is possible that Cassio does know, and only pretends ignorance," though it is "perhaps more probable . . . that, in writing Act I, Shakespeare had not yet thought of making Cassio Othello's confidant, and that" later "he neglected to alter the passage in Act I."[2] This view, with specific acknowledgments to Bradley, is shared by C. H. Herford and R. M. Alden.[3] Professor Kittredge, however, makes at least one reservation. He agrees, in view of Desdemona's later remarks, that in Act I, "Cassio either does not know of the elopement or does not choose to disclose his knowledge to Iago . . . . nothing in the play indicates

[2] *Shakespearean Tragedy* (London, 1929), pp. 433–434.
[3] American Arden edition, *Othello* (Boston, 1924), p. xix, n. 1.

that" in Act I "he was . . . aware of the marriage."[4] But Kittredge does not hold, with Bradley, that Desdemona's recollection is "probably . . . an afterthought" on Shakespeare's part.

Now this matter of afterthoughts in dramatic composition brings us back squarely to Shakespeare's practice in exposition; i.e., to borrow a differentiation from G. P. Baker's study of modern *Dramatic Technique*,[5] Shakespeare's practice in "preliminary" and in "later" exposition.

As regards his preliminary exposition: only the uncritical now insist that Shakespeare was never guilty of "oversight." The first act of *Othello* is perhaps a case in point, even though everyone agrees that on the whole it is a great technical achievement. According to the American Arden editors, indeed, "every line of the first act has its function in the economy of the entire drama."[6] Yet the fact is that Cassio's early question *may* have survived by an oversight on Shakespeare's part—like Iago's cryptic opening remark about the wifeless Cassio, "A fellow almost damn'd in a fair wife,"[7] and like the Duke's mysterious "Marcus Luccicos," to whom he writes "post-post-haste" in I.iii.44–46, only to have the man drop absolutely out of sight forever after, exactly as does Claudio's uncle after the opening scene of *Much Ado* (I.i.18). Since Shakespeare sometimes worked in haste and was never a mechanically perfect manufacturer of well-made plays, it is possible that he simply neglected to excise Cassio's opening question.

Does it necessarily follow, however, that Desdemona's account of Othello's wooing was an afterthought? Granville-Barker,[8] among others, has noted that in spite of the compelling rush of

---

4 *Othello* (Boston, 1941), p. 133.

5 Boston, 1919, pp. 142, 176.

6 P. xxxviii.

7 *Othello* I.i.21. Probably Shakespeare's uncorrected recollection of the Captain's wife in Cinthio (cf. H. Granville-Barker, *Prefaces to Shakespeare, Fourth Series* [London, 1947], p. 3, n.; and others). Concerning Shakespeare's oversights, see above, Chapter V, pp. 91–94, 79, n.2.

8 *Ibid.*, pp. 10 ff., 15 ff.

action in the opening of *Othello,* Shakespeare's shaping of the story requires him to point a fresh center of interest after he has transported his characters to Cyprus. Preliminary exposition, as all technicians agree, must be adequate but concise, lest it grow tedious while the action languishes. Since, as Bradley clearly recognized, Othello's first-act account of his wooing had to be "condensed" ("it was no part of his business to trouble the Senators with the details of his courtship"),[9] it would seem possible that Shakespeare may purposely have held some expository data in reserve, for effective use, later, in developing his story and characters. Through this delayed exposition, at all events, Desdemona comes out immensely in Act III. Even in Act I, this "maiden never bold," "of spirit so still and quiet," speaks out courageously in defense of her choice. But she strikes a new note in Act III. Her delightfully mischievous[10] account of Othello's wooing, like Ophelia's smiling rejoinder to Laertes' lecture on maidenly reserve, lends, for the moment at least, fresh zest to the scene, fresh piquancy to the character drawing. It brings out Othello too. It is pleasant to learn, at long last, that he was "dispraisingly" required to woo with a will and with a good friend's aid, instead of merely telling his lady a pretty tale and allowing her to love him for the dangers he had passed! In short, whether Desdemona's speech was Shakespeare's afterthought or forethought, it is a tremendously effective bit of delayed exposition. If Shakespeare had thought of changing anything, he might have changed Cassio's first-act query, but not Desdemona's belated recollection—since this speech also provides the perfect impetus for Iago's opening moves in the great temptation scene:

> Did Michael Cassio, when you woo'd my lady
> Know of your love? (III.iii.94-95)

Thus Desdemona's speech not only enriches characterization but also serves the other great purpose of exposition, to further

---

9 *Shakespearean Tragedy,* p. 433.
10 Cf. Granville-Barker, p. 40.

the plot. These two familiar expository functions unite, to serve plot and characterization at once, in some instances of delayed exposition to be noticed later in this chapter—for example, in Iago's long wooing of Emilia to steal the handkerchief, and in the slow revelation of Angelo's past in *Measure for Measure*. We shall see other instances which primarily illustrate one expository function or the other; e. g., characterization in Shylock's memory of Leah in *The Merchant of Venice*, or plot in Bertram's surprise recollection of fair Maudlin in *All's Well*.[11]

The delayed exposition in Desdemona's speech, curiously enough, is at least roughly analogous to a passage in the second act of Ibsen's *A Doll's House*, where Nora pleads with her husband to reinstate the villain, Krogstad. In each case the play is half over before the audience learns the real inwardness of Othello's friendship with Cassio or of Helmar's "rash friendship" of former days with Krogstad.[12] The point is worth noting because writers on modern drama so frequently intimate that delayed exposition was Ibsen's special contribution to dramatic technique, if not positively his own invention. Earlier dramatic theorists tend to ignore this aspect of the subject—Freytag, for example, holding that *all* exposition is purely and simply introductory explanation: "at the beginning . . . in the . . . first ripple of the short waves which . . . precede the storms of the drama."[13] Later writers recognize the function of delayed exposition: in Ibsen but not in Shakespeare. In *Othello*, writes Brander Matthews,[14] "When the first act . . . is over, we know *all* that we need to know." I have italicized the debatable word *all*. A somewhat similar generalization, in another context, appears in Wolfgang

11 Cf. my notes 21, 5, etc., and text, and see p. 133, below.

12 *Eleven Plays of Henrik Ibsen*, Modern Library edition (New York, n.d.), pp. 212–213.

13 As in the "fine beginnings" of *Romeo and Juliet*, *Hamlet*, *Macbeth*, and *Richard III*. Gustav Freytag, *Technique of the Drama*, trans. E. J. MacEwan (Chicago, 1898), pp. 118–120.

14 *A Study of the Drama* (New York, 1910), pp. 181, 187.

Clemen's excellent later study, *The Development of Shakespeare's Imagery*. "In a truly great drama," he writes, "nothing is left disconnected, everything is carried on."[15] Yet the fact is, as repeatedly noted in this book, that *Othello*, a truly great drama, has several loose ends.

As regards essential exposition, Brander Matthews adds that

No dramatic author can evade [this] necessity. . . . He can put it into tense dialogue supported by swift action in the opening scenes of the first act, as Shakespeare does in *Othello*. He can postpone it for a while and scatter it through a whole play, as Ibsen does in *Ghosts*.

This observation concerning *Ghosts* glances significantly at the usefulness of "postponed," i. e., *delayed* exposition. Professor Clemen has established the fact that a "Shakespearean image often points beyond the scene in which it stands to preceding or following acts; it almost always has reference to the whole play. It appears as a cell in the organism of the play." Further, Clemen quotes Dover Wilson: the dramatist's "art" is "progressive revelation."[16] By the same token, does it not follow that the first act may not in every case tell us all it is well to know, that often we learn most effectively by the gradual revelation of delayed exposition?

William Archer,[17] meanwhile, made even larger claims for Ibsen. The latter's work exhibited

an extraordinary progress in the art of so unfolding the drama of the past as to make the gradual revelation no mere . . . prologue to the drama of the present but an integral part of its action.

*Ghosts*, in particular, carries this method

to the extreme. . . . It is scarcely an exaggeration to call the play all exposition and no drama. . . . In other words, the exposition is all drama, it

[15] Dramabooks edition (New York, 1962), p. 6.
[16] *Ibid.*, pp. 3-6; J. Dover Wilson, *What Happens In Hamlet* (Cambridge, 1935), p. 230.
[17] *Play-Making* (Boston, 1925), pp. 102, 106–107.

*is* the drama. . . . The discovery of this method[18] . . . was Ibsen's great technical achievement.

Sophocles among the ancients had certainly been aware of the art of delayed exposition; witness *Oedipus the King.* Among the moderns, to be sure, Ibsen's pre-eminence in delayed exposition is not to be denied. Indeed it goes almost without saying that by virtue of the modern emphasis upon psychological-realistic character study, the exposition has tended to become all drama, *is* the drama, not only in *Ghosts* and *Magda* but in *Mourning Becomes Electra* and *A Streetcar Named Desire, The Death of a Salesman* and *After the Fall.* For better and for worse, modern drama has carried the method to extremes far removed from Shakespeare's unhectic, victorious storytelling. I have shown, however, that in *Othello* he did use delayed exposition to speed his plot and to enrich his characterization. Once stated, the principle, or at least the device, will easily be recognized as a moving force in many of his plays and in those of his contemporaries. A few additional illustrations must suffice.

We have seen that when the first act of *Othello* is over, the exposition is not really complete. Of sundry other bits of late exposition in this play, I will mention a few. (1) Iago's revelation in II.i.316 that he suspects not only Othello but also Cassio of guilty familiarity with his wife, Emilia ("For I fear Cassio with my nightcap too"). (2) In *The Merchant of Venice,* the Prince of Morocco, "a Tawny Moor," opens his wooing scene with an outspoken confession of his color-consciousness ("Mislike me not for my complexion"), which Portia politely, if not quite truthfully, minimizes.[19] In the opening scenes of *Othello,* Roderigo, Iago, and Brabantio successively speak abusively of Othello behind his back ("the thick lips," "an old black ram") or to his face (his "sooty bosom"), but from him we get no indica-

---

[18] Archer admits, however, that, according to Dryden, Greek tragedy had anticipated this method (p. 107, n.).

[19] See above, p. 20.

tion of any basic sensitivity, no notion of inferiority on this score; on the contrary, he is clearly aware of his worth, of his descent from men of royal siege, and is justly "proud" of his achievements. Not until the third scene of the third act, following Iago's specific allusion to Othello's "complexion," do we hear from his own lips that he knows he is vulnerable here: "Haply for I am black. . . ." (3) Not until the fourth scene of the third act do we —and Desdemona!—learn from Othello of the talismanic virtue of her handkerchief (which has already been lost, stolen, and delivered to Iago): of its power, according to his mother, of holding her husband's love, and in turn, her son's love for his wife. Desdemona says "Is't possible?" Obviously, she had not heard previously of the sentiment and the magic in the web of it. Almost incredible it is that any husband would have failed, until too late, to tell any wife the story of so valued a token! If, however, Othello *had* told Desdemona earlier, she would doubtless have taken care not to lose it—and so the whole handkerchief episode might have been lost! (4) The preceding scene, again, contains Emilia's remark *after* she has filched the handkerchief (III.iii.292–293)—"My wayward husband hath a hundred times/ Woo'd me to steal it."

This bit of retrospection inevitably calls to mind a famous passage in *Hamlet,* and, with it, a score of other retrospective expository remarks in the tragedies and histories, especially in the great soliloquies, which belatedly show us something of the inwardness of Hamlet and King Claudius, Julius Caesar and Richard II, Lady Macbeth and King Lear, as they were before the curtain rises. Thus we see young Hamlet borne "a thousand times" on poor Yorick's back, and remembering, in Ophelia's grave, that he had loved her more than forty thousand brothers— after King Claudius, in prayer, has at long last revealed the true witchery of his strong guilt and grace, his inexorable self-judgment and his abiding passion: "My crown, mine own ambition, and my queen." So also the doors of the past open in lightning flashes upon the living and the great dead: upon Caesar in his better days, as Antony and even Brutus remember him, "the foremost man of all this world"; on Henry IV, near death, admitting that he won his crown by "crooked" ways (2 *Henry IV* IV.v.185), and upon Richard II, counting the strokes of the clock just as his time runs out—"I *wasted time,* and now doth time waste me" (V.v.49); upon King Lear, storm-tossed in mad grief, remembering to pity the "houseless" poor, raging, with a lifetime's cumulative anger, against flattery, uncleanness, injustice; upon Lady Macbeth, long after she had sought to banish all human kindness from her breast:

> Had he not resembled
> My father as he slept, I had done't.

Professor A. C. Sprague reminds me of another case in point. "Is it Shakespeare's richness of knowledge," he writes,

which leads him so often to enlarge the narrow moment of life that a play affords, by dipping back into the past? . . . What I'm thinking of is your *Hamlet* reminiscence of Yorick. It's scarcely exposition really, in the ordinary sense, but something that enlarges, and gives a greater sense of life. In Act IV of *Macbeth,* in a flash, we hear that Macduff once loved the tyrant well ["This tyrant . . ./you have lov'd him well; /He hath not touch'd you yet" (IV.iii.12–14)]. Not that anything springs from this, or that it is necessary to explain anything; but it is there, and sets the imagination to work.

I find, somewhat later in the scene to which Mr. Sprague refers, another instance of this sort of dipping back into the past. This later instance of delayed exposition provides additional information concerning the gracious Duncan and his wife, Malcolm's parents, though this does not set one's imagination to work as does the recollection that Macduff once loved Macbeth. When Malcolm has pronouced himself lacking in all "the king-becoming graces" (IV.iii.91) and, hence, unfit to govern, Macduff, agreeing, wonders how Malcolm could thus "blaspheme his breed" (IV.iii.108):

> Thy royal father
> Was a most sainted king; the queen that bore thee
> Oft'ner upon her knees than on her feet
> Died every day she liv'd. . . .
> Thy hope ends here. (IV.iii.108–111, 114)

I should also like to note in this connection something like the converse of these effects of delayed exposition, these backward flashes into the past. Delayed exposition may also serve to achieve forward-looking direction. And here I owe to another friend and former colleague, the late Professor Walter Morris Hart, a further illustration from *Macbeth*. The earlier version of this essay, Professor Hart wrote, confirmed "the view that much is to be gained by reading the earlier parts of Shakespeare's plays in the light of what one learns *later on*. For example, every appearance, every word and act of Banquo, gains in significance when read in the light of Macbeth's confession of his inferiority complex; it helps to provide Macbeth with a motive for killing Duncan when it appears that chance in any case might crown him king." By the same token, Professor Sprague[20] has recently written of the opening scene of *1 Henry IV*, "like many of Shakespeare's opening scenes, this one is continually looking towards the future."

Though I have dealt chiefly, thus far, with delayed exposition in the tragedies, the principles of this technique as noted above (pp. 125, 127–130) are readily recognizable also in many others of his plays: for example, in such histories as *2 Henry IV* and *Richard II* and in such comedies as *Measure for Measure*, *The Merchant of Venice*, and *All's Well*. Compendious discussion of the technique in these plays would hardly be desirable even if space permitted. A few illustrations, however, may be useful: to indicate, especially, that delayed exposition played a significant

[20] *Shakespeare's Histories* (London: The Society for Theatre Research, 1964), p. 53.

part also in Shakespeare's comedies and in some of the plays of his contemporaries.

1. Lady Macbeth's allusion to her father is akin to Shylock's belated recollection of his dead wife, whose ring Jessica gave away for a monkey: "I had it of Leah when I was a bachelor." And the opening puzzlement of *The Merchant of Venice*—Antonio's "In sooth, I know not why I am so sad"—is resolved by the delayed exposition of II.viii.50: "I think he [Antonio] only loves the world for him," that is to say, for his bosom friend Bassanio, whom Antonio, as he had feared, was about to lose to Portia.

2. Delayed exposition in *Much Ado* establishes the true history of Benedick and Beatrice. II.i.289 informs us that "once before" the play opened, Benedick had "won" Beatrice's "heart . . . with false dice."[21] Not till III.i.109 does Beatrice bid "Contempt farewell! and maiden pride, adieu," dropping, at last, the show of sprightly shrewishness she had put on for protective coloring.

3. Early in *Twelfth Night* (I.ii.11–17, 24–30, 52–54), we meet the helpful Captain who, besides telling Viola about the noble duke, Orsino, optimistically reports that he saw her brother, Sebastian, ride the waves like Arion on the dolphin's back. This scene closes with Viola paying the Captain to conceal her identity and provide her disguise. Not until the last scene of the play do we learn what happened when the good Captain carried out Viola's instructions. He immediately took charge and care (she tells Orsino) of her "maid's garments," but, "upon some action . . . at Malvolio's suit" was kept "in durance" until the curtain is about ready to go down—while the whirligig of time brought in his revenges against Malvolio in *his* dark chamber (V.i.281–283)! Viola's brother Sebastian, meanwhile, had first appeared

---

21 Previously (I.i.146) Beatrice had said only "I know you of old." In II.ii.13–18 Borachio plots with Don John to disgrace Hero by having Margaret, "at her lady's chamber window" at night, mistaken for Hero. Not till V.i.245 do we learn that Borachio managed this by "court[ing] Margaret *in Hero's garments.*"

in II.i.23–24. There we hear only that Antonio, who became his bosom friend, took him "from the breach of the sea" shortly after Viola was supposedly drowned. The middle of the play (III.iii.26–37) brings somewhat obscure word of an earlier "sea-fight" in consequence of which Antonio, having then fought against Orsino's galleys, might have to "pay dear" if captured in Orsino's domain. Not until the last scene of the play (V.i.72–99) are we informed that (1) in Orsino's book Antonio had been set down as a "notable pirate," a "salt-water thief"; (2) Antonio and Sebastian had been close companions ("both day and night did we keep company") for "three months," three long, undramatic months, stretching—uncalendared!—between the opening of the play and its denouement.

4. In the opening of *Measure for Measure*, the Duke hints that he means to watch—perhaps to unmask—his deputy, the "precise" Angelo, by giving him power:

> Hence shall we see,
> If power change purpose, what our seemers be. (I.iii.53–54)

Not till III.i.221–239 is "this well-seeming" Angelo's past re-vealed—his desertion, before the play opened, of his betrothed, Mariana, on the pretense of finding her dishonorable; in reality, because she had lost her brother and her dowry. In IV.i.8–9 we learn from Mariana that the duke had long since befriended her in her trouble, proved himself

> a man of comfort whose advice
> Hath often still'd my brawling discontent.

5. In the closing scene of *All's Well*, Bertram, commanded by the King to marry Maudlin, Lafeu's daughter, in place of his supposedly dead wife, Helena, suddenly attempts to "excuse" his rejection of Helena on the ground that he had "*At first . . .* stuck my choice upon" fair Maudlin (V.iii.42–55). The King, curiously enough, says that Bertram is "well excus'd." It should be noted, however, that similar tricks of delayed exposition—

usually for the sake of surprise, sometimes for retrospective motivation—served the plots of many Elizabethan plays, from *Gorboduc* to *The Silent Woman*, *The White Devil*, *The Duchess of Malfi*, and *The Cardinal*.[22]

6. Less tricky, possibly a mere afterthought, but certainly another clear case of delayed exposition, is Orlando's observation in the closing scene of *As You Like It*, just before Rosalind brings all her couples to the ark and just after the good Duke has "remember[ed] some lively touches of my daughter's favour" in the supposed Ganymede. Says Orlando:

> My lord, *the first time* that ever I saw him
> Methought he was a brother to your daughter. (V.iv.26–29)

Before concluding, I wish to return briefly to *Othello* and to *Hamlet*. Criticism, as a rule, has ignored the matters discussed here. Still, on re-checking my notes on delayed exposition in *Othello*, I find that at least one distinguished scholar has incidentally mentioned another case in point. Othello, writes Professor Kittredge, "has a frank and open nature and is 'not easily jealous'—for we must accept what Shakespeare makes him say of himself in the manifestly expository passage at the end of the play ['Soft you, a word or two before you go. . . .']."[23]

Another scholar and producer, *per contra*, sees something "very like" delayed exposition at the very beginning of a great

---

[22] In *Gorboduc* IV.ii.111, Porrex explains that he killed Ferrex because his brother had secretly tried to poison him. In *The Silent Woman*, the *woman's* "part of the plot" is "conceal[ed]" even from the actors till V.iv.277 (see also II.iv.49). The villains of *The Duchess of Malfi* (IV.ii.293–295) and of *The Cardinal* (III.i.27–28) belatedly explain that money was one substantial motive of their evil-doing, whereas it was "hot lust" in *The White Devil* (IV.iv.111). These and similar instances of withheld or "gradual revelation" (cf. above, nn. 16–18 and text) are, in effect, cases of delayed exposition—at least insofar as they provide retrospective explanatory glimpses, however theatrical, of the characters' early motives.

[23] V.ii.338–356; Kittredge, *Othello*, p. xi.

play. "I have thought of a noble example of a 'delayed exposition' *within an exposition*," writes Professor Nevill Coghill.

> Of course you have . . . noticed the two opening words of *Hamlet*, Bernardo's "Who's there?"
>
> It is clear from what follows *later* that (a) Bernardo is relieving Francisco on sentry-go, and (b) that Bernardo (but not Francisco) *had* seen a ghost on that precise sentry-go the night before.
>
> This explains (by delayed exposition) why the wrong man (Bernardo) gives the challenge. It's an unheard-of thing for a relieving sentry to challenge a sentry on guard, and these two words in themselves show that there is "something rotten in the state of Denmark." And from this tiny detail of action and the *subsequent* exposition, a producer perceives at once how to set the scene on an Elizabethan stage; thus:
>
>> Enter Francisco, pacing to and fro, on guard, and *halting* for a few seconds at the end of his beat.
>>
>> During one of these halts, enter Bernardo, who sees an armed, motionless figure before him. Bernardo has seen *and is expecting to see* a ghost, and cries out in horror "Who's there?" thinking that Francisco *is* the ghost. (Of course a discerning producer will place Francisco *exactly* where the ghost will later appear, and in exactly the same stance. Their armour should be something of the same sort.)
>
> The play in fact opens with a kind of *scream*, Bernardo half-drawing his sword, I suppose; but is instantly reassured by Francisco's authoritative reply, "Nay, answer me! Stand and unfold your*self*." Bernardo's ejaculation (of the pass-word?) "Long live the King!" is one of intense relief.[24]

By the same token, *Hamlet*, like *Othello*, ends as it begins, with a touch of delayed exposition. This comes in the belated revelation of the mutual esteem between the Prince of Denmark and his ambitious successor, Fortinbras:

*Haml.* Fortinbras. . . . has my dying voice.
So tell him . . . (V.ii.367–368; cf. IV.iv.48–50)
*Fort.* Bear Hamlet like a soldier to the stage;
For he was likely, had he been put on,
To have prov'd most royally . . . (V.ii.407–409)

---

[24] Mr. Coghill touched upon other aspects of this subject in his essay, "Shakespeare As A Dramatist," in *Talking of Shakespeare*, ed. John Garrett (London, 1954), pp. 23ff.

# PART THREE

# Literary Influence
## Shakespeare and Milton

# 8

## Shakespearean Recollection in Milton

### A Summing Up

SCHOLARSHIP HAS ALWAYS DELIGHTED to render unto Shakespeare and Milton individually the tribute which is their natural due. Strangely enough, however, it long neglected the relationships between them. Specifically, so far as I know, no systematic investigation of the range and quantity of Shakespearean recollection in Milton, much less of its quality, has been available until our own times. Such an investigation I attempted in three earlier essays. The first of these, "The Shaksperian Element in Milton," appeared in 1925.[1] Next, this was revised and, with substantial additions, for some of which I was indebted to the collections of other scholars, reprinted in my *Shakspere's Silences* (Cambridge, Mass., 1929).[2] This version of the study examined approximately 250 passages in Milton's work, early and late, which seemed significantly reminiscent of Shakespeare, that is to say, of thirty-five of his plays. To these findings I added, in "Shakespeare and Milton Once More" (*SAMLA Studies in Milton*, ed. J. Max Patrick, Gainesville, Florida, 1953)[3] nearly fifty fresh passages from Milton further illustrating his habitual closeness to Shakespeare. The present chapter re-examines and

---

[1] *PMLA*, XL, 645–691.

[2] Pp. 139–208, here revised and supplemented, by permission of the publisher, Harvard University Press.

[3] Pp. 80–99, here revised and integrated by permission of the publisher, University of Florida Press.

combines my previous materials with some new items, and provides essential bibliographical and other addenda. By and large, this study marks one facet of Shakespeare's abiding influence upon his aftertimes at home and abroad.[4]

That there are numerous points of contact between Shakespeare and Milton has, of course, been common knowledge, as has the fact that many likenesses between our poets were noted long ago by Thomas Warton, Warburton, Newton, and others. By 1800 many of these "coincidencies of fancy's sweetest children" had been collected and enlarged upon by Todd in his Variorum edition of Milton,[5] and later such scholars as Verity,[6] Hanford,[7] and others[8] added much valuable material. Even so, the sum total of probable Shakespeare-Milton relationships hitherto generally recognized remained fragmentary, and the task of assembling and testing the evidence was long put off. No doubt the inherent difficulties served as a deterrent. For Milton's "in-

[4] For discussion cf. E. C. Dunn, *Shakespeare in America* (New York, 1939); my *Shakspere's Silences*, pp. 3–5, *Shakespeare and Democracy* (Knoxville, 1941), pp. 5–6, 45 ff., and "Whittier and the English Poets," *New England Quarterly*, XXIV (1951), 53 ff.; and James G. McManaway, "Shakespeare in the United States," *PMLA*, LXXIX (1964), 513–518.

[5] First edition, London, 1801; revised and enlarged, 1809. References below are to this revised edition.

[6] In his editions of *Paradise Lost, Samson Agonistes, Comus, Lycidas and Other Poems*, and *A Midsummer Night's Dream*.

[7] Especially in his article on "The Dramatic Element in *Paradise Lost*," *Studies in Philology*, XIV (1917), 178–195.

[8] Among modern editions of Milton, those of Hanford and Merritt Y. Hughes are especially useful for notes on the pros and cons of Shakespearean and other literary influence on Milton. Related aspects of our subject are touched upon in many works early and late besides those mentioned above; notably, among others, in Sir Arthur Quiller-Couch's *Shakespeare's Workmanship* (New York, 1917), and in William Haller's "What Needs My Shakespeare," *Shakespeare Quarterly*, III (1952), 3 ff. A substantial list of recent items appears in Gordon R. Smith's *Classified Shakespeare Bibliography, 1936–1958* (University Park, Penn., 1963), p. 368. See also below, p. 141, n. 11. I have drawn freely upon these materials, especially upon those made available by the late Professor George Coffin Taylor in his "Shakspere and Milton Again," *Studies in Philology*, XXIII (1926), 189–199, and upon unpublished notes kindly sent me by Professor S. F. Gingerich and Dr. Wilmon Brewer. Items not otherwise credited (see below, p. 143) are my own.

stinct of eager assimilation"[9] from all the world of great books necessarily makes somewhat difficult, not to say hazardous, the attempt to assign a definite source[10] to any given thought or phrase of his. And even though it be granted that certain of these are evidently colored by Shakespearean reminiscence, it is not always possible to point to the exact passage in Shakespeare from which they are derived; for it is characteristic of the working of Milton's creative imagination that he fused—or transfused, into something new and strange—the rich and varied stores of his memory. Yet one must recognize, on the other hand, that surprisingly similar phrases or ideas may be spontaneously and independently generated by any two poets, and that other similarities may grow out of the poets' use of common sources.[11]

To be sure, when one reads in *Paradise Lost* that

Adam . . . wept
*Though not of woman born*; compassion quelled
*His best of man* and *gave him up to tears*  (IX.495–497)[12]

---

[9] Cf. W. V. Moody, Cambridge Poets *Milton* (Boston, 1899), p. 95.

[10] Some cases of obviously casual analogy are easily recognizable. For example, it is probably mere chance that Shakespeare and Milton give qualified approval, respectively, to "self-love" and to "self-esteem" (*Henry V* II.iv.74–75; *PL* VIII. 571–572). Again, Shakespearean reminiscence is not needed to account for the fact that Milton matches Shakespeare's animadversions upon the multitude (the "giddy and unsure . . . vulgar heart," the "fond Many" of 2 *Henry IV* I.iii.89–91) with the Saviour's sharp reflection in *PR* III.49–51 upon "the people" as "a herd confused,/A miscellaneous rabble who extol/Things vulgar." Some cases, however, are not so clear. In the text below, for example, I have reluctantly omitted a striking likeness between a famous line from *Hamlet* (I.iv.56) and an equally famous line from *PL* (II.148), though it can hardly be denied that Belial's "thoughts that wander through eternity" are, in one sense, strikingly analogous to Hamlet's "thoughts beyond the reaches of our souls." In this case it is not safe to assume that Milton necessarily remembered Shakespeare—but it is not easy to make up one's mind. Cf. n. 11 and below, pp. 158 f., under *Hamlet* B(5) (b).

[11] Two studies which emphasize common sources as the explanation of certain Shakespeare-Milton likenesses are G. C. Taylor's "Patristic Conventions Common to Shakespeare and Milton," *Studies in Philology*, XXVIII (1931), 625 ff., and John E. Hankins' "Pains of the Afterworld in Milton and Shakespeare," *PMLA*, LXXI (1956), 482 ff.

[12] Except as otherwise noted, the texts used here are *The Complete Works of Shakespeare*, ed. G. L. Kittredge (Boston, 1936), and *The Poems of John Milton*,

one is moved to recall the coming of Birnam Wood to Dunsinane which cowed the better part of man in Macbeth because his opponent, Macduff, was not of woman born; that Adam gave himself up to tears reminds us that Exeter in *Henry V* did exactly this in mourning the loss of a comrade at Agincourt.[13] Moreover, in this case suspicion virtually becomes certainty because many other passages in Milton prove definitely that he knew and cherished *Macbeth* and *Henry V*. Other cases are less obvious. Indeed, many Shakespearean lines cited by Milton's commentators, early and late, are neither close parallels nor even slight reminiscences, but merely illustrations of current Elizabethan idioms.[14] The student in search of actual evidence of Shakespearean reminiscence in Milton must therefore thread his way warily through the commentators. Again, commentators and editors usually content themselves with line-by-line notes or glosses upon Milton's text. When they quote Shakespearean "parallels" they rarely put two and two together. Yet to eliminate mere conjecture so far as may be, it is necessary to set side by side, not one or two possible reminiscences from, say, *The Merchant of Venice* or *Julius Caesar*, but all probable or possible echoes of any given play in all of Milton's work, so far as they can be discovered. This method, here adopted, makes it possible to test any single case by the whole body of the evidence. The cumulative effect of the evidence thus adduced frequently serves to establish the probability of Milton's indebtedness to Shakespeare in cases that, taken by themselves, might well be thought doubtful; whereas the absence of cumulative evidence

---

ed. J. H. Hanford, 2nd ed. (New York, 1953). Just which of the early editions of Shakespeare *Milton* may have used—or perhaps unconsciously collated?—can hardly be determined; but textual variations in Shakespeare do not substantially affect Milton's Shakespearean reminiscence.

13 See below, pp. 169, 193.

14 See, for example, Verity's notes on *PL* I.206, VI.374, etc., and Todd's on *PL* VIII.62, *Il Penseroso* 35, etc.

suggests that other cases, not without interest in themselves, must be set aside as somewhat remote possibilities.[15] This method will also bring out points of contact between our poets which seem hitherto to have escaped the commentators—or, at worst, an occasional fresh "coincidency" which, since it concerns Shakespeare and Milton, may be of interest even if it is only a coincidence. Again, this systematic survey will indicate how many of Shakespeare's plays Milton remembered and which ones he remembered best.

The method of presentation in the summaries below, further, is intended to indicate something of the nature and quality of Milton's Shakespearean recollection. Of many possible classifications only two seemed finally practicable. Some of the plays remained in Milton's memory not by virtue of their underlying dramatic concepts but solely by the spell of the Shakespearean word or the fascination of their imagery. Such echoes or likenesses—of epithet, phrase, or figure: all essentially *verbal* or *figurative*, and very often both in one—I have brought together, play by play, in Group A. Reminiscences or striking likenesses more essentially *dramatic* in nature—echoes of dramatic theme or mood, situation, or characterization—are presented play by play, in so far as they occur, in Group B. The underlying assumption here is that the presence of recognizable verbal or figurative echoes of any one play in Milton establishes fair ground for considering the possibility that such a play *may* also have influenced Milton's dramatic workmanship. Most of the material below I have independently collected, but it goes without saying that I owe many specific items, and much general aid and comfort, to Milton's editors and commentators. All passages observed by them are noted *passim*.[16] New matter—that is, material not spe-

---

[15] In this connection see, for example, notes 149 and 195, below.

[16] Usually by initials appended to the passages from Milton: B = Bowle; D = Dunster; N = Newton; S = Steevens; W = Thomas Warton; T = Todd (whose Variorum edition of 1809 may be consulted for citations from these writers);

cifically credited to earlier students—has, as a rule, been entered at the end of each of the two groups.

In addition to supplying a reasonably broad and systematic basis for the study of the quantitative and qualitative aspects of Shakespeare's influence upon Milton, this study will, I hope, be useful in another way. It should help to dispel a venerable misconception which has blinded many students; namely, the belief that the Elizabethan poets, especially the dramatists, influenced Milton only in his youth; that in his maturity they ceased to interest or inspire him; so that, as Thomas Warton[17] has it, "his warmest poetical predilections were at last totally obliterated by civil and religious enthusiasm" or crowded out of his memory because classical standards and Puritan doctrine claimed him for their own. The critics would seem to have been misled by Milton's bitter comment (in the preface to *Samson Agonistes*) upon the "infamy" into which "tragedy . . . with other common Interludes" had fallen in the Restoration theater, when the sons of Belial held the stage. They fail to remember that in the preface to *Paradise Lost* he justifies his choice of blank verse partly on the ground that "our best English tragedies" had "rejected rime." Some time ago a writer in one of our journals[18] declared categorically, after a "very careful examination" of the prose and verse of this very Milton who thus cites the authority or example of the Elizabethan dramatists, that his "connections with [Elizabethan] dramatic literature were very slight." This astonishing conclusion was perhaps a result of the traditional failure of the critics[19] to see a distinction which this study is intended to em-

---

Br. = R. C. Browne (*English Poems by John Milton*, Clarendon Press, 1923); G. C. T. = George Coffin Taylor ("Shakspere and Milton Again," see above, n. 8); H = Hanford (see above, n. 7); M = Masson (*Poetical Works of John Milton*, 1890); V = Verity (see above, n. 6).

[17] Cf. Todd, VII, 181.

[18] Professor Louis Wann, "Lycidas and Barnavelt," *Modern Language Notes*, XXXVII (1922), 473, n.

[19] See also, for example, Professor Hales's "Milton's *Macbeth*," *Nineteenth Century*, XXX (1891), 919–932, still a valuable paper, though it repeats something

phasize; namely, that while Milton, as time went on, lost patience with the stage and theater, he always retained imaginative sympathy with the profound and challenging beauty of Elizabethan dramatic poetry. He gave the best possible proof of this by remembering it. A glance at the many Shakespearean reminiscences in *Paradise Lost, Paradise Regained,* and *Samson,* recorded below, will remind readers that not the least glory of these last and greatest of Milton's works lies in their subtle overtones of memory—their echoes of Shakespeare (and his fellows)[20] recollected in tranquillity, amid the din of evil tongues in evil days.

## I. THE TRAGEDIES

### *1. Titus Andronicus.*[21]

The first Shakespearean tragedy which unmistakably left its mark upon Milton's memory is, as one would expect, not *Titus Andronicus* but *Romeo and Juliet.* It has been thought, however, that a line in *L'Allegro* resembles a phrase in the earlier play:

---

of the old mistake. "Milton in his younger days . . . read Shakspere with immense appreciation." But the *Samson* preface, according to Hales, is not to be explained by Milton's disgust with the Restoration theater. Only the Greek drama was "meet and right" in his eyes. "The modern drama seemed a somewhat dubious growth . . . with which as an author he meant to have little to do, however he might peruse it as a reader." The evidence below will indicate that Milton *as an author,* even though he did not write dramas in the manner of the Elizabethans, had much to do with them by virtue of his memory. A notable exception to the usual critical blindness appeared in the excellent paper already referred to (see n. 7) by Professor Hanford. "There is no evidence," says Hanford, "that Milton ever outgrew his early love of Elizabethan drama. . . . What passes out of Milton is but the more sensuous and esthetic essence of Elizabethan poetry. . . . [His] sympathy with the English renaissance in its moral, philosophical, and human phases deepens with advancing years. Classicism moulds and modifies the Elizabethan influences. Puritanism makes them wear a special expression. But neither Classicism nor Puritanism can efface them."

20 Cf. *PMLA,* XLIII (1928), 569–570.

21 See also below, p. 180, n. 99.

## A.

(1) II.iii.15:
The green leaves quiver with the cooling wind.
And make a *chequer'd shadow* on the ground.

*L'Allegro* 95–96:
Many a youth and many a maid
Dancing in the *chequered shade*.—
(Richardson; cf. T)

### 2. *Romeo and Juliet*.[22]

In Milton's first Latin elegy occurs his familiar description of "the pomp of the changing theater" as he saw it in the days of his youth. Some of the stock characters of Roman comedy pass in review, and "awful tragedy" shakes her "bloody sceptre":

> Bitterness mingles with sweet tears as I see some hapless boy, torn from his love, leave all his joys untasted, and fall lamentable; or when the fierce avenger of crime recrosses the Styx out of the shades. (Moody's translation, lines 40–43)

"By the youth," writes Thomas Warton,[23] "he perhaps intends Shakspeare's Romeo. In the second either Hamlet or Richard the Third. He then draws his illustrations from the ancient tragedians." That the hapless boy was Romeo several later scholars[24] have independently conjectured, and on the face of it no conjecture could be more plausible than that young Milton must have felt the spell of Shakespeare's immortal tragedy of youth. There is evidence—fairly substantial, though less far-reaching than in the case of the greater tragedies—to indicate that he did not soon forget it.

## A.

(1) II.iii.1:
The grey eye'd *morn smiles* on the *frowning night*.

*PL* V.124:
When fair *Morning* first *smiles* on the world.— (T)

---

[22] Some commentators see likenesses (over and above those listed here) between the play, I.iv.19–21, and *PL* IV.181 (S); II.ii.28, and *PL* III.229 (G. C. T.).

[23] Cf. Todd, VII, 181.

[24] Cf., for example, E. N. S. Thompson, *Essays on Milton* (New Haven, 1914), pp. 14–15.

*Ibid.* III. 424:
Dark, waste, and wild, under the
   *frown of Night.*— (T) [25]

(2) II.iii.9–10 *(from the same
   speech as* [1]):
The earth that's *nature's mother* is
   her tomb,
What is her *burying grave* that is
   her *womb.*

*PL* II.910–911:
            This wild Abyss,
The *womb of Nature* and perhaps
   *her grave.*— (T)

(3) I.iv.37:
For I am *proverb'd* with a grandsire
   phrase.

*Samson* 203:
Am I not sung and *proverbed* for a
   fool?— (D; cf. G. C. T.) [26]

(4) I.iv.100–101:
            The *wind,* who *wooes*
Even now the frozen bosom of the
   North. . . .

*On the Nativity* 37–38:
She [Nature] *woos* the *gentle air.*[27]

(5) III.ii.1–21:
Gallop apace, you fiery-footed steeds,
Towards Phoebus' lodging; such a
   wagoner
As Phaethon would whip you to the
   west
And bring in *cloudy night* immedi-
   ately.
Spread thy close curtain, love-per-
   forming night,
That runaway eyes may wink . . .
   *Come, civil* night,
Thou *sober-suited matron all in
   black* . . . .
*Hood* my unmann'd blood, baiting
   in my cheeks,
With *thy black mantle.* . . . *Come,*

*Il Penseroso* 122:
Till *civil-suited* Morn appear.— (T)
*Ibid.* 31-33:
*Come,* pensive Nun, devout and
   pure . . .
*All in a robe of darkest grain* . . .

*PL* II.962:
*Sable-vested Night,* eldest of things.

*The Passion* 29–30:
*Befriend* me, *Night,* best Patroness
   of grief,
Over the pole thy *thickest mantle*
   throw.

*PL* IV.598–609:
Now came still Evening on, and
   Twilight gray

---

[25] Verity compares with the "black-*brow'd night*" of *A Midsummer Night's
Dream* III.ii.387, "the rugged *brow* of *night*" of *Il Penseroso* 58.

[26] See below, n. 86 and text. Taylor also compares *Romeo and Juliet* V.iii.35,
with *Samson,* 952–953, but the resemblance between these lines rests upon a commonplace which editors find also in Euripides and Massinger.

[27] See also *Macbeth* I.vi.1–3, 5–6.

loving black-brow'd night,
Give me my Romeo.

Had in her *sober livery* all things
    clad.
Silence accompanied. . . . Hesperus
    that led
The starry host, rode brightest, till
    the Moon
Rising *in clouded majesty*, at length
Apparent queen, unveiled her peer-
    less light
And o'er the dark her *silver mantle*
    threw.[28]

(6)  II.ii.161–164:
Bondage is hoarse and may not
    speak aloud;
Else would I tear the cave where
    *Echo* lies,
And make her *airy tongue* more
    hoarse than mine
With repetition of my Romeo's
    *name*.

*Comus 205–209 (just before the Lady
    sings her Echo song, she recalls*):
A thousand fantasies . . .
Of calling shapes and beckoning
    shadows dire,
And *airy tongues* that syllable men's
    *names*
On sands and shores and desert
    wildernesses.

(7)  IV.i.45  (*Juliet to the Friar*):
Come weep with me—*past hope,
    past cure, past help!*

*Samson 120–121*
(*The Chorus first sees Samson*):
As one *past hope*, abandoned,
And by himself given over.

(8)  IV.i.81, 84; iii.40–45:
Or shut me nightly in a *charnel
    house* . . .

*Comus 470–473*:
Such are those thick and gloomy
    shadows damp

---

[28] Of the five passages from Milton here noted, the likeness in language between the first and Juliet's "sober-suited matron, civil night" is the only one that
has been generally recognized: Of the other passages the last two are of especial
interest—the lines from *The Passion* because that poem was written within a few
years of the *Elegia Prima* (in which Milton, as we have seen, probably alludes to
Romeo). The last passage may be more doubtful, but I think it is at least possible,
in view of Milton's habit of repeating himself in repeating Shakespeare, to recognize in this beautiful evening scene, written late in Milton's life, a memory, however shadowy, of Juliet's "cloudy night"—of the sober-suited matron's mantle
turned silver, as it were, in the star-light of memory. (This in spite of the fact that
other poets employ the same figure, Todd, for example, citing Phineas Fletcher
[*Purple Island* VI.54], "night's black livery," and Spenser [*Epithalamion* 315–332],
"Now welcome, Night . . . And in thy sable mantle us enwrap." The phrase "sable
night" occurs also in *Lucrece*. See below, p. 221.

Or bid me go into a *new-made grave.* . . .
As in a vault . . .
. . . where, as they say,
At some hours in the night *spirits resort.*

Oft seen in *charnel vaults* and sepulchres,
Lingering, and sitting by *a new-made grave*
As *loth to leave the body* that it loved.

## B.

(1) Like Romeo and Juliet's good friar, the Genius of the Wood in *Arcades* makes his rounds at early dawn to visit and cherish his plants and flowers.

II.iii.1–18:
The grey-ey'd morn smiles on the frowning night . . .
And flecked darkness like a drunkard reels
From forth day's path. . . .
Now, ere the sun advance his burning eye . . .
I must up-fill this osier cage of ours
With baleful weeds and precious-juiced flowers.
. . . from [earth's] womb children of divers kind
We sucking on her natural bosom find;
Many for many virtues excellent. . . .
For naught so vile that on the earth doth live
But to the earth some special good doth give.

*Arcades* 48–60:
. . . all my plants I save from nightly ill . . .
And from the boughs brush off the evil dew,
And heal the harms of thwarting thunder blue,
Or what the cross dire-looking planet smites. . . .
And early ere the odorous breath of morn
Awakes the slumbering leaves, or tasselled horn
Shakes the high thicket, haste I all about,
Number my ranks, and visit every sprout
With puissant words and murmurs made to bless.

## *3. Julius Caesar.*

### A.

(1) II.ii.18:
*Graves* have *yawn'd* and yielded up their dead.

*PL* X.635:
Sin and Death and *yawning grave.*—
(T)

(2) III.i.273:
Cry *'Havoc!'* and let slip the *dogs of war.*

*PL* X.616–617 (*on Sin and Death coming to earth*):
See with what heat these *dogs of Hell* advance
To waste and *havoc* yonder World.— (V)

(3) II.i.230:
Enjoy the honey-heavy *dew of slumber.*

*PL* IV.614:
The timely *dew of sleep.*— (V) [29]

(4) IV.iii.226:
The *deep of night* is crept upon our talk.

*PL* IV.674:
Unbeheld in *deep of night.*— (V) [30]

(5) IV.i.19–26:
        These honors . . .
He shall but bear them *as the ass bears gold . . .*
And having brought our treasure where we will
Then take we down his load and *turn him off*
*(Like to the empty ass).* . . .

*Samson* 537–539:
A deceitful concubine, who shore me
*Like a tame wether,* all my precious fleece;
Then *turned me out,* ridiculous, despoiled.— (G. C. T.)

## B.

(1) Both Caesar and Samson respond with haughty refusal to the demand that they present themselves publicly to the Roman Senate and the Philistine lords, respectively:

II.ii.59–64:
*Decius.* I come to fetch you to the Senate House . . .
*Caesar.* Tell them that *I will not come to-day.*
Cannot, is false; and that I dare not, falser;
*I will not come.*

*Samson* 1318, 1332, 1342 (*Samson, bidden to appear before the "illustrious lords" of the Philistines*):
Return the way thou camest; *I will not come . . . .*
Joined with extreme contempt! *I will not come.*— (G. C. T.)

---

[29] Verity compares also *Richard III* IV.i.84: "The golden dew of sleep."
[30] Cf. also *Merry Wives* IV.iv.40: "In deep of night to walk by this Herne's oak"—(V). See also below, *Lear*, A (4), p. 166, top.

(2) Compare Cassius' description of Caesar, and Samson's of himself:

I.ii.135:

He doth bestride the narrow world *Like a Colossus,* and we *petty* men Walk under his huge legs and peep about To find ourselves dishonorable graves.

*Samson* 529–531:

Fearless of danger, *like a petty god,* I walked about, admired of all and dreaded On hostile ground, none daring my affront.

(3) The lofty elegiac close of *Samson* is strikingly like the noble closing tribute to Brutus:

V.v.56, 68–75:

Brutus only overcame himself . . . This was the *noblest* Roman of them all . . . . His life was gentle, and the elements So mix'd in him that Nature might stand up And say to all the world, 'This was a man.'

*Samson* 1709–1710, 1721–1724:

Samson hath quit himself / Like Samson . . . . Nothing is here for tears, nothing to wail Or knock the breast, no weakness, no contempt, Dispraise, or blame, nothing but well and fair, And what may quiet us in a death so *noble.*

*4. Hamlet.*

A.

(1) I.i.44:

Most like; it *harrows* me with *fear* and wonder.

*Comus* 565:

Amazed I stood, *harrowed* with grief and *fear.*— (S)

(2) I.iv.52:

Thou, dead corse, again *in complete steel.*

*Comus* 421 (*on chastity*):

She that has that is clad *in complete steel.*— (T)

(3) I.v.17–20:

Make . . . each particular *hair* to stand on end Like quills upon the *fretful porpentine.*

*Samson* 1136–1138:

Though all thy *hairs* Were bristles . . . Of chafed wild boars or *ruffled porcupines.*— (N)

(4) I.i.118–123:
*Disasters* in *the sun* . . . *the moist star*
Upon whose influence Neptune's empire stands
Was sick almost to doomsday with *eclipse* . . . .
As . . . prologue to the *omen coming on.*

*PL* I.594–599:
    *The sun* new-risen
Looks through the horizontal misty air
Shorn of his beams, or from behind *the moon*
In *dim eclipse, disastrous* twilight sheds
On half the nations, and with *fear of change*
Perplexes monarchs.— (T) [31]

(5) III.iv.45–51:
    O, such a *deed* . . . .
    Heaven's face doth glow,
Yea, *this solidity and compound mass*
With tristful visage as against the doom
Is *thought-sick* at the act.

*PL* IX.782–784:
*Earth* felt *the wound,* and Nature from her seat
*Sighing* through all her works, gave signs of woe
That all was lost.— (Davies) [32]

(6) I.ii.10–13 (*Claudius, opening speech*):
As 'twere with a defeated joy,
With an auspicious and a dropping eye,
In equal scale *weighing delight with dole.*

*PL* IV.892–894:
    Change
Torment with ease, and soonest *recompense*
*Dole with delight.*— (T)

(7) II.ii.485–486:
With *eyes like carbuncles* . . . Pyrrhus
Old grandsire Priam seeks.

*PL* IX.499–500 (*the serpent*):
    His head
Crested aloft, and *carbuncle his eyes.*
    — (T)

---

[31] Verity compares a somewhat similar figure in *Hamlet* I.i.126, and *PL* X.412–414. See also *King Lear* I.ii.112, 130: "*eclipses* in the sun and moon"; "our *disasters.*"

[32] For this "sublime passage of the Earth's sympathizing with Adam and Eve when they ate the forbidden fruit," Milton may have been indebted to the lines quoted from Hamlet's remonstrance to his mother upon her crime. (Davies, *Dramatic Miscellanies.*)

(8) II.ii.508–509:[33]
    The dreadful *thunder*
Doth *rend* the region . . . .

(9) I.v.63–64:
And *in the porches of my ears* did
    *pour*
The *leperous distilment.*

(10) III.iii.97–98 (*Claudius pray-
    ing*):
My *words fly up*, my thoughts re-
    main below,
Words without thoughts never *to
    heaven* go.

(11) I.iii.78–80:
    *To thine own self be true* . . .
Thou canst not then be *false* to any
    man.

(12) III.iv.51–52 (*the Queen to
    Hamlet*):
    *Ay me! What act*
That roars so loud and *thunders* in
    the index?

(13) III.ii.19–20:
*Suit the action to the word, the word
    to the action.*

(14) III.i.51–53:
The *harlot's cheek*, beautied with
    plast'ring art,
Is not more ugly to the thing that
    helps it

*PL* XII.181–182:
    *Thunder* mixed with hail
. . . must *rend* the Egyptian sky.— (V)

*Comus* 839–840:
And *through the porch* and inlet
    of *each sense*
*Dropt* in *ambrosial oils.*— (N)

*PL* XI.14–15:
*To Heaven* their *prayers*
*Flew up*, nor missed the way.— (V)
*On the Religious Memory of Mrs.
    Catherine Thomason* 5–13 (*Her
    good "works and alms"*):
Stayed not behind, nor in the grave
    were trod;
But. . . . *up they flew* . . .
*Before the Judge.*

*Samson* 823–824 (*Samson to Dalila;
    cf. 784*):
Bitter reproach though true
*I to myself was false ere thou to me.*

*PL* X.813–815 (*Adam on the fear of
    eternal punishment*):
    *Ay me! That fear*
Comes *thundering* back with dread-
    ful revolution
On my defenceless head.

*PR* III.9–10:
*Thy actions to thy words accord, thy
    words*
*To thy large heart* give utterance
    due.

*PR* IV.343–344:
. . . their *swelling epithets* thick laid
As *varnish* on a *harlot's cheek.*— (D)

---

33 Passages (7) and (8) are both from the player's ranting speech.

Than is my deed to my most *painted*
   word.

(15) I.ii.133–134:
How *weary*, stale, *flat*, and unprof-
   itable
*Seem* to me all the uses of this
   world!

*Samson* 594–596:
So much I feel *my genial spirits*
   *droop*,
My hopes all *flat*; Nature within
   me *seems*
In all her functions *weary* of herself.— (M) [34]

(16) V.ii.358:
Absent thee from *felicity* awhile,
And in this harsh world draw thy
   breath *in pain*,
To tell my story.

*Epitaph on the Marchioness of Win-*
   *chester* 61–68:
Whilst thou, bright Saint, high sitt'st
   in glory,
Next her, much like to thee in story,
[Joseph's mother, who] at her next
   birth, much like thee
*Through pangs* fled to *felicity*.[35]

(17) Immediately below[36] I present evidence to show that Milton
remembered the "thoughts, deeds, and words" of certain outstanding characters of this play, including the words of the
Ghost in his opening colloquy with Hamlet. If my ear does not
deceive me, the cadence[37] of another great line in the Ghost's
speech seems to have echoed and re-echoed in Milton's memory,
and thereafter, with Miltonic variations, in the memory of other
English poets.

I.v.76–77 (*the elder Hamlet was*):
Cut off even in the blossoms of my
   sin,
*Unhous'led, disappointed, unanel'd.*

*PL* II.185; V.899:
*Unrespited, unpitied, unreprieved.*
   . . .
*Unshaken, unseduced, unterrified.*
*PR* III.429:
*Unhumbled, unrepentant, unre-*
   *formed.*

---

[34] Cf. below, pp. 157–158, 173.

[35] This *Epitaph* also echoes unmistakably a song from *Cymbeline* (cf. p. 213).

[36] Under B, p. 155.

[37] I think it was Shakespeare's cadence that took the ear of the later poets. This
in spite of the fact, noted by Thyer and Todd (see Todd, II, 387), that some of the

Note also: Pope's "unwept, unhonoured, uninterr'd";[38] Scott's "unwept, unhonour'd, and unsung";[39] Byron's "unknell'd, uncoffin'd, and unknown";[40] and Browning's "ignoble, insufficient, incomplete."[41] One word more as regards the cadence. In Shaw's *Dark Lady of the Sonnets* the Beefeater asks, "What manner of thing is a cadence, sir?" To which the Man (Shakespeare) replies, once for all, "A thing to rule the world with, friend."[42]

B. The characteristics, thoughts, deeds, and words of certain outstanding persons of the play have left their mark upon Milton's characters:

(1) The Ghost.

(a) I.v.2–4 (*his return to torture*):
My *hour* is almost come
When I to sulph'rous and *torment-ing* flames
Must render up myself.

*PL* II.88–92 (*Moloch, on "the pain of unextinguishable fire"*):
When the scourge
Inexorably, and the *torturing hour*[43]
Calls us to penance.— (T)

(b) I.i.145–146 (*his invulnerability*):
It is as the *air, invulnerable,*
And our vain blows malicious mockery.

*PL* VI.344–349:
*Spirits . . .*
Cannot but by annihilating die,
*Nor* in their liquid texture *mortal wound*
*Receive*, no more than can the fluid air.— (V) [44]

---

Greek tragedians and some English poets before Shakespeare had—with sundry differing cadences—used "this way of introducing several adjectives beginning with the same letter, without any conjunction"—as in Spenser's "unbodied, unsoul'd, unheard, unseen" (*FQ* VII.vii.46) and Fairfax's "unseen, unmark'd, unpitied, unrewarded" (*Tasso* II. xvi). Later editors who comment on the *Hamlet* passage in connection with *PL* II.185 include Browne, Verity, and F. A. Patterson (*The Student's Milton*, New York, 1933).

[38] *Iliad* XXII.484.
[39] *Lay of the Last Minstrel* VI.i.
[40] *Childe Harold* IV.179.
[41] *Luria* IV.190.
[42] G. B. Shaw, *Misalliance, The Dark Lady, Fanny's First Play* (London, 1914), p. 135.
[43] Cf. below, *A Midsummer Night's Dream*, A (6), p. 197.
[44] Cf. below, *Macbeth*, B (3) (c), p. 172, and *Tempest* III.iii.62–63.

(c) I.i.158–164 (*not "abroad" in the Christmas season*):
*Some say* that ever 'gainst that season comes
Wherein our Saviour's birth is celebrated,
The bird of dawning singeth *all night* long;
And then, they say, *no spirit can walk abroad,*
The nights are wholesome, then no planets strike,
*No fairy takes, nor witch hath power to charm.*

*Comus* 432–437:
*Some say, no evil thing that walks by night*
In fog, or fire, by lake or moorish fen,
Blue meager hag, or stubborn *unlaid ghost*[45]
That breaks his magic chains at curfew time,
No goblin or swart *fairy* of the mine
Hath hurtful power o'er true virginity.[46]

## (2)  King Hamlet's picture.

III.iv.55–59:
See what a *grace* was *seated on this brow;*
Hyperion's curls; the *front* of Jove himself;
A *station* like *the herald Mercury,*
New *lighted* on a heaven-kissing *hill.*

*PL* II.301–304 (*Beëlzebub in Pandemonium*):
                In his rising seemed
A pillar of state; deep *on his front*
Deliberation sat and public care
And princely counsel . . .— (V)

*Ibid.* V. 275–276, 285–286 (*Raphael reaches Eden*):
At once on the eastern *cliff* of Paradise
He *lights.* . . . Like *Maia's son he stood*
And shook his plumes.— (N)

*PR* II.216–218 (*Satan on Christ*):
How would one look from his *majestic brow*
*Seated* as *on the top* of Virtue's *hill*
Discountenance her, despised[47] . . . .
                — (D)

---

[45] Cf. below, *Cymbeline,* A (2), p. 213.

[46] In writing this passage, "Milton had Shakspeare in his head"—Warton (cf. Todd, VI, 313, and Taylor, p. 190).

[47] That is, the lure of woman.

(3) Claudius:[48] his prayer, and Satan's, frustrated by persistence in sin.

III.iv.64–66:

> What then? What rests?
> *Try what repentance can.* What can
> it not?
> Yet what can it when one cannot
> repent?

*PL* IV.79–82:

> O then at last relent: *is there no
> place
> Left for repentance,* none for par-
> don left?
> None left but by submission; and
> that word
> Disdain forbids me.— (N)

(4) Polonius, crying out from behind the arras just before he is slain, is alluded to[49] in the *Apology for Smectymnuus*, perhaps to remind Milton's opponents that tedious old fools behind the arras are sometimes in grave danger of sudden annihilation:

III.iv.22–23:

> *Polonius [behind].* What ho! help,
> help, help!
> *Hamlet [draws].* How now! A rat?
> Dead, for a ducat, dead!

*Apology (Prose Works,* ed. J. A. St.
John, III, 140):

> *This Champion from behind the
> Arras cries out* that those toothless
> satires were of the Remonstrant's
> making . . . .

(5) Hamlet.—The influence of three of his speeches seems especially recognizable in Milton.

(a) I.ii.129–146 (*themes: world-
weariness, suicide, woman's inconstancy*):

> O that this too, too solid flesh would
> melt . . . .
> Or that the Everlasting had not fix'd
> His canon 'gainst self-slaughter. O
> God! God!
> How weary, stale, flat and unprof-
> itable

*PL* X.1001–1002 (*Eve in despair,
after the fall, suggests suicide*):

> Let us seek Death, or, he not found,
> supply
> With our own hands his office on
> ourselves.

*Ibid.* X.1025–1028 (*Adam replies
that death*):

> So snatched will not exempt us from
> the pain

---

[48] See also entry A (10) of this play, p. 153.

[49] As Furnivall, and others, have observed (see John J. Munro, *Shakspere Allusion Book* [London, 1909], I, 475, and Milton's *Prose Works,* ed. J. A. St. John [London, 1904–1909], III, 140, n.).

Seem to me all the uses of this world . . . .
Let me not think on't. *Frailty, thy name is woman.*

We are by doom to pay; rather such acts
Of contumacy will provoke the highest
To make death in us live.

*Samson* 595–596, 783, 1010–1012
   (*Samson, world-weary; the Chorus on Woman*):
      Nature within me seems
In all her functions weary of herself.— (M) [50]
Nor should'st thou have trusted that to *woman's frailty* . . . .
It is not virtue, wisdom, valour, wit . . .
That woman's love can win or long inherit.[51]

(b) Hanford[52] has shown that the "To be or not to be" soliloquy is closely related to Adam's self-communion after the fall.

> How gladly would I meet
> Mortality my sentence, and be Earth
> Insensible, *how glad would lay me down*
> *As in my mother's lap!* There I should *rest*
> *And sleep secure;* his dreadful voice no more
> Would thunder in my ears, no fear of worse
> To me and to my offspring would torment me
> With cruel expectation. *Yet one doubt*
> *Pursues me still, lest all I cannot die,*
> Lest that pure breath of life, the spirit of Man
> Which God inspired, cannot together perish
> With this corporeal clod; then in the grave
> Or in some other dismal place, who knows
> But I shall die a living death? (*PL* X.775–788)

Undeniably the passage owes much, in language and sentiment, to the Book of Job, but "the weighing of the problem, the shrink-

50 See below, on *Macbeth*, B (3) (e), p. 173.
51 See below, on *Cymbeline*, B (2), p. 214.
52 See above, p. 140, n. 7, and cf. *Measure for Measure*, pp. 210–211, below.

ing on the brink of the unknown, the sense of mystery which puzzles the will—'to die, to sleep! To sleep? Perchance to dream!' —all this is Hamlet." It may be worth while to add that other characters in *Paradise Lost* likewise reflect this characteristic "weighing of the problem": that Adam, tossed "in a troublous sea of passion" (like Hamlet's "sea of troubles," or Isaiah's)[53] has comrades in perplexity. Moloch knows that he wants war, but cannot shut his eyes to certain alternatives and questions:

> What fear we then? . . .
> His utmost ire . . .
> Will either quite consume us . . .
> Or, if our substance be indeed divine
> . . . we are at worst
> On this side nothing. (*PL* II.94–101)

Belial, like Hamlet for at least one great moment, argues that the ills we have,

> Though full of pain, this intellectual being,
> Those thoughts that wander through eternity (*Ibid.* II.146–147),

are preferable to annihilation in the unknown, for who knows whether oblivion—that "beastly oblivion" of which Hamlet speaks—would bring peace:

> . . . who knows
> . . . whether our angry Foe
> Can give it, or will ever? (*Ibid.* II.151–153)

Eve, finally, meditates upon the now and the hereafter with Hamlet-like question and iteration even before she tastes the apple. God, says she,

> Forbids us good, forbids us to be wise!
> Such prohibitions bind not. *But if Death*
> *Bind us with after-bands,* what profits then
> Our inward freedom? (*Ibid.* IX.759–762)

---

[53] *Hamlet* III.i.59; *Isaiah* lvii.20; cf. Verity on *PL* X.718.

And after eating she continues the debate before deciding to let Adam share the fruit.

(c) II.ii.309–322 (*on the dust and divinity of the world, of man, and of woman*):

*This goodly frame,* the earth, seems to me a sterile promontory . . . this brave o'erhanging firmament . . . a foul and pestilent congregation of vapours. *What a piece of work is a man!* how noble in reason! how infinite in faculty! in form and moving how express and admirable! in action how like an angel! in apprehension how like a god! the beauty of the world! *the paragon of animals!* And yet, to me, what is *this quintessence of dust?* Man *delights* not me,—no, nor *woman* neither. . . .

*PL* VIII.15:
When I behold *this goodly frame* this World . . . .— (T) [54]

*Samson* 667:
God of our fathers! *what is man . . . .*

*PL* VII.505–511:
There wanted yet *the master-work, the end*
Of all yet done—a creature who not prone
And brute as other creatures, but endued
With sanctity of reason, might erect
His stature, and upright with front serene
Govern the rest, self-knowing, and from thence
Magnanimous to correspond with Heaven.

*Ibid.* VII.524–525:
                    Man,
*Dust* of the ground . . . .

*PR* II.153, 191–192 (*Belial in council suggests that Christ be tempted with woman*):
[*Belial*] Set *women* in his eye . . .
[*Satan*] These . . . / *Delight* not all.

All readers of Milton are familiar with the opening echo here noted, but the probability that he recalled Hamlet's speech as an organic whole has escaped notice. The last phrase, "Man delights not me . . ." would seem to have left its mark, however slightly and strangely, upon *Paradise Regained*, and the rest re-

---

[54] "This universal frame, thus wondrous fair" (*PL* V.154–155). Undoubtedly both Shakespeare and Milton drew upon the eighth Psalm, but Milton is nonetheless indebted to Shakespeare.

appears in *Samson* and *Paradise Lost* in the weighing of man in the balance—man as the quintessence of dust, and man as the paragon of animals, the master-work, the end.

(6) The passionate attachment, strengthened by mutual guilt, between King Claudius and Gertrude, is analogous to that between Adam and Eve after the fall. The two men state the case in similar terms.

IV.vii.14:
She's so *conjunctive* to my *life* and *soul*
That, as the star moves not but in his sphere,
*I could not but by her.*

*PL* IX.952–958:
. . . I with thee have fixed my lot
. . . if death
Consort with thee, *death is to me as life* . . .
*Our state cannot be severed; we are one.*

## 5. *Othello.*[55]

### A.

(1) II.iii.57–60:
Three . . . noble swelling spirits . . .
Have I to-night fluster'd with *flowing cups*.[56]

*PL* V.443–445:
Meanwhile . . . Eve . . . their *flowing cups*
With pleasant liquor crowned.— (V)

(2) II.iii.212:
Though he had twinn'd with me, both *at a birth* . . . .

*PL* VII.453–455:
The earth . . . *teemed*[57] *at a birth*
Innumerous living creatures.— (V)

(3) III.i.52:
To take the safest *occasion* by the front . . . .

*PR* III.172–173:
Zeal and duty are not slow,
But on *occasion's forelock*[58] watchful wait.— (D)

(4) III.iii.355–357:
And O you mortal *engines*, whose rude throats

*PL* VI.585–587 (*cannon, invented in hell, directed against the heavenly hosts*):

---

[55] See also below, on *Macbeth*, B (3) (d), p. 172, n. 80, and *Cymbeline*, B (3), pp. 214–215.

[56] Verity notes also *Henry V* IV.iii.55: "Be in their *flowing cups* freshly remembered."

[57] Cf. *Macbeth* IV.iii.176: "Each minute *teems* a new" grief.

[58] Fortune's forelock, however, is mentioned also in the *Distichs of Cato*, and by the Greek and Latin poets.

Th' immortal *Jove's dread thunder*
  counterfeit,
Farewell!

    All Heaven appeared
From those *deep-throated engines*
  belched.– (N) [59]

*PL* VI.490–491 (*Satan boasts*):
  They shall fear we have disarmed
The *Thunderer* of his only *dreaded*
  *bolt*.

(5) V.ii.277–281:
Whip me, ye devils. . . .
*Blow* me about in *winds*! roast me
  in sulphur!
Wash me in steep-down gulfs of
  liquid *fire*!
O Desdemona, Desdemona! dead!

*PL* III.487–488; II.598–603:
A violent cross *wind* . . .
*Blows* them transverse ten thousand
  leagues awry.
. . . the bitter change/Of *fierce ex-*
  *tremes* . . .
From beds of raging *fire* to starve
  in *ice*
. . . thence hurried back to fire.[60]

## B.

(1) Hanford[61] finds in the situation of Adam and Eve in relation to Satan "an essential repetition of that of Othello, Desdemona, and Iago," and observes that Satan resembles Iago in his malignity, his motive-hunting, and his half-pity for his victims. (I may note incidentally that Walter Savage Landor in one of the *Imaginary Conversations*, between Southey and Landor, on the comparative merits of Shakespeare and Milton, touches upon the same point: "*Landor*.—Othello was loftier than the citadel of Troy; and what a Paradise fell before him!" Professor Bradley also alludes to the general likeness here referred to.[62] Hanford calls attention especially to the similarity between Satan's great soliloquy and Iago's, upon first beholding their unconscious victims:

---

[59] Cf. below, *Henry V*, A (4), p. 193.

[60] Milton's lines are also close to *Measure for Measure* III.i.83–85, 118–128.

[61] See above, p. 140, n. 7.

[62] Though he remarks that "to compare Iago with the Satan of *Paradise Lost* seems almost absurd, so immensely does Shakespeare's man exceed Milton's fiend in evil" (*Shakespearean Tragedy*, p. 207).

| | |
|---|---|
| II.i.201–202: | *PL* IV.505–535: |
| O you are well tun'd now! | Sight hateful, sight tormenting! . . . |
| But I'll set down the pegs that make | these two |
| this music . . . . | Imparadised in one another's arms. |
| | . . . Live while ye may, |
| | Yet happy pair; enjoy till I return |
| | Short pleasures; for long woes are to |
| | succeed. |

I believe there is another curious recollection of Iago in *Paradise Regained* in the scene in which the tempter tries upon Christ an argument similar to that which Iago had urged home to Roderigo:

| | |
|---|---|
| I.iii.322, 344, 353: | *PR* II.427–431: |
| *Virtue! a fig . . . Put money in thy* | *Get riches first, get wealth . . .* |
| *purse; . . . fill thy purse with* | They whom I favour thrive in |
| *money.* | wealth amain |
| | While *virtue*, valour, wisdom, sit in |
| | want. |

(2)  Many are the sayings of the wise,
    In ancient and in modern books enrolled,
    Extolling patience as the truest fortitude. . . . (*Samson* 652–654)

This venerable commonplace—the bestowal upon sufferers of proverbial comfort (or "sentences" of "studied argument") which attempts to patch grief with proverbs—Shakespeare dramatized both early and late.[63] Samson's refusal to listen to Manoa's attempt to comfort him, whether or not it owes anything directly to Shakespeare, may be worth comparing with Brabantio's negative response to the Duke's sentences:

| | |
|---|---|
| I.iii.199–208; 216–219: | *Samson* 504–505, 588: |
| *Duke.* Let me . . . lay a sentence. . . . | *Man.* Repent the sin; but, if the |
| When remedies are past, the griefs | punishment |
| are ended . . . . | Thou canst avoid, self-preservation |
| Patience her injury a mockery makes, | bids . . . . |

---

63 Cf. *Comedy of Errors* II.i.15–41; *Much Ado* V.i.17, etc.

The robb'd that smiles steals something from the thief . . .

*Bra.* These sentences . . . are equivocal.

But words are words; I never yet did hear

That the bruis'd heart was pierced through the ear.

His might continues in thee not for naught . . .

*Ibid.* 590, 648:

All otherwise to me my thoughts portend . . . .

Hopeless are all my evils, all remediless.

*Ibid.,* 652–654 (quoted p. 163); 660–662:

*Chor.* With the afflicted in his pangs . . .

Little prevails, or rather seems a tune

Harsh and of dissonant mood.

(3) A twice-repeated phrase of Othello's to Desdemona, in response to her plea for Cassio just before Iago undermines Othello's faith in her—and possibly another famous phrase from Othello's last speech, again concerning his love for Desdemona —seem to be echoed in Samson's reproach to Dalila.

III.iii.70–83; V.ii.344:

*Desd.* What, Michael Cassio,

That came a-wooing with you . . . to have so much to do

To bring him in? . . .

*Oth.* . . .Let him come when he will!

*I will deny thee nothing!*

*Desd.* Why, this is not a boon.

'Tis as I should entreat you wear your gloves. . . .

*Oth.* I will *deny thee nothing!*

. . . one that *lov'd* not wisely, but *too well.*

*Samson* 876–881:

I before all the daughters of my tribe

And of my nation chose thee from among

My enemies, *loved* thee, as *too well* thou knew'st,

*Too well,* unbosomed all my secrets to thee,

Not out of levity, but overpowered

By thy request, who could *deny thee nothing.*

## 6. King Lear.

I believe, for several reasons, that Professor Firth was right in suggesting that the almost disproportionately large "space devoted in" Milton's *"History of Britain* to the story of Lear and Cordelia,[64] is probably a tribute to Shakespeare."[65] Milton's entry, for example, concerning his proposed drama on the subject of *Macbeth*,[66] gives strong support to Firth's suggestion that no small part of "Milton's interest in the legendary and anecdotal side of history" was that of a literary artist in search of material.[67] Furthermore, Milton's frequent and varied echoes of *King Lear*, as indicated below, prove that this tragedy engraved itself indelibly upon his memory.

## A.

(1) I.i.84–85 *(Cordelia)*:

> Our joy,
> *Although the last, not least.*

*PL* III.276–278:

> Dear
> To me are all my works, nor *Man*
>    the least.
> *Though last* created.[68]— (N)

(2) III.iii.12–13; III.iv.16:

> These injuries . . . will be revenged
>   *home . . . .*
> But I will punish *home.*

*PL* VI.621–622:

> The terms we sent were full of . . .
> force urged *home.*— (V)

(3) I.iv.248–249:

> His *notion* weakens, his discernings
> Are lethargized.

*PL* VII.176–179:

>   The acts of God . . .
> So told as earthly *notion* can receive.
>   — (V) [69]

(4) IV.vii.34–35:

> In the most terrible and nimble
>   stroke

*Arcades* 51–52:

> And heal the harms of thwarting
>   thunder *blue*

---

[64] That is, 2½ in a total of 20 pages devoted to the sketch of British legendary history, from Albion, son of Neptune, to the coming of Caesar (cf. Milton's *Prose Works*, ed. St. John, V, 164–185).

[65] C. H. Firth, "Milton as an Historian," *Proceedings of the British Academy,* 1907–1908, p. 232.

[66] See below, p. 168.

[67] Firth mentions also Milton's remark (in the *History, Prose Works*, V, 344) to the effect that the amatory adventures of King Edgar were "fitter for a novel than a history."

[68] Cf. *Julius Caesar* III.i.189: "Though *last, not least,* in love."

[69] Cf. *Macbeth* III.i.83: "To half a soul and to a *notion* crazed."

Of quick, *cross* lightning . . . .
(Cf. *Julius Caesar* I.iii.46–51:

               I . . .
Have bar'd my bosom to the thun-
   derstone
. . . when the *cross blue* lightning
   seem'd to open
The breast of heaven.)

Or what the *cross* dire-looking planet
   smites.— (T)

(5) III.i.4–9 (*Lear*):
Contending with the fretful elements
. . . tears his white hair
Which the *impetuous* blasts, with
   eyeless *rage*
Catch in their fury and make nothing of.

*PL* I.174–175:
           The thunder
Winged with red lightning and *impetuous rage.*— (G. C. T.)

## B.

(1) IV.i.67–72 (*Gloucester to Poor
Tom, on giving him his purse;
the heavenly "ordinance" requir-
ing that the rich give of their
superfluity to the poor*):
Heavens, deal so still!
Let the *superfluous* and *lust-dieted
man,*
That slaves your ordinance, that will
   not see
Because he does not feel, feel your
   power quickly;
So distribution should undo *excess,*
And each man have enough.

*Comus* 768–773 (*the Lady, refuting
Comus' argument against temper-
ance*):
If every just man that now pines
   with want
Had but a moderate and beeseeming
   share
Of that which *lewdly-pampered Lux-
ury*
Now heaps upon some few with vast
   *excess,*
Nature's full blessings would be well
   dispensed
In *unsuperfluous* even proportion.
   — (T)

(2) Professor Taylor has shown[70] that certain descriptive details
of the storm in *Lear* reappear in *Paradise Lost*. In dramatic purpose this storm, as I have previously observed, is virtually identi-

[70] "Shakspere and Milton Again," p. 191.

cal with the tempest in *Paradise Regained*. In the center of one stands Lear, "bare-headed"; in the other, Christ, "ill shrouded," endures, unappalled, the malice of Satan. In each case the violent uproar in nature is a symbol of spiritual malignity. Details—which are not of prime importance in this case—are different in some respects, alike in others. All storms have their clouds and winds, lightning and thunder, but not all their "oak-cleaving" thunderbolts; nor are all storms of such intensity as to threaten to annihilate the cosmos:

III.ii.1–7, 60:

Blow, winds, and crack your cheeks! Rage! Blow!
You *cataracts* and hurricanoes, *spout*
. . .
You sulph'rous and thought-executing fires,
Vaunt-couriers of *oak-cleaving* thunderbolts,
*Singe my white head!* And thou, all-shaking *thunder,*
Strike flat the thick rotundity o' th' world!
Crack Nature's moulds . . . .

*Kent.*—Alack, *bare-headed?*

(Cf. also, for verbal likenesses with *Paradise Regained* and *Paradise Lost*, the following lines from *The Tempest* and *Cymbeline*.)

*Tempest* V.i.41–48:
I have bedimm'd
The noontide sun, call'd forth the *mutinous winds,*
And 'twixt the green sea and the azur'd vault
Set roaring war; to *the dread rattling thunder*
Have I given *fire*, and *rifted Jove's stout oak*

*PL* II.174–178:
                What if . . . this firmament
Of Hell should *spout* her *cataracts* of fire,
Impendent horrors, threatening hideous fall
One day *upon our heads?*— (G. C. T.)

*PR* IV.408–421:
                Either tropic now
'Gan *thunder,* and both ends of heaven . . .
Fierce rain with lightning mixed, water with *fire*
In ruin reconciled; *nor slept the winds*
Within their stony caves, but rushed abroad
From the four hinges of the world, and fell
On the vexed wilderness, whose *tallest pines*
Though rooted deep as high, and *sturdiest oaks*
*Bowed* their stiff necks, loaden with stormy blasts,
Or *torn up sheer. Ill* wast thou *shrouded* then
O patient Son of God!

*With his own bolt* . . . and by the
spurs *pluck'd up*
The *pine* and cedar.
*Cymbeline* IV.ii.174–176:
    The rud'st wind
That by the *top* doth take the *moun-
tain pine*[71]
And make him *stoop* to th' vale.

*PL* I.612–614:
        When *heaven's fire*
Hath scathed the *forest oaks* or
    *mountain pines,*
With *singëd top* . . . .

## 7. *Macbeth.*

The closing entry in the list of ninety-nine subjects which
Milton jotted down in the course of his reading between 1639
and 1642, while he was pluming his wings for a greater flight
than any he had yet attempted, runs as follows:

> Kenneth, who having privily poison'd Malcolm Duffe that his own son
> might succeed, is slain by Fenella. Scotch Hist., pp. 157, 158.
> Mackbeth. Beginning at the arrivall of Malcolm at Macduffe. The matter
> of Duncan may be express't by the appearing of his ghost.[72]

Professor Hales[73] has suggested that Milton may have thought of
writing an independent drama on the theme of Macbeth for two
reasons: first, because his "profound respect for historic fact"
may have been outraged by Shakespeare's free and easy treatment
of history in this play, and second, because Milton, being inclined
to deal with the problem of evil "in the spirit of the dogmatist,"
would have wished to emphasize the "wilfulness of Macbeth's
ruin" more than did Shakespeare. The entry, however, suggests
another consideration—perhaps as important as any—upon which
Hales touches only in passing. Milton was thinking "of immor-
tality" when he was jotting down these several plans for the
great poem he meant to write, and his was not the nature to
emulate anything but excellence itself. The very fact, then, of

---

[71] See also *Merchant of Venice* IV.i.75–77; Variorum *Cymbeline*, ed. Furness,
pp. 308, 290–291 and notes; and, below, *Macbeth* A (1), p. 169.
[72] So printed by Todd, V, 503, from the Trinity College MS.
[73] See above, n. 19.

his proposing to treat this theme, suggests that Shakespeare's *Macbeth* must have impressed him profoundly. His writings prove that it did, though happily no new *Macbeth* is among them.

A.

(1) I.iii.75–78:
    Say . . . why
Upon this *blasted heath* you stop our way
With such prophetic greeting.

*PL* I.614–615 (*The mountain pines*):
    Their stately growth, though bare,
Stands on the *blasted heath.*— (D)

(2) III.ii.53:
*Night's black agents* to their preys do rouse.[74]

*Comus* 432:
No *evil thing that walks by night.*
    — (W)

(3) V.viii.30–31; 17–18:
*Though* . . . thou oppos'd, *being of no woman born* . . .
Accursed be the tongue that tells me so,
For it hath cow'd *my better part of man.*

*PL* XI.495–497:
    Adam . . . wept
*Though not of woman born,* compassion quelled
*His best of man.*[75]— (Whalley)

(4) III.iv.128–129:
How say'st thou, that Macduff denies his person
At our *great bidding?*

*PL* XI.314:
Therefore to His *great bidding* I submit.— (T)

(5) II.i.50–51:
        Wicked dreams abuse
*The curtain'd sleep.*

*Comus* 554:
The litter of *close-curtained sleep.*— (T)

(6) III.ii.40–43:
        Ere the bat hath flown
His cloister'd *flight,* ere to black Hecate's summons
The shard-borne beetle with his *drowsy* hums
Hath rung Night's yawning peal . . . .

*Comus* 552–554:
Till an unusual stop of sudden silence
Gave respite to the *drowsy-flighted* steeds
That draw the litter of close-curtained sleep.[76]

[74] See item (6) for an echo from Macbeth's speech immediately preceding this.

[75] See below, *Henry V,* A (1), p. 193.

[76] Warton (cf. Todd, VI, 331) thinks there can be no doubt that in painting his drowsy-flighted steeds, Milton "had his eye upon 'the jades' " who, in the

(7) III.i.42-44:
To make *society*
The *sweeter* welcome, we will keep ourself
Till supper time *alone*.

(8) I.vi.1-6:
The *air*
Nimbly and sweetly recommends itself
Unto our gentle senses.
. . . the heaven's breath
Smells *wooingly* here.

(9) III.ii.22-23:
Duncan is in his grave;
After *life's fitful fever* he sleeps well.

*PL* IX.249-250:
For *solitude* sometimes is best *society*,
And short retirement urges *sweet* return.

*On the Nativity* 32-33, 37-38:
Nature . . ./ Had doffed her gaudy trim. . . .
Only with speeches fair
She *woos* the *gentle air*.[77]

*Comus* 3-9:
. . . bright aerial spirits live insphered . . .
Above the smoke and stir[78] of this dim spot
Which men call Earth, and with low-thoughted care,
Confined and pestered in this pinfold here,
Strive to keep up a *frail and feverish being*,
Unmindful of the crown that Virtue gives.

Wordsworth and Keats, in turn, remembered Shakespeare *and* Milton ("life's fitful fever" and "the smoke and stir of this dim

---

*2 Henry VI* (IV.i.3-6), "drag the tragic melancholy night," and with "their drowsy, slow, and flagging wings/Clip dead men's graves." No one has ventured to put forward the claims of the great passage from *Macbeth* here suggested as an at least equally probable source of Milton's adjective. If there was a Shakespearean source, this, indeed, would seem the more probable, in proportion to its immense superiority to the *Henry VI* passage, and Milton's far more intimate relationships with *Macbeth*. Incidentally the *Macbeth* passage supports the Cambridge MS. reading, "drowsy-flighted," as against the "drowsy-frighted" of all other earlier editions of *Comus*. Cf. also *King John* III.iii.38, on the midnight bell, sounding "into the drowsy ear of night."

[77] A similar passage in *Romeo and Juliet* I.iv.100 is noted above, p. 147.

[78] Verity (*Comus*, 1921, p. 46) thinks that Milton's "smoke and stir" is "an echo perhaps of Horace's famous . . . '*fumum et opes strepitumque Romae.*'"

... Earth") in "Tintern Abbey" ("the fretful stir/Unprofitable, and the fever of the world") and in the "Ode to a Nightingale" ("The weariness, the fever, and the fret/Here, where men sit and hear each other groan").

B.

(1) Hales notes that *Macbeth* and *Paradise Lost* both treat of the origin of evil and the ruin of man; and Hanford points to the similarity between the relations of Adam and Eve and those of Macbeth and his lady, growing out of "Milton's adoption of romantic love as an essential motive."

(2) The weird sisters.

(a) Like the witches in *Macbeth*, Comus and his rout have many guileful spells

> To inveigle and invite the unwary sense
> Of them that pass unweeting by the way, (*Comus* 538–539)

and Thyrsis has heard them, night by night, howling

> Like stabled wolves or tigers at their prey,
> Doing abhorred rites to Hecate. (*Ibid.* 534–535)

(b) III.v.23–24 (*Hecate to the witches*):
Upon *the corner of the moon* There hangs a vap'rous drop profound.

*Comus* 1013–1017 (*Thyrsis' song*):
I can ... soar as soon To *the corners of the moon*.— (V)

(c) IV.i.138–139; III.v.20–21; IV.i. 30–31; V.i.55:
Infected be *the air on which they ride,* And damn'd all those that trust them.
I am *for th' air*; this night I'll spend Unto a dismal and a fatal end.
Finger of *birth-strangled babe* Ditch-deliver'd by a drab.
Here's *the smell of the blood* still.

*PL* II.540–541 (*Satan's crew*):
*Ride the air* In whirlwind.— (V)
*Ibid.* II.662–665:
The night-hag ... *riding through the air* she comes,
Lured with *the smell of infant blood*, to dance With Lapland witches, while the laboring moon Eclipses at their charms.— (V)

### (3) Macbeth.

(a) Professor Hales points out that, just as Malcolm's preferment to the principality of Cumberland is the signal for the unleashing of Macbeth's evil ambition (I.iv.48–50), so does the appointment of the Son as Vice-regent of Heaven mark the beginning of Satan's rebellion (*PL* V.609, 679).

| (b) II.ii.36: | *PL* IV.883 (*Satan comes to Eden*): |
|---|---|
| Macbeth does *murder sleep.* | To *violate sleep.*— (N) |

(c)[79] His supposed physical invulnerability is like that of the spirits in *Paradise Lost*:

| V.viii.8–12. | *PL* VI.344–349: |
|---|---|
| Thou losest labour. | Spirits . . . |
| As easy mayst thou the *intrenchant air* | Cannot but by annihilating die, Nor in their liquid texture mortal |
| With thy keen sword impress as make me bleed. | wound Receive, no more than can *the fluid* |
| Let fall thy blade on vulnerable crests; | *air.*— (N; cf. G. C. T.) |
| I bear a charmed life. | |

(d) Mental and spiritual torment besets Macbeth, Lady Macbeth, and Samson:

| V.iii.40–45; i.82; iii.55–56: | *Samson* 611–627 (*Samson describes his torment of the "inmost mind" after his fall as a*): |
|---|---|
| Canst thou not minister to a *mind diseas'd,* | Dire inflammation which no cooling herb |
| Pluck from the memory a *rooted sorrow,* | Or medicinal liquor can asswage.— |
| Raze out *the written troubles of the brain,* | (T) [80] |

---

79 Cf. above, *Hamlet*, B (1) (b), p. 155.

80 Editors find similar expressions in Æschylus, Sidney, and Spenser, but nowhere else is the likeness in thought and word so unmistakable as in Shakespeare and Milton. See also *Othello* III.iii.330–333:

> Not poppy nor mandragora . . .
> Shall ever medicine thee to that sweet sleep
> Which thou ow'dst yesterday.

With Milton's "medicinal liquor" compare Shakespeare's "medicinal gum," *Othello* V.ii.351 (N).

And with some sweet oblivious *anti-dote*
*Cleanse the stuff'd bosom* of that
   perilous stuff
Which weighs upon the heart?

*Doctrine and Discipline of Divorce,*
Preface (*Prose Works*, ed. St. John,
III, 184):
This present truth . . . undertakes
the cure of an *inveterate disease*
crept into the best part of human
society; and to do this with no
smarting corrosive but a smooth and
pleasing lesson which, received,
hath[81] the virtue to soften *rooted
and knotty sorrows.*[82]

*More needs she the divine than the
   physician.*

*Reason of Church Government,* Ch.
3 (*Prose Works*, II, 497). (*The
minister's function is to*):
Recover . . . man, both soul and
body, to an everlasting health . . .
Two . . . evil[s] he has to cope with,
ignorance and malice . . . Against the
latter . . . he . . . beginning at the
prime causes and *roots* of the *disease,*
sends in these two divine ingredients
of most *cleansing* power to *the soul,*
admonition and reproof; besides
which two there is *no drug or anti-dote* that can reach *to purge the
mind.*

What *purgative drug*
Would scour these English hence?

## (e) Final despair, Macbeth and Samson:

V.v.49–50:
I gin to be *aweary* of the sun
And wish the estate of the world
   were now undone.—

*Samson* 595–598:
   *Nature within me* seems
In all her functions *weary* of herself,
My race of glory run and race of
   shame,
And I shall shortly be with them
   that rest.[83]

---

81 Some editors read "both."

82 Todd quotes the part of this passage beginning with "a smooth and pleasing
lesson," but no one hitherto seems to have noticed the equally close parallel in
*The Reason of Church Government.* (See text immediately below.)

83 See above, on *Hamlet,* B (5) (a), p. 157.

(4)  V.viii.46–50  (*Siward inquires concerning his son's death in battle*):
Had he his hurts before?
Ross.      Ay, on the front.
Siward.    Why then, God's soldier be he!
Had I as many sons as I have hairs,
I would not wish them to a fairer death.
And so his knell is knoll'd.

(5)  I.iv.7–8  (*Cawdor dies bravely*):
                Nothing in his life
*Became him* like *the leaving* it. (Cf. p. 151.)

*Samson* 1579–1589, 1708–1724 (*Manoa asks the Messenger about Samson's death*):
How died he? death to life is crown or shame. . . .
*Messenger.* Unwounded of his enemies he fell. . . ./ The edifice . . .
Upon their heads and on his own he pulled. . . .
*Manoa.* Come, come, no time for lamentation now,
. . . Samson hath quit himself
Like Samson, and heroicly hath finished
A life heroic. . . .
*Nothing* is here . . . but *well* and *fair,*
. . . in a *death* so *noble.*

## 8.  Timon of Athens.

### A.

(1)  IV.iii.3–5:
*Twinn'd* brothers of one womb,
Whose procreation, residence, and birth,
Scarce is *dividant.*

*PL* XII.83–85:
            True liberty
. . . Always with right reason dwells
*Twinned* and from her hath no *dividual* being.— (D)

(2)  V.i.203–205:
            With other *incident throes*
That *nature's fragile vessel* does sustain
*In life's uncertain voyage.*

*Samson* 656:
All *chances incident* to *man's frail life.*— (G. C. T.)

(3)  I.i.26–37:
*Painter.* A picture, sir. . . . is't good?
*Poet.*        I will say of it
It *tutors nature.*

*PR* II.295:
Nature's own work it seemed, *Nature taught Art.*— (M; cf. G. C. T.) [84]

---

[84] Masson and Taylor cite also *Winter's Tale* IV.iv.90–91—"Art . . . adds to nature," but Dunster's references (see Todd) to Spenser and Tasso suggest that this phrase is a commonplace.

### B.

(1) Timon and Samson are both bitterly disillusioned in their friendships:

*(at first Timon thinks himself "wealthy in my friends"* [II.ii.193], *only to recognize, before long)*:
"the monstrousness of man
When he looks out in an ungrateful shape" (III.ii.79–80).
*(he rails bitterly at these fair-weather friends)*: "such summer birds are men," "mouth-friends," "trencher friends" (III.vi.34, 99, 106).

*Samson* 187–193:

... I learn
Now of my own experience, not by talk
How counterfeit a coin they are who "friends"
Bear in their superscription (of the most
I would be understood). In prosperous days
They swarm, but in adverse withdraw their head
Not to be found, though sought.

### *9. Antony and Cleopatra.*

### A.

(1) II.v.43:
If thou say Antony lives ...
I'll set thee in *a shower of gold*, and hail
*Rich pearls* upon thee.

*PL* II.3–4:
The *gorgeous East*[85] with richest hand
*Showers* on her kings *barbaric pearl and gold.*— (V)

(2) II.ii.217–223:
A *strange invisible perfume hits the sense*
Of the adjacent wharfs. The city cast
Her people out upon her; and Antony,
Enthron'd i' th' market-place, did sit alone
Whistling to *th' air*, which, but for vacancy,
Had gone to gaze on Cleopatra too
*And made a gap in nature.*

*Comus* 555–560:
At last a soft and solemn-breathing sound
Rose *like a steam of rich distilled perfumes*
And *stole upon the air*, that even *Silence*
Was took ere she was ware, and wished she might
*Deny her nature* and be never more,
Still to be so *displaced.*— (G. C. T.)

---

[85] This phrase appears in *Love's Labour's Lost*, A (3); see below, p. 195.

(3) I.v.72:
My *man of men.*

*PR* I.122:
This *man of men.*—(G. C. T.)

(4) IV.xv.51–52:
The *miserable change* now at my
end
Lament nor sorrow at.

*Samson* 340–341:
O *miserable change*! is this the man,
That invincible Samson?—(G. C. T.)

(5) V.ii.215–217:
Scald rhymers [will]
Ballad us out o' tune. The quick
comedians
Extemporally will stage us . . .

*Samson* 203–204:
Am I not sung and proverbed for a
fool
In every street?[86]

(6) I.v.24–27:
He's speaking now,
Or murmuring 'Where's my serpent
of old Nile?'
For so he calls me. Now I feed my-
self
With most *delicious poison.*

*Comus* 524–527 (*The enchanter*):
. . . to every thirsty wanderer
By sly enticement gives his baneful
cup,
With many murmurs mixed, whose
*pleasing poison*
The visage quite transforms of him
that drinks.[87]

(7) My citation of evidence, under B immediately below, shows
that the character of Cleopatra made "deep impression" upon
Milton. One aspect of her fascination is unforgettably described
in the great speech of Enobarbus concerning her inexhaustible
but unsatiating allure. This, by a curious transference, seems
to reappear in the remarks of Adam to Raphael, concerning
his insatiable desire to hear more of the Angel's gracious discourse of God and man.

II.ii.240–243:
Age cannot wither her nor custom
stale
Her infinite variety. Other women
*cloy*
*The appetites* they feed, but *she
makes hungry*

*PL* VIII.211–216:
". . . sweeter thy discourse is to my
ear
Than fruits of palm-tree, pleasantest
to thirst
And hunger both . . . *they satiate
and soon fill,*

[86] Todd here cites *Job* xxx.9: "And now I am their song, yea . . . their by-
word," but it seems to me just as likely that Milton had in mind the scurrilous
Elizabethan street ballads "sung to filthy tunes" mentioned also by Falstaff (*1
Henry IV* II.ii.48). See also above, *Romeo and Juliet*, A (3), p. 147.
[87] Cf. below, p. 184, under *King John.*

| | |
|---|---|
| *Where most she satisfies.* | Though pleasant, but thy words, with grace divine Imbued, *bring to their sweetness no satiety.*" |

## B.

(1) Hanford notes the similarity of the response made by Antony and Adam, respectively, when Cleopatra and Eve, having betrayed their lords, seek to calm them with "soft words." I may add that Samson's response to Dalila's peace overtures[88] is identical with the others:

| IV.xii.30: | *PL* X.867: |
|---|---|
| Ah, thou spell! Avaunt! | Out of my sight, thou Serpent! |
| | *Samson* 725, 748: |
| | My wife, my traitress, . . . Out, out, hyaena! |

(2) The vicissitudes of life familiarize both Cleopatra and Eve with the thought of seeking easy methods to end it:

| V.ii.358–359: | *PL* X.1003–1006: |
|---|---|
| Her physician tells me She hath pursu'd conclusions infinite Of *easy ways to die.* | Why stand we longer shivering under fears That . . . have the power Of *many ways to die* the shortest choosing, Destruction with destruction to destroy?— (G. C. T.) |

(3) The blind Samson's challenge to single combat, addressed to the giant Harapha (an incident which Milton did not find in his Scriptural source), resembles in its dramatic point that which the baffled Antony sends to Octavius. Both challenges are scornfully declined:[89]

| IV.i.4–6: | *Samson* 1226: |
|---|---|
| Let the old ruffian know I have many other ways to die; meantime Laugh at his challenge. | To fight with thee no man of arms will deign. |

---

[88] See also below, on *Cymbeline*, B (2), p. 214.
[89] See above, on *Julius Caesar*, B (1), p. 150.

### 10. Coriolanus.

### A.

(1) III.i.239–240:
Romans . . . they are not,
Though *calv'd* i' th' porch o' th'
Capitol.

*PL* VII.463:
The grassy clods now *calved.*— (V)

(2) V.ii.73:
The glorious *gods* sit in hourly
*synod.*

*PL* VI.156–157:
The *gods* in *synod*[90] met
Their deities to assert.— (V)

(3) III.ii.105–106:
You have *put* me now to *such a part*
which never
I shall discharge to th' life.

*PL* IX.665–667:
The Tempter . . . with shew of zeal
and love . . .
*New parts put on.*[91]— (V)

(4) IV.v.66–68: (*the face of Corio-*
*lanus*):
Bears a command in 't; *though thy*
*tackle's torn*
Thou show'st a noble *vessel.*

*PL* II.1041–1044:
                         Satan
. . . like a weather-beaten *vessel* holds
Gladly the port, *though* shrouds and
    *tackle torn.*— (G. C. T.)

(5) II.ii.87–89:
                    *It is held*
That *valour* is the *chiefest virtue,*
and
*Most dignifies the haver.*

*PL* XI.691–694:
*To overcome in battle,* and subdue
Nations . . . *shall be held the highest*
    *pitch*
*Of human glory.*— (G. C. T.)

## II. THE HISTORIES

### 11. 1 Henry VI.[92]

### A.

(1) IV.ii.42–44:
*He fables not;* I hear the enemy.

*Comus* 800–801:
*She fables not;* I feel that I do fear
Her words.— (W)

---

[90] A word "specially used by Shakspere of an assembly of the gods. . . . So Milton" (Verity). See also *PL* II.391, etc.

[91] A figure drawn from the theater. Verity compares also *PR* II.239–240.

[92] See below, n. 99.

*12. 2 Henry VI.*[93]

A.

(1) IV.ii.195:
Spare none but such as go in *clouted
    shoon.*

*Comus* 634–635:
        The dull swain
Treads on it daily with his *clouted
    shoon.—* (N) [94]

(2) I.i.75:
Brave peers of England, *pillars of
    the state.*

*PL* II.299–302:
Beëlzebub . . . rose . . .
*A pillar of state.—* (N) [95]

*13. 3 Henry VI.*

A.

(1) II.iii.9:
Our hap is loss, our *hope* but sad *de-
    spair!*

*PL* II.142–143:
    Thus repulsed, our final *hope*
Is flat *despair.—* (Malone)

*14. Richard III.*

Milton remarks, in a well-known passage of his *Eikonoklastes*:[96]

The poets . . . have been . . . so mindful of decorum as to put never more
pious words in the mouth of any person than of a tyrant. I shall not instance an abstruse author . . . but one whom we well know was the closet
companion of these his solitudes, William Shakspeare, who introduces the
person of Richard the Third speaking in as high a strain of piety and
mortification as is uttered in . . . this book [the *Eikon Basilike*]:

> I do not know that Englishman alive
> With whom my soul is any jot at odds
> More than the infant that is born to-night.
> I thank my God for my humility. [II.i.69–72]

Other stuff of this sort may be read throughout the whole tragedy . . . .

---

[93] See also above, n. 76.

[94] Warton adds the passage from *Cymbeline* IV.ii.213–214: "I . . . put/My
*clouted brogues* from off my feet."

[95] I reproduce this parallel for what it may be worth. Todd finds this phrase
also in Gascoigne.

[96] *Prose Works*, ed. St. John, I, 326–327.

Obviously[97] Milton is here attacking not Shakespeare but Charles I. His close and frequent recollections of *Richard III* prove that this play impressed him strongly.

## A.

(1) I.i.9:
*Grim-visag'd War* hath smooth'd his wrinkled front.

*PL* VI.236:
The ridges of *grim war.*— (T)

(2) IV.iii.54:
Then *fiery expedition* be my *wing*.

*Samson* 1283–1285:
With *winged expedition* . . . he *executes*[98]
His errand on the wicked.— (T)

(3) I.ii.228–229:
Was ever woman in this humour *woo'd*?
Was ever woman in this humour *won*?

*PL* VIII.503 (*Eve, conscious of her worth*):
That would be *wooed*, and not unsought be *won.*— (T) [99]

(4) II.iii.28:
The queen's sons and brothers, *haught and proud* . . . .

*Psalm* LXXX.31–35:
Thou . . . drov'st out Nations, *proud and haut.*— (T)

(5) I.iii.264:
Our *aëry* [eyry] *buildeth* in the *cedar's top*.

*PL* VII.423–424:
The eagle and the stork
On cliffs and *cedar-tops* their *eyries build.*— (V)

(6) V.iii.311:
Our strong arms be our conscience, *swords* our *law*.

*PL* XI.671–672; IX.653–654:
So violence
Proceeded, and oppression, and *sword-law.*— (T)
. . . we live
Law to ourselves; our reason is *our law*.

(7) V.iii.175:
*God and good angels* fight on Richmond's side.

*PL* II.1033:
*God and good angels* guard.— (T)

97 Though the contrary has sometimes been supposed. For discussion, see Masson, *Life of Milton*, III, 515.
98 Cf. *Richard II* I.iii.79: "Be *swift* like lightning in the *execution*."
99 Shakespeare, as Verity notes, was especially fond of this proverbial phrase. It reappears in *1 Henry VI* V.iii.77; *Titus Andronicus*, II.i.82–83, and Sonnet 41.

(8) I.iv.58–59:

With that (methought) *a legion of foul fiends*
*Environed* me, and *howled* in mine ears.

(9) I.iv.37–39:
    Still the envious flood
Stopp'd in my soul, and would not let it forth
To find the *empty, vast, and wand'ring air.*[100]

PR IV.422–423:

*Infernal ghosts,* and hellish furies, round
*Environed* thee; some *howled,* some yelled, some shrieked.— (D)

*PL* II.404–409 (*Satan, bound for earth, tempts*):
    With *wandering* feet
The dark, unbottomed, infinite Abyss . . .
Upborne with indefatigable wings
*Over the vast Abrupt,* ere he arrive.
    . . .

(10) III.vii.94:
So *sweet* is zealous *contemplation.*

*Comus* 376–377:
    *Sweet* retired solitude,
. . . With her best nurse, *Contemplation.*

(11) [101] II.ii.151–152:

My *other self,* my counsel's consistory,
My oracle, my prophet.

*PL* VIII.450:
    . . . thy *other self,*[102]
Thy wish exactly to thy heart's desire.

B.[103]

(1) Hanford points out that Satan resembles Richard III in that both of them, unable to partake of the delights they see about them, with irresistible determination adopt evil as their good:

I.i.18–31:

I, that am curtail'd of this fair proportion . . .
To entertain these fair, well-spoken days,
I am determined to prove a villain
And hate the idle pleasures of these days.

*PL* IX.119–121; IV.110:
    The more I see
Pleasures about me, so much more I feel
Torment within me . . . .
Evil, be thou my Good.

---

[100] This passage, like item (8), is from Clarence's description of his dream.
[101] Taylor compares also V.iii.185 ("Then fly. What, from myself?") with *PL* IV.20–22, 75—a likeness in thought to which I had previously referred in another connection. (See *PMLA,* XL, 669, n. 57, and cf. below, n. 105.)
[102] The "classical" *alter ego?*
[103] See also below, n. 120.

(2) I am inclined to think that the resemblance between Richard III and Milton's *dramatis personae* goes further.[104] Thus, I think it likely that the opening soliloquy of Comus—in which he descants upon the beastly "deformities" with which he has surrounded himself, and, more especially, upon the power of those dazzling spells and glozing words of his which win the easy-hearted to their doom—owes something to Milton's memories of Richard's opening soliloquy and of the one which follows soon after. In all three of these soliloquies the speaker sets forth his evil purpose not only with the utmost frankness, but with the keenest enjoyment of his power for mischief and of his sense of intellectual superiority over his prospective victims:

I.i.30–41; ii.228–238:

*I am determined to prove a villain*
. . .
Plots have I laid, inductions dangerous . . .
And if King Edward be as true and just
As I am subtle, false and treacherous,
This day should Clarence closely be mew'd up . . .
*Dive, thoughts, down to my soul;*
*here Clarence comes . . . .*
Was ever woman in this humour woo'd?
Was ever woman in this humour won? . . .
To take her in her heart's extremest hate . . .
The bleeding witness of my hatred by . . .
And I no friends to back my suit

*Comus* 150–169:

    Now to my charms,
And to my wily trains; I shall ere long
Be well stocked with as fair a herd as grazed
About my mother Circe. Thus I hurl
My dazzling spells into the spongy air,
Of power to cheat the eye with blear illusion
And give it false presentments . . .
*I, under fair pretence of friendly ends,*
*And well-placed words of glozing courtesy,*
*Baited with reasons not unplausible,*
*Wind me into the easy-hearted man*
*And hug him into snares . . . .*
*But here she comes; I fairly step aside,*

---

104 Blackstone's conjecture, however (cf. Todd, II, 423), that Milton might have got "the hint" for his allegory of Sin and Death (*PL* II.648) from *Richard III* I.iii.293,—"sin, death, and hell have set their marks on him,"—is not to be taken seriously. The source, as Verity notes, is Scriptural—*James* i.15.

withal
*But the plain devil and dissembling*
  *looks,*
And yet to win her, all the world to
  nothing?

And hearken, if I may her business
  hear.

(3) The brazen wit with which Richard so jauntily assails his
prospective victims also inspires the efforts of Comus and Satan
(in *PR*) to bedazzle their intended victims.

IV.i.79–80; I.ii.49–50, 81–84, 114–115
*(though ultimately, as Anne reports,*
*her)*:

                           woman's heart
Grossly grew captive to his honey
  words,
*(originally, seeing through him, she*
*had repelled his advances with a*
*sharp riposte for his every thrust)*:
*Richard.* Sweet saint, for charity, be
  not so curst.
*Anne.* Foul devil, for God's sake
  hence, and trouble us not! . . .
*Richard.* Fairer than tongue can
  name thee, let me have
Some patient leisure to excuse myself.
*Anne.* Fouler than heart can think
  thee, thou canst make
No excuse current but to hang thyself. . . .
*Richard.* But, gentle Lady Anne,
To leave *this keen encounter of our*
  *wits*. . . .

*Comus* 789–791 *(the Lady refuting*
*Comus)*:
Enjoy your *dear wit and gay rhetoric*
That hath so well been taught her
  dazzling fence;
Thou art not fit to hear thyself con-
  vinced.

*PR* IV.2–5:
The Tempter stood . . .
Discovered in his fraud, thrown from
  his hope
So oft, and the persuasive rhetoric
That sleeked his tongue.

## 15. *King John.*

### A.

(1) III.i.77–80:
To solemnize this day the glorious
  *sun*

*PL* III.606–611:
What wonder then if fields and re-
  gions here

Stays in his course, and *plays* the *alchymist*,
Turning with splendor of his *precious* eye
The meagre cloddy earth to *glittering gold.*

Breathe forth elixir pure, and rivers run
*Potable gold,* when, with one virtuous touch
*The arch-chemic Sun . . .*
Produces . . .
Here in the dark so many *precious things.*— (N)

(2) V.vii.46 (*King John, dying*):
*Within me is a hell.*

PL IV.18–21 (*Satan in Eden*):
Horror and doubt . . . from the bottom stir
*The hell within him.*— (T) [105]

(3) I.i.213:
Sweet, sweet, *sweet poison* for the age's tooth.

*Comus* 47:
. . . the *sweet poison* of misusëd wine.[106]

## B.

(1) Adam's reflections upon death, already referred to above,[107] remind one also of Constance's great apostrophe in this play. Both characters refuse all comfort but the last:

III.iv.25–36:
Death, death! O *amiable lovely death!* . . .
Come, grin on me, . . . Misery's love
. . .
O, *come* to me!

PL X.854–856:
   *"Why comes* not *Death,"*
Said he, "with *one thrice-acceptable stroke*
To end me?"

## 16. Richard II.

### A.

(1) V.i.5–6:
Here let us *rest, if* this rebellious earth
*Have any resting.*

PL I.183–185:
   Let us . . .
There *rest, if* any *rest* can harbor there.— (B)

---

[105] Cf. *PL* IV.75–80; I.254 ("Which way I fly is Hell, myself am Hell," and "the mind is its own place"), and see below, *A Midsummer Night's Dream*, A (7), p. 198. The thought is the common property of all poets from Dante to Marlowe.

[106] Cf. above, p. 176, under *Antony and Cleopatra*, item 6.

[107] P. 157, *Hamlet*, B (5) (a).

(2) III.ii.24–25 (*Richard on touching English earth*):
*This earth shall have a feeling*, and these stones
Prove armed soldiers.

*Comus* 796–797 (*the Lady, on her cause*):
Dumb things would be moved *to sympathize,*
And *the brute Earth* would lend her nerves and shake.– (S)

(3) III.iii.62–66:
King Richard doth . . . appear
As doth *the blushing discontented sun*
From out the fiery portal of the east,
When he perceives *the envious clouds* are bent
To dim his glory . . . .

*PL* I.592–596:
Nor appeared [Satan]
Less than Archangel ruined, and the excess
Of glory obscured: as when *the sun new-risen*
Looks through *the horizontal misty air*
Shorn of his beams. . . .– (D)

(4) I.iv.33 (*Bolingbroke and the commons*):
[They] had the tribute of his *supple knee.*

*PL* V.787–788:
Will ye submit your necks, and choose to bend
The *supple knee?*– (T)

(5) I.iii.129–130:
      The *eagle-winged pride*
Of sky-aspiring and ambitious thoughts.

*PL* VI.762:
At his right hand *Victory*
Sat *eagle-winged.*– (T)

(6) II.iii.65:
Evermore *thanks*, the exchequer of the poor.

*PR* III.127–129:
      *Thanks,*
The slightest, easiest, readiest recompense
From them who could return him nothing else.

(7) II.i.252–255 (*on the treasure wasted by Richard*):
*Wars hath not wasted it*, for warr'd he hath not
But *basely* yielded . . . .
More hath he spent in *peace* than they *in war.*

*PL* XI.784:
*Peace* to *corrupt* no less than *war* to *waste.*

(8) II.iv.9–15:
. . . *meteors* fright the fixed stars of heaven;
*The pale-fac'd moon* looks bloody

*PL* I.594–599:
      . . . the sun new-risen
Looks through the horizontal misty air

on the earth,
And lean-look'd prophets whisper
    *fearful change*. . . .
These signs forerun the death or
    *fall of kings*.

Shorn of his beams, or from behind
    the moon
In *dim eclipse* disastrous twilight
    sheds
On half the nations, and with *fear
    of change*
*Perplexes monarchs*.

(9) II.iv.18–20:
Ah, Richard! . . .
I see thy glory, *like a shooting star,
Fall* to the base earth from the
    firmament.[108]

*PL* IV.555–556; I.740–746:
Thither came Uriel, gliding through
    the even
On a sun beam, *swift as a shooting
    star*.[109]
(Mulciber, "thrown by angry Jove"
over "the crystal battlements" of
heaven):
Dropped from the zenith *like a fal-
    ling star,*
On Lemnos the Aegæan isle.

## B.

(1) Milton echoes the patriotic theme of the play, as set forth in John of Gaunt's speech:

II.i.40, 46:
    This scept'red *isle* . . .
This *precious stone* set in the silver
    sea.

*Comus* 21–23:
    All the sea-girt *Isles*
That, like to *rich and various gems,
    inlay*
The unadornëd bosom of the deep.
    — (W)

(2) Adam and Eve start upon their exile from Paradise very much in the mood and language of Mowbray, upon facing exile from England:

---

[108] See also below, p. 200, item (17), and p. 201, item (c).

[109] Todd (II, 364) suggests that Milton might have "adapted" this simile directly from Theocritus (*Idyll* XIII.49), but it seems likely that he remembered it more immediately as a favorite of Shakespeare's.

I.iii.206–207:
> Now no way can I stray
> Save back to England, *all the world's*
>   *my way.*

PL XII.645–647:
> Some natural tears they dropped,
>   but wiped them soon;
> *The world was all before them,*
>   where to choose
> Their place of rest.— (Johnson)

Again, the Archangel's comforting exhortation to Eve, who is lamenting the prospect of exile, resembles in effect Gaunt's fatherly counsel as Bolingbroke goes into exile from his English paradise:

I.iii.275–276:
> All places that the eye of heaven
>   visits
> Are to a wise man ports and happy
>   havens . . . .

PL XI.290–292:
> Thy going is not lonely; with thee
>   goes
> Thy husband; him to follow thou
>   art bound:
> Where he abides, think there thy
>   native soil.— (V) [110]

## *17. 1 Henry IV.*

A.[111]

(1) III.i.220–221 *(the dawn)*:
> *The hour* before the heavenly-har-
>   ness'd team
> Begins his *golden progress* in the
>   east.

PL XI.173–175:
> The *morn* . . . begins
> Her *rosy progress* smiling.— (N)

(2) I.i.9–10:
> *Hostile* paces . . . like the meteors of
>   a *troubled heaven.*

PL II.533–534:
> *War* appears
> Waged in the *troubled sky.*— (N) [112]

---

[110] The thought, as editors note, is sufficiently familiar. It appears in *Euphues*, and elsewhere.

[111] See also *1 Henry IV* V.iv.85–86: "Thou art . . . *food for* . . . *worms*, brave Percy," and *PL* X, 983–986: "Our own begotten. . . . *Food for* so foul a monster" [death]—but cf. *Job* xxiv.20.

[112] Todd quotes two somewhat similar—but not especially significant—sets of parallelism in figure—*1 Henry IV* V.iv.65, and *PL* VI.313; *1 Henry IV* III.i.15, and *PL* I.728.

(3) IV.iii.68–73:
The more and less . . . followed him
Even *at the heels* in golden multitudes.

*PR* II.419:
What followers, what retinue canst thou gain,
Or *at thy heels* the dizzy multitude?
— (G. C. T.)

(4) I.ii.235–238:
*Like bright metal on a sullen ground,*
My reformation, glitt'ring o'er my fault,
Shall show more goodly and attract more eyes
Than that which hath no *foil to set it off.*

*Lycidas* 78–79:
Fame is no plant that grows on mortal soil,
Nor in the *glistering foil*
*Set off* to the world. . . .— (W)

(5) I.iii.59–62:
And that it was great pity, so it was,
This villanous saltpetre should be *digg'd*
*Out* of the *bowels of* the *harmless earth.*

*PL* I.685–690: (*men, following Mammon's example*):
Ransacked the Centre, and with impious hands
Rifled the *bowels of* their mother *Earth*
For treasures better hid. . . . — (G. C. T.)
And *digged out* ribs of gold.

## B.

(1) Dalila, in defense of her treachery, asserts her wifely claims upon Samson—as against those of war and danger without—in terms which resemble those of Lady Hotspur to her Harry:[113]

II.iii.40–67:
O, my good lord, why are you thus alone?
For what offence have I this fortnight been
*A banish'd woman from my Harry's bed?*

*Samson* 800–809:
Why, then, revealed? . . . I knew that liberty
Would draw thee forth to perilous enterprises,
While I at home sat full of cares and fears,

---

[113] And, to a lesser extent, those of Portia to Brutus—"Y've ungently, Brutus, stole from my bed" (*Julius Caesar*, II.i.237–238).

Tell me, sweet lord, what is 't that
takes from thee
Thy stomach, pleasure, and thy gold-
en sleep? . . .
Why hast thou . . . given my treasures and my rights of thee
To thick-ey'd musing and curst melancholy? . . .
Some heavy business hath my lord
in hand,
And I must know it, else he loves me
not.

*Wailing thy absence in my widowed*
*bed;*
Here should I still enjoy thee day
and night
Mine and love's prisoner,[114] not the
Philistines',
Whole to myself, unhazarded
abroad,
Fearless at home of partners in my
love.

(2) It seems to me that Milton, in depicting the relations between Jehovah and the rebellious angels, did not altogether
forget those between Henry IV and his rebellious lords as represented here and in Part II of this play. At all events, the two
poets hold identical views as to the difficulty of reconciliation
between mighty opposites and concerning the penalties of war.

(a) V.ii.4–23 (*Worcester, like Satan,*
*persists in rebellion because rec-*
*onciliation seems to him impossi-*
*ble*):
It is not possible, it cannot be . . . .
He will suspect us still, and find a
time
To punish this offence . . . .
For treason is but trusted like the
fox . . . .
We . . . shall pay for all.

*PL* IV.98–99:
For never can true reconcilement
grow
Where wounds of deadly hate have
pierced so deep.

(b) Belial, like Morton and Lord Bardolph in *2 Henry IV*,
urges his comrades to take their punishment calmly since they
had taken the chance of war with a full knowledge of the
penalties.

---

114 Todd says nothing as to the passage as a whole, but compares this line with
Juliet's to Romeo—whom, at parting, she would "pluck . . . back again" like "a
wanton's bird . . . So loving-jealous of his liberty" (*Romeo and Juliet* II.ii.177–182).

| *2 Henry IV* I.i.166–168; 180–184: | *PL* II.204–208: |
|---|---|
| You cast the event of war . . . | I laugh when those who at the spear are bold |
| And summ'd the account of chance before you said, | And venturous, if that fail them, shrink and fear |
| Let us make head. . . . | What yet they know must follow— to endure |
| We all that are engaged to this loss Knew that we ventur'd on such dangerous seas | Exile, or ignominy, or bonds, or pain, |
| That if we wrought our life 't was ten to one | The sentence of their conqueror. |
| And yet we ventur'd, for the gain propos'd | |
| Chok'd the respect of likely peril fear'd . . . . | |

(3) Milton gives Satan one trait which in the play belongs not to the chief rebel but to the king himself—a cringing humility[115] assumed for the purposes of the moment: in hopes of dispossessing the incumbent of the throne.

| III.ii.50–52: | *PL* IV.958–961 (*Gabriel to Satan*): |
|---|---|
| And then I stole all courtesy from heaven | Who more than thou |
| And dress'd myself in such humility | Once fawned, and cringed, and servilely adored |
| That I did pluck allegiance from men's hearts . . . . | Heaven's awful Monarch? wherefore, but in hope |
| | To dispossess him, and thyself to reign? |

(4) I have noted above[116] an echo, in *PL* II.533–534, of King Henry's memorable opening speech. I now find that two additional phrases, both from that part of the same great speech in which the king pays tribute to the Master, were in young Milton's mind in 1629—a year before his lines "On Shakespeare"—when he wrote his ode *On the Nativity.*

| I.i.18–27: | *On the Nativity* 23–25, 151–153: |
|---|---|
| Therefore, friends, As far as to the sepulchre of Christ— | The star-led Wizards haste with odors sweet! |

---

115 See also *Richard II* I.iv.24–36, and the *Eikonoklastes* passage, above, p. 179.
116 P. 187.

Whose soldier now, under whose
blessed cross
We are impressed and engag'd to
fight . . .
To chase these pagans in those holy
fields
Over whose acres walk'd those
*blessed feet*
Which fourteen hundred years ago
were nail'd
For our advantage on the *bitter
cross.*

O run, prevent them with thy hum-
ble ode,
And lay it lowly at his *blessed feet.*
. . .
The Babe lies yet in smiling infancy
That on the *bitter cross*[117]
Must redeem our loss.

*18. 2 Henry IV.*—See also above, *1 Henry IV*, B(2), pp. 189–190.

**A.**

(1) IV.ii.20–22 (*the Archbishop*):
The very opener and intelligencer
Between the grace, *the sanctities of
Heaven*
And our dull workings.

*PL* III.60 (*Jehovah*):
About him all *the sanctities of Heav-
en*
Stood thick as stars.— (V)

(2) IV.v.184–186:
        God knows, my son
By what *by-paths* and *indirect*
crook'd ways
I met this crown.

*PL* XI.629–631:
"O pity and shame that they who
to live well
Entered so fair should *turn aside* to
tread
*Paths indirect,* or in the midway
faint!"— (V)

(3) III.i.5–8:
        O sleep, O *gentle sleep,*
Nature's soft nurse, how have I
frighted thee
That thou no more wilt weigh my
eyelids down
And *steep my senses in forgetfulness?*

*PL* VIII.287–289:
        There *gentle sleep*[118]
First found me, and with soft oppres-
sion *seized*
My *drowsèd sense.*

---

117 Neither "blessed feet" nor "bitter cross" is Biblical. R. C. Browne noticed
"the bitter cross" (I, 258: "Cf. Shakespeare, 'For our advantage on the bitter
cross' "), but not the significant compound echo in "his blessed feet."

118 The phrase appears also in *Richard II* I.iii.133.

(4) III.i.9–13. In connection with (3) above, note the compound echo which harks back to the same great speech at the opening of *2 Henry IV* III.

Why rather, sleep, liest thou in
  *smoky cribs,*
Upon uneasy pallets stretching thee
  . . .
*Than in the perfum'd chambers of*
  the great,
Under the canopies of costly state.
  . . .

*Comus* 321–325:
. . . I . . ./ trust thy honest-offered
  courtesy,
Which oft is sooner found in *lowly*
  *sheds*
With *smoky rafters, than in tapestry*
  *halls*
*And courts* of princes.

### B.[119]

(1) Masson and other commentators have suggested that Milton's "double-mouthed" Fame, as described in *Samson Agonistes*, is first cousin to Shakespeare's Rumour, "painted full of tongues." And Rumour "with a thousand tongues" speaks also in Milton's *In Quintum Novembris*. Though Milton's Fame may owe something to Ovid, Virgil, and Chaucer, the family resemblance between it and Shakespeare's loud-mouthed bearer of false or contradictory reports seems unmistakable:

Induction, 1–16 (*enter Rumour,*
  *painted full of tongues*):
*Rum.* Open your ears, for which of
  you will stop
The vent of hearing when *loud*
  *Rumour speaks* . . . .
The *acts* commenced on this ball of
  earth.
Upon my tongues continual slanders
  ride,
The which in every language I pro-
  nounce,
Stuffing the ears of men with false
  reports.

*Samson* 970–974:
Fame, if not double-faced, is *double-*
  *mouthed,*
And with *contrary blast proclaims*
  most *deeds;*
On both his wings, one black, the
  other white,
Bears greatest names in his wild
  aerie flight.— (M, Keightley, Br.)
*In Quintum Novembris* 191–193:
*Millenisque* loquax auditaque visa-
  que *linguis*
Cuilibet effundit temeraria; veraque
  mendax

___
[119] See above, *1 Henry IV*, B (2) (b), pp. 189–190.

... Rumour is *a pipe*
*Blown by surmises,* jealousies, con-
    jectures ....

Nunc minuit, modo confictis ser-
monibus auget.— (Cf. M)

(2) There can be little doubt that Milton shared and remembered Shakespeare's views of the burdens and responsibilities of true kings, as expressed in *Henry IV* and *Henry V*.[120]

III.i.31; IV.v.23:
Uneasy lies the head that wears a
    *crown.*

O polish'd perturbation, *golden*
    *care!*
*That keep'st the ports of slumber*
    *open wide* ....

*PR* II.458–459:
    A crown,
*Golden* in shew, is but a wreath of
    thorns,
Brings dangers, troubles, *cares,* and
    *sleepless nights*
To him who wears the regal diadem.

## 19. Henry V.

### A.

(1) IV.vi.30–32:
But I had not *so much of man* in me,
And all my mother came into mine
    eyes
*And gave me up to tears.*

*PL* XI.496–497:
        Compassion quelled
His *best of man, and gave him up to*
    *tears.*— (Whalley) [121]

(2) II.Prologue 8:
For now *sits Expectation* in the air.
    . . .

*PL* VI.306–307:
        *Expectation stood*
In horror.— (N) [122]

(3) IV.iii.25:
Nor care I who doth *feed upon my*
    *cost.*

*PR* II.421:
Longer than thou *canst feed them*
    *on thy cost.*— (D)

(4) III.Prologue 33:
The *devilish cannon.*

*PL* VI.553; IV.17:
His *devilish enginry* ...
A *devilish engine.* .... — (V; cf. G. C.
    T.)

---

120 Though, as Hanford has shown (*PMLA*, XXXVI, 310–311), Shakespeare was by no means the sole formative influence that shaped Milton's ideal of kingship. On *Henry V*, see below. Compare also *Richard III* I.iv.78–83—"Princes have but their titles for their glories. . . ."

121 See above, *Macbeth*, A (3), p. 169.

122 Todd, however, finds the phrase ("Expectation . . . took stand") in Fletcher's *Bonduca*, III.i. Verity cites *Troilus and Cressida*, Prologue 20–22: "Now expectation, tickling skittish spirits. . . . Sets all on hazard."

(5) Opening Prologue, 15–18:

O, pardon! since a crooked figure may

Attest in little place a million;

And let us, *ciphers to this great accompt,*

On your imaginary forces work.

*A Free Commonwealth (Prose Works,* ed. St. John, II, 138):

For what can [the King] more than another man? who, *even in the expression of a late court poet,* sits only *like a great cipher* set to no purpose before a long row of other significant figures.[123]

## B.

(1) In *Paradise Lost* as well as in *Paradise Regained* there are passages strikingly like those in which Henry V speaks of the burdens which rest upon kings,[124] and of the idol Ceremony:

IV.i.247–259:

*Upon the King!* let us our lives, our souls,

Our debts, our careful wives,

Our children, and our sins lay on the King!

*We must bear all....* What infinite heart's-ease

Must kings neglect, that private men enjoy!

And what have kings, that privates have not too,

Save ceremony, save general ceremony?

And what art thou, *thou idol Ceremony?*

What kind of god art thou, that suffer'st more

Of mortal griefs than do thy worshippers?

*PR* II.462–465:

*On his shoulders each man's burden lies;*

For therein stands the office of a king

His honour, virtue, merit, and chief praise,

That *for the public all this weight he bears.*— (Keightley)

*PL* V.354–357:

*The tedious pomp that* waits

*On princes,* when their rich retinue long

Of horses led and grooms besmeared with gold

Dazzles the crowd and sets them all agape.

## 20. Henry VIII.

### A.

(1) III.ii.352–357:

This is the state of man; to-day he puts forth

*Samson* 1574–1577:

What windy joy ... had I conceived . . .

---

[123] I owe this reference to Dr. Wilmon Brewer.

[124] See above, on *2 Henry IV,* B (2), p. 193.

*The tender leaves of hopes,* to-mor-
    row blossoms, . . .
The third day comes a frost, a killing
    *frost,*
And . . . *nips* his root.

Abortive as *the first-born bloom of*
    *spring*
*Nipt* with the lagging rear of win-
    ter's *frost!*— (Warburton) [125]

(2) II.i.77–78:
Make of your prayers one sweet
    sacrifice
And *lift my soul to heaven.*

*PL* IV.687–688:
        Their songs
Divide the night, and *lift our*
    *thoughts to Heaven.*— (T) [126]

## III. THE COMEDIES

### 21. *Love's Labour's Lost.*

### A.

(1) I.i.171:
This *child of fancy,* that Armado
    hight.

*L'Allegro* 133:
Sweetest Shakespeare, *Fancy's child.*
    — (T) [127]

(2) IV.iii.340–343:
Is not love . . . as sweet and *musical*
*As* bright *Apollo's lute?*

*Comus* 476–478:
How charming is divine Philosophy
Not harsh and crabbed . . .
But *musical as is Apollo's lute.*— (B)

(3) IV.iii.222–223:
Like a rude and savage man *of Ind,*
At the first opening of *the gorgeous*
    *east.*

*PL* II.2–4 (*Satan's throne*):
Outshone the wealth of Ormus **and**
    **of Ind**
Or where *the gorgeous East* with
    richest hand. . . .— (T) [128]

(4) V.ii.904:
*Daisies pied* and violets blue.

*L'Allegro* 75:
Meadows trim with *daisies pied.*—
    (W and M) [129]

[125] Newton compares *Love's Labour's Lost* I.i.100–101:
        Berowne is like an envious sneaping frost
        That bites the first-born infants of the spring.

[126] This likeness is perhaps not especially significant. Todd also quotes Drum-
mond, "And lift a reverent eye and thought to heaven."

[127] If this is, as Todd says, an "obvious parallel," there is a deal of unconscious
irony in it.

[128] Editors compare Spenser, *Fairie Queene* III.iv.23, on "the wealth of th' East
and pompe of Persian kings," but these lines are not nearly so close to Milton's
as are Shakespeare's. See above, *Antony and Cleopatra,* A (1) p. 175.

[129] "Almost certainly a recollection of Shakespeare" (Masson).

(5) II.i.246–247 (*Boyet's description of the King, smitten by the Princess's charms*):
His face's own margent did quote *such amazes*
That all eyes saw his eyes enchanted *with gazes.*

*On the Nativity* 69–70:
The stars with *deep amaze*
Stand fixed *with* steadfast *gaze.*[130]

## 22. *Two Gentlemen of Verona.*
### A.

(1) I.i.45–46:
    The most forward bud
Is eaten by *the canker* ere it blow.

*Lycidas* 45:
As killing as *the canker* to the rose.
    — (W) [131]

(2) V.iv.51–53:
    Better have none
Than plural faith, which is too much by one.
Thou *counterfeit* to thy *true friend!*

*Samson* 189–191:
How *counterfeit* a coin they are who "*friends*"
Bear in their superscription (of the most
I would be understood).— (D)

(3) III.i.219–220:
O, I have *fed upon this woe* already,
And now excess of it will make me *surfeit.*

*Samson* 1558–1562 (*the Messenger to Manoa*):
Gaza yet stands, but all her sons are fallen. . . .
*Feed on that* first, there may in *grief* be *surfeit.*— (Br.)

## 23. *A Midsummer Night's Dream.*[132]
### A.

(1) II.i.249–251:
I know *a bank* . . .

*Comus* 543–545:
    *A bank*

[130] This curious likeness in rhyme-words, if it is nothing more, has escaped the commentators.

[131] Cf. *Twelfth Night* II.iv.114 "concealment, like a worm i' th' bud." Warton and Todd hold that "frequent repetition of this image" by Shakespeare "suggested it to Milton."

[132] "A play," says Verity, "constantly imitated by Milton." Appendix I, on "Milton and *A Midsummer Night's Dream*," in Verity's edition (Cambridge University Press, 1923) of the play, is an important contribution to our subject.

Quite *over-canopied with luscious woodbine*. . . .

With ivy *canopied*, and interwove
*With flaunting honeysuckle.*— (W)[133]

(2) II.i.69:
The farthest *steep of India.*

*Comus* 139:
The nice Morn, on the *Indian steep.*
— (V)

(3) II.i.28–29, 141:
And now they never meet *in grove or green*
By *fountain clear* or *spangled* star-light *sheen* . . . .
And see our *moonlight revels.*

*PL* I.781–785:
                    *Faery elves*
Whose *midnight revels, by a forest side*
Or *fountain* some belated peasant sees,
Or dreams he sees, while overhead the *Moon*
Sits arbitress.— (V)

*Comus* 1003:
Far above in *spangled sheen.*— (W.
   A. Wright)

(4) II.i.25:
To *trace the forests* wild.

*Comus* 423:
*Trace* huge *forests* and unharboured heaths.— (Holt White) [134]

(5) III.ii.380–384:
      Yonder shines *Aurora's har-binger;*
At whose approach, *ghosts* wand'ring here and there
Troop home to churchyards:
   *damned spirits* all
That in crossways and floods have burial,
Already to their *wormy beds* are gone.

*Song on May Morning* 1:
The bright morning star, *Day's har-binger.*— (V)

*On the Nativity* 232–234:
   The flocking *shadows* pale
   Troop to the infernal jail;
Each fettered *ghost* slips to his sev-eral grave.— (V)

*Death of a Fair Infant* 31:
Thy beauties lie in *wormy bed.*— (W)

(6) V.i.37:
To ease the anguish of a *torturing hour.*

*PL* II.90–92:
                    The scourge
Inexorably and the *torturing hour*
Calls us to penance.— (Thyer)

---

[133] Cf. also *A Midsummer Night's Dream* II.i.15 and *Lycidas* 146; and the whole flower passage in *Lycidas* (140–150) with Oberon's flowers.

[134] See *A Midsummer Night's Dream*, Furness, Variorum, p. 51, and cf. Verity.

(7) II.i.243:
I'll follow thee, and *make a heaven of hell.*

*PL* I. 254:
The mind is its own place, and in itself
Can *make a Heaven of Hell,* a Hell of Heaven.— (V) [135]

(8) V.i.398–399:
Through the house give *glimmering light*
By the dead and drowsy fire.

*Il Penseroso* 79–80:
Where *glowing embers* through the room
Teach *light* to counterfeit *a gloom.*
— (W) [136]

(9) III.ii.389–393:
I with the Morning's love have oft made sport . . .
Even till *the eastern gate,* all *fiery red,*
Opening on Neptune, with fair blessed beams,
Turns into yellow gold his salt green streams.

*L'Allegro* 59–61:
Right against *the eastern gate,*
Where the great Sun begins his state,
Robed *in flames* and amber light.—
(V)

(10) II.i.107–108, 128–129:
Hoary-headed frosts
Fall in the *fresh lap* of the crimson rose. . . .
The sails conceive
And grow big-bellied with the *wanton wind.*

*Lycidas* 136–138:
Ye valleys low, where the mild whispers use
Of shades, and *wanton winds,* and gushing brooks,
On whose *fresh lap* the swart star sparely looks.— (V)

(11) I.i.74–78:
Thrice blessed they that master so their blood
To undergo such maiden pilgrimage;
But earthlier happy is *the rose distill'd*[137]

*Comus* 737–744:
List Lady, be not coy, and be not cozened
With that same vaunted name *Virginity* . . . .
If you let slip time, like a neglected *rose,*

---

[135] See above, *King John*, A (2), p. 184.

[136] "Much the same image" as Shakespeare's, says Warton, but he cites also Spenser, *Fairie Queen* I.i.14: "A little glooming light, much like a shade." Malone quotes from *Lucrece* 1378–1379: "Ashy lights,/ Like dying coals burnt out in tedious nights."

[137] See below, *Sonnets*, p. 222.

Than that which, *withering* on the
  *virgin* thorn,
Grows, lives, and dies in single
  blessedness.

It *withers* on the stalk with lan-
  guished head.— (W; cf. T and
  M) [138]

(12) I.i.184–185:
More tuneable than lark *to shep-*
  *herd's ear*
When wheat is green, *when haw-*
  *thorn buds appear.*

*Lycidas* 45–49:
As killing as the canker to the rose
  . . .
*When first the white-thorn blows,*
Such, Lycidas, thy loss *to shepherd's*
  *ear.*— (T; cf. M)

(13) II.i.161–164:
But I might see young Cupid's fiery
  shaft
*Quench'd* in the *chaste beams* of *the*
  *watery moon,*
And *the imperial vot'ress passed on*
*In maiden meditation,* fancy-free.
Yet mark'd I where *the bolt of Cu-*
  *pid* fell. . . .

*Comus* 428–445 (*She that has chas-*
  *tity*):[139]
Where very desolation dwells
*She may pass on with unblenched*
  *majesty* . . . .
Hence . . . the huntress Dian . . .
*Fair silver-shafted Queen for ever*
  chaste,
  . . . set at nought
The frivolous *bolt of Cupid.*

(14) II.i.99–100 (*because of the*
*fairies' dissension*):
. . . the *quaint* mazes in the *wanton*
  green
For lack of tread are undistinguish-
  able.

*Arcades* 44–47:
  . . . I am the Power
Of this fair wood . . . and curl the
  grove
With *ringlets quaint* and *wanton*
  *windings* wove.— (W)

(15) III.i.163–164 (*Titania to Bot-*
*tom*):
And I will *purge* thy *mortal gross-*
  *ness* so
That thou shalt like an airy spirit
  go.

*Arcades* 72–73:
. . . the heavenly tune, which none
  can hear
Of *human mould* with *gross un-*
  *purgëd ear.*— (W)

---

[138] This figure, "is a favorite with . . . Shakespeare, Spenser, Daniel, Drayton,
Fletcher" (Masson). See below, p. 210, n. 160.

[139] On the dangers that beset chaste beauty in the night, Verity compares *A
Midsummer Night's Dream* II.i.217–219, with *Comus* 393–403.

(16) I.i.184–185:
*More tuneable than* lark to shepherd's ear.

PR I.479–480:
. . . pleasing to the ear
And *tuneable* as sylvan pipe or song.
— (D)

PL V.151:
*More tuneable than* . . . lute or harp.

(17) II.i.153, 7:
And certain *stars shot* madly from their spheres.

*Swifter* than the moonës sphere.

Comus 80–81:
*Swift* as the sparkle of a *glancing star*
I *shoot* from heaven.[140]

## B.[141]

### (1) Puck.

(a) Reminiscences of Puck's mischief-making and of his "capricious good-will" appear in *L'Allegro, Comus,* and *Paradise Lost*:

II.i.33–41; 16:
You are that *shrewd and knavish sprite*
Call'd Robin Goodfellow. Are not you he
That *frights* the maidens of the villagery . . .
And sometime make the drink to bear no barm,
*Mislead night-wanderers,* laughing at their harm?
Those that *Hobgoblin* call you and sweet Puck,
*You do their work,* and they shall have good luck . . . .

PL IX.638–640:
Some *evil spirit* . . .
*Misleads* the amazed *night-wanderer* from the way.— (T)

Comus 39:
*Threats* the forlorn and *wandering passenger.*

L'Allegro 105–110:
How *the drudging goblin sweat*
To earn his cream-bowl duly set . . .
His shadowy flail hath threshed the corn
That ten day-labourers could not end;

---

[140] Cf. above, p. 186, item 9. Todd (VI, 253) compares *Venus and Adonis* 815: "Look how a bright star shooteth from the sky."

[141] Verity remarks that the passage in *PL* X.896–908, on the "innumerable mischiefs" wrought by "female snares," reads "like a commentary" on the proverbial line, "The course of true love never did run smooth" (*A Midsummer Night's Dream* I.i.134). Masson quotes approvingly Todd's comparison of *A Midsummer Night's Dream* V.i.12, with Milton's *Elegia Quinta* 19.

Farewell, thou *lob* of *spirits.*

Then lies him down, the *lubbar fiend.*— (M)¹⁴²

(b) The Attendant Spirit in *Comus,* says Moody,¹⁴³ "in his closing song reminds us of . . . Puck":

II.i.175–176:
I'll put a girdle round about the earth in forty minutes.

*Comus* 1013–1014:
I can fly or I can run Quickly to the green earth's end.

(c) The opening speech of Thyrsis confirms the resemblance:

III.ii.100:
I go, I go; look how I go, *Swifter* than arrow from the Tartar's bow.

*Comus* 80–81:
*Swift* as the sparkle of a glancing star I shoot from heaven.

(2) Verity¹⁴⁴ notes that toward the close of the *Vacation Exercise* the fairies dance upon the hearth—"in token of favor and blessing to children in nativity"—very much as Oberon bids them do for the heirs-to-be of the three couples at the end of the play:

V.i.408–428:
Now, until the break of day,
Through this house each *fairy stray.*
To the best bride-bed will we,
Which by us shall *blessed* be,
And the issue there create
Ever shall be fortunate . . . .
[Unblemished] *in nativity* . . .
Every fairy take his gait,
And each several *chamber* bless,
Through this palace with sweet peace . . . .
*Trip* away, make no stay.

*Vacation Exercise* 59–64:
Good luck befriend thee, Son, for *at thy birth*
The *fairy ladies danced upon* the hearth;
Thy drowsy Nurse hath sworn she did them spy
Come *tripping to the room* where thou didst lie,
And, sweetly singing round about thy bed,
Strew all their *blessings* on thy sleeping head.

(3) Change of seasons, as an affliction visited upon man, follows in *A Midsummer Night's Dream* upon the disturbance of the

---

¹⁴² The "drudging goblin," writes Masson, "is Shakespeare's Puck," though in some respects Milton's description of him is closer to Jonson's (in the masque, *Love Restored*).

¹⁴³ Page 37.

¹⁴⁴ Page 148; cf. G. C. Taylor, p. 190.

fairies' sports by Oberon's jealous brawls; in *Paradise Lost* upon man's tasting the apple.

II.i.88–116:

*The winds,* piping to us in vain,
As in revenge have suck'd up from the sea
*Contagious fogs. . . . the moon,* the governess of floods,
*Pale* in her anger washes all the air
That rheumatic *diseases* do abound
. . .
*The seasons alter.* Hoary-headed frosts
Fall in the fresh lap of the crimson rose,
And on *old Hiems thin and icy* crown
An odorous chaplet of sweet summer buds
Is as in mockery set. The spring, the summer,
The childing autumn, *angry winter,* change
Their wonted liveries; and the mazed world,
By their increase, now knows not which is which.
And *this* same progeny of *evils comes*
*From our . . . dissension.*
(Compare also *As You Like It* II.i. 5–11:
Here feel we but *the penalty of Adam,*
*The seasons' difference;* as, the icy fang
And churlish chiding of the *winter's wind . . .*
Even till I *shrink with cold.*[145])

PL X.651–666, 677–695, 736:
The Sun
Had first his precept so to move, so shine
As might affect the Earth with cold and heat
Scarce tolerable, and from the north to call
*Decrepit winter. . . .* To *the blanc Moon*
Her office they prescribed. . . . To *the winds* they set
Their corners when with bluster to confound
Sea, air, and shore . . . . to bring in *change*
*Of seasons* to each clime. Else had the spring
Perpetual smiled on Earth with vernal flowers . . . .
Avoided *pinching cold* . . . .
These changes . . . slow, produced
*Vapour, and mist,* and exhalation hot,
Corrupt and *pestilent* . . . .
*For this we may thank Adam.*

---

145 For discussion, see *As You Like It,* Furness, Variorum, p. 65, and John E.

(4) Shakespeare's memorable concept of the shaping power of the creative imagination is recalled in the thought and phrasing of a passage in *Paradise Lost.*

V.i.14–17:

... as *imagination* bodies forth
The forms of *things* unknown, the poet's pen
Turns them to *shapes,* and gives to *airy* nothing
A local habitation and a name.

*PL* V.100–105 (*Adam lectures Eve on the nature of the soul's faculties, of which Reason is "chief," and*):
                              *Fancy* next
Her office holds; of all external
   *things* . . .
She forms *imaginations, airy shapes.*[146]


## 24. *Merchant of Venice.*

### A.

(1) V.i.294–295:
Fair ladies, you *drop manna* in the way of starved people.

*PL* II.112–114:
   His tongue
*Dropt manna* and could make the worse appear
The better reason.— (N)


(2) V.i.60–65:
There's not *the smallest orb* which thou beholdst
But *in his motion* like an angel *sings* . . .
But whilst *this muddy vesture* of decay
Doth *grossly* close us in, *we cannot hear* it.

*Arcades* 72–73 (*on the music of the spheres*):
. . . *the heavenly tune,* which *none can hear*
Of *human mould,* with *gross unpurgèd ear.*— (W) [147]


Hankins, "The Penalty of Adam," in *Shakespearean Essays,* ed. Alwin Thaler and Norman Sanders (Knoxville, Tenn., 1964), pp. 41 ff. Cf. G. C. Taylor, p. 192.

[146] Cf. above, p. 148, item 6.

[147] "I think this was more immediately . . . suggested by Shakespeare" than by Plato (Warton). Verity compares another passage from Lorenzo's speech—"Look how the floor of heaven/Is thick inlaid with patines of bright gold," (V.i.58–59)—with Milton's "road of Heaven, star-paved" (*PL* IV. 976). See also (2) above and p. 199, item 15.

(3) II.vii.65:
All that *glisters* is not gold.

*PL* VIII.90–94:
> Great
> *Or bright infers not excellence.* The
> Earth . . . so small
> Nor *glistering,* may of solid good
> contain
> More plenty than the Sun that bar-
> ren shines.— (V)

(4) IV.i.196–197:
Earthly power doth then show likest
God's
When *mercy* seasons *justice.*

*PL* X.58–60, 77–78:
> I intend
> *Mercy* colleague with *justice,* send-
> ing thee
> Man's friend, his Mediator. . . . I
> shall temper . . .
> *Justice* with *mercy.*— (T) [148]

(5) V.i.56–57, 60–65, 79:
Soft *stillness and the night*
*Become* the touches of sweet *har-*
*mony.* . . .
There's not the *smallest orb* which
thou behold'st
But in his motion like an angel
sings . . .
Such harmony is in immortal souls;
But *whilst this muddy vesture of*
*decay*
Doth *grossly close it in, we cannot*
hear it. . . .
. . . the *sweet power* of *music.*

*Arcades* 61–64, 68–73:
> . . . in deep of night . . . then *listen* I
> To the *celestial sirens' harmony,*
> That sit upon the nine enfolded
> *spheres.* . . .
> Such *sweet compulsion* doth in *mu-*
> *sic* lie
> To . . . keep unsteady Nature to her
> law,
> And the low world in measured
> motion draw
> After *the heavenly tune,* which *none*
> *can hear*
> Of human mould with *gross un-*
> *purgèd* ear.— (W)

*Comus* 457–458:
> And in clear dream and solemn
> vision
> Tell her of things that no *gross ear*
> can hear.

---

[148] Compare also *Measure for Measure* II.ii.75–78:
> How would you be
> If he which is the top of judgment should
> But judge you as you are? O, think on that
> And mercy then will breathe within your lips.

## 25. *The Taming of the Shrew.*

### A.

(1) I.ii.204–205:
Have I not heard great ordinance in
    the field
And *heaven's artillery* thunder in
    the skies?

*PL* II.714–715:
    As when two black clouds
With *Heaven's artillery* fraught,
    come rattling on.— (T) [149]

(2) II.i.174:
*Morning roses newly wash'd with
    dew.*

*L'Allegro* 22:
*Fresh-blown roses washed in dew.*—
    (W)

## 26. *The Merry Wives of Windsor.*[150]

### A.

(1) V.v.55–56:
Raise up *the organs of her fantasy,*
Sleep she as sound as careless in-
    fancy.

*PL* IV.800–802 (*Eve, tempted by
    Satan*):
Squat like a toad . . .
Assaying by his devilish art to reach
*The organs of her fancy.*— (T) [151]

## 27. *As You Like It.*

### A.

(1) IV.iii.109–113:
A green and gilded *snake* . . . un-
    link'd itself
And *with indented glides* did slip
    away.

*PL* IX.494–498:
The . . . *serpent* . . .
Addressed his way—not *with indent-
    ed wave,*
Prone on the ground, as since. . . .
    — (N)

(2) I.iii.110–112:
Alas, what *danger* will it be to us,
*Maids* as we are, to travel forth so
    far.

*Comus* 393–402:
*Beauty* . . . had need the guard
Of dragon-watch with unenchanted
    eye . . . .

[149] Milton's use of this familiar figure, which, as commentators observe, appears also in Crashaw, Vaughan, and Dryden, does not in and by itself prove that he remembered the play. But the parallelism (2) which immediately follows in the text, supports the conjecture that he did, even though Todd finds similar expressions in Greene, and elsewhere. By the same token the single, unsupported parallelism noted under *The Merry Wives* is hardly sufficient to prove that Milton remembered this play.

[150] See above, n. 30.

[151] See n. 149.

*Beauty* provoketh thieves sooner than gold.

*Danger* will [not] wink on Opportunity
And let a single helpless *maiden* pass.— (W)

(3) III.ii.10:
The fair, the chaste, and *unexpressive* she.

*On the Nativity* 116–117:
Harping ... with *unexpressive* notes. — (M) [152]

*Lycidas* 176:
The *unexpressive* nuptial song.— (W)

(4) II.vii.137–142:
*Duke.* This wide and universal theatre
Presents more woeful pageants than *the scene*
Wherein we play in.
*Jaques. All the world's a stage*
And all the men and women merely players;
They have *their exits and their entrances.*

*Colasterion, ad fin. (Prose Works,* III, 460):
I had rather, *since the life of man is likened to a scene,* that all *my entrances and exits* might mix with such persons only whose worth erects them and their actions to a grave and tragic deportment, and not to have to do with clowns and vices.[153]

(5) See above, *A Midsummer Night's Dream,* B (3), p. 202.

(6) III.ii.420–425, 446:
*Rosalind.* Love is merely a *madness.*
. . . Yet I profess curing it. . . .
*Orlando.* I *would not be cured.* . . .

*Elegy* VII 87–88, 99:
O utinam spectare semel mihi detur amatos
Vultus, et coràm tristia verba loqui.
. . .
Deme meos tandem, verùm nec deme, furores.
(Oh, that I may have the privilege of seeing once again that beloved face

---

152 "Warton fancies that Shakespeare may have coined" the word "unexpressive," "but search may find older instances" (Masson). The *N.E.D.* records no earlier occurrence of the word.

153 A passage called to my attention by Dr. Wilmon Brewer. The *totus mundus* commonplace does not adequately account for the likeness here.

and of telling her my sad tale.
. . . Take away *my madness,* I pray;
or rather, *do not take it away.*—N.
G. McCrea's translation.) [154]

## 28. *Twelfth Night.*[155]
### A.

(1) II.iv.21–22:
It gives a very echo to *the seat*
Where *love* is throned.

*PL* VIII.589–591:
*Love* . . . hath his *seat*
In reason.— (V)

(2) III.i.89:
My *legs* do better *understand* me than
I understand what you mean.

*PL* VI.621–625 (*Belial, punning on terms of weight sent from the cannon's mouth*):
Who receives them right
Had need *from head to foot* well
*understand.*— (T) [156]

(3) I.v.82:
*Infirmity,* that *decays the wise* . . . .

*Lycidas* 70–71:
Fame is the spur that the clear spirit doth raise
(That last *infirmity of noble mind*).
. . .[157]

## 29. *Troilus and Cressida.*
### A.

(1) III.iii.239:
Great Hector in his *weeds of peace.*

*L'Allegro* 119–120:
Throngs of knights and barons bold
In *weeds of peace* high triumphs hold.— (T)

---

[154] Quoted from Patterson, pp. 93–94.

[155] See above, n. 131.

[156] Todd and Verity suggest that Milton borrowed this "miserable equivocation" from Shakespeare, and quote also, *Two Gentlemen* II.v.28: "My staff understands me." The pun, however, had had a wide currency. Jonson and others laughed frequently at the "grave *understanders* of the pit."

[157] R. C. Browne (I, 301) compares Tacitus (*Hist.* IV.5): "Etiam sapientibus cupido gloriae novissima exuitur."

(2) IV.i.8:
Witness the *process of your speech.*

*PL* VII.176–178:
The acts of God . . . to human ears
Cannot without *process of speech* be told.— (T)

(3) IV.iv.120–121:
The *lustre* in your *eye, heaven in* your cheek
Pleads your fair usage.

*PL* VIII.488:
Grace was in all her steps, *heaven in her eye.*— (N) [158]

## B.

(1) Dalila is "as false as Cressid," and, as Professor Taylor[159] observed, she virtually—like Cressida—pronounces this verdict against herself, in words that recall Cressida's own:

III.ii.190–203:
*Cressida.* Prophet may you be!
If I be *false,* or swerve a hair from truth,
*When time is old and hath forgot itself . . .*
And mighty states characterless are grated
To dusty nothing—yet let *memory*
From false to false, *among false maids in love*
*Upbraid my falsehood!* . . .
Yea, let them say, to stick *the heart of falsehood,*
*'As false as Cressid.'*

*Samson* 955–957, 975–979:
*Samson.*—Bewail thy *falsehood,* and the pious works
It hath brought forth *to make thee memorable*
*Among illustrious women, faithful wives . . . .*
*Dalila.*—My name, perhaps, among the circumcised
In Dan, in Judah, and the bordering Tribes,
*To all posterity* may stand defamed,
With maledictions mentioned, and *the blot*
*Of falsehood* most unconjugal traduced.

(2) The giant Harapha surveys Samson limb by limb, in the same spirit and for the same purpose as Achilles "perusing" Hector, to vaunt his own superiority:

---

[158] Todd, however, quotes from *Philaster,* "Heaven is in your eyes," and, less closely, from Phineas Fletcher.

[159] "Shakspere and Milton Again," p. 195.

IV.v.231–233, 237–259:
*Achilles.* Now, Hector, I have fed
mine eyes on thee;
*I have with exact view perus'd thee,*
Hector,
And *quoted joint by joint.* . . . I will
the second time
As I would buy thee, *view thee limb
by limb* . . . .
Tell me, you heavens, in which part
of his body
Shall I destroy him, whether there,
or there, or there . . . .
*Hector.* His insolence draws folly
from my lips;
But I'll endeavour *deeds* to match
these *words*.

*Samson* 1082–1091:
*Harapha.*—Much have I heard
Of thy prodigious might and feats
performed,
Incredible to me, in this displeased,
That I was never present . . . where
we might have tried
Each other's force . . .
*And now am come to see* of whom
such noise
Hath walked about, and *each limb
to survey,*
If thy appearance answer loud re-
port.
*Samson.* The way to know were not
to *see*, but *taste.*— (G. C. T.)

## *30. All's Well that Ends Well.*
### A.

(1) I.i.99–100 (*Helena upon her
"bright particular star"*):
In his bright *radiance* and *collateral*
light
Must I be comforted.

*PL* X.85–86 (*Christ rising to judge
Man*):
From his *radiant* seat he rose
Of high *collateral* glory.— (T)

(2) III.iii.5–6 (*Bertram accepting
his commission*):
We'll strive to bear it for your worthy sake
To *th' extreme edge of hazard.*

*PR* I.94–95 (*Satan on the coming of
Christ*):
Ye see our danger on *the utmost
edge of hazard.*— (Br.)

(3) I.i.136–138 (*Parolles to Helena*):
*It is not politic in* the commonwealth of *nature to preserve virginity.* Loss of virginity is rational
increase.

*Comus* 720–738 (*Comus to the
Lady*):
        If all the world
Should in a fit of temperance, feed
on pulse . . .
We should . . . live like *Nature's* bas-
tards, not her sons,
*Who would be quite surcharged with
her own weight* . . . .

List, Lady be not coy and be not
cozened
With that same vaunted name, *Virginity.*[160]

(4) IV.iii.83–84:
The *web* of our life is of a *mingled
yarn, good and ill together.*

*Areopagitica (Prose Works,* II, 67):
*Good and evil* . . . in . . . this world
grow up *together* almost inseparably; and the knowledge of *good* is
. . . *interwoven* with the knowledge
of *evil.*[161]

## *31. Measure for Measure.*[162]
### A. and B.

(1) III.i.83–85, 118–128 (*Claudio on
death*):
　If *I* must *die,*
I will *encounter darkness as a bride,*
And hug it in mine arms.

*PL* X.775–778:
　　*How gladly would I meet
Mortality,* my sentence, and *be earth
Insensible!* how glad would *lay me
down
As in my mother's lap!*—(G. C. T.) [163]

*Ibid.* II.146–151:
Sad cure . . .To perish . . .
In the wide womb of uncreated
Night

---

[160] This theme, of course, had wide currency in the literature of the Renaissance. It was a favorite with the sonneteers, including Shakespeare, and appears prominently in Marlowe's *Hero and Leander,* Jonson's *Volpone,* and elsewhere. See above, n. 138 and text. But, though the theme was a commonplace, Shakespeare's treatment of it—for which see also *Romeo and Juliet* I.i.222–225—is not likely to have escaped Milton.

[161] The figure of good and evil woven together as in textual warp and woof is not Scriptural. See above, pp. 9 f. I do not deny that the likeness here *may* be a coincidence.

[162] See also above, n. 148.

[163] I have reproduced Professor Taylor's italics. The mood and figure here seem to me somewhat different, but the phrase "be earth Insensible" deserves comparison (together with the passage next quoted from *Paradise Lost*) with Claudio's "sensible warm motion."

Ay, but to die, and go we know not where
To lie in cold obstruction and to rot;
*This sensible warm motion* to become
A kneaded clod, and *the delighted spirit*
*To bathe in fiery floods, or to reside*
*In thrilling region of thick-ribbed ice*;
To be imprison'd in the viewless *winds*
*And blown with restless violence round* about[165]
*The pendent world.* . . . 't is too horrible.

*Devoid of sense and motion.*— (T) [164]
*Ibid.* II.598–601:
The bitter change . . . Of fierce extremes . . .
From *beds of raging fires to starve in ice*
*Their* soft ethereal *warmth.*— (N) [166]
*Ibid.* III.487–489 (*when unworthy seekers of heaven reach Limbo*):
A *violent* cross *wind* from either coast
*Blows them transverse*, ten thousand leagues awry
Into the devious air.
*Ibid.* II. 1051–1052:
This *pendent world.*— (T) [167]

Masson[168] observed that "Claudio's celebrated speech . . . was familiar to Milton," but the astonishingly organic quality of these recollections has never, I think, been concretely set forth. Specifically, the likeness between the close of the speech and Milton's description of the violent winds of Limbo seems to have escaped the commentators. The cumulative effect of the indications here supports the conjecture that Milton remembered Shakespeare in this as in other details.

[164] "Milton evidently alludes to Shakspeare, in the expression as well as the sentiment" (Todd).

[165] This antithesis is a familiar one (editors cite examples from *Job*, Dante, Surrey, etc.), but in this context the likeness is none the less worth noting.

[166] Verity compares this and the preceding line with *PL* II. 178–182:

> We perhaps . . .
> Caught in a fiery tempest, shall be hurled,
> Each on his rock transfixed, the sport and prey
> Of racking whirlwinds.

The Limbo passage quoted in the text seems to me the more apposite.

[167] For another parallelism, based upon a common (Biblical) source, cf. *Measure* II.ii.122; *PL* VIII.77–78; and *Psalms* ii.4.

[168] Milton's *Poetical Works*, III, 424.

## 32. Pericles.

### A.

(1) II.ii.4–7:
Our daughter,
In honor of whose birth *these tri-
umphs* are,
Sits here, like *beauty's child, whom
nature gat*
*For men to see,* and seeing *wonder
at.*

*Comus* 745–747:
*Beauty* is *Nature's brag,* and *must
be shown*
In courts, at feasts, and *high solem-
nities,*
Where most may *wonder at* the
workmanship.— (T) [169]

(2) Act I, Prologue, 21–24:
This king unto him took a feere,
Who died and left a female heir,
*So buxom, blithe, and* full of face
As heaven had lent her all his grace.

*L'Allegro* 19-24:
Zephyr with Aurora playing,
As he met her once a-Maying . . .
Filled her with thee, a daughter
fair,
*So buxom, blithe, and* debonair.—
(W)

## 33. Cymbeline.

### A.[170]

(1) II.iii.22:
Hark hark, *the lark at heaven's gate
sings.*

*PL* V.197–198:
Ye birds
That *singing* up to *Heaven gate*
ascend.— (T) [171]

[169] Todd, however, quotes also a passage, equally close to Milton, from Dray-
ton's *Legend of Matilda*:
Nature thee ordayned
As her brav'st Piece . . .
(Wherein her former workmanship she stayned) . . . .
Hoard not thy beauty when thou has such store.

[170] See above, notes 94, 71, and text. Todd compares also the following passages:

*Cymbeline* II.iv.87–88 (*Imogen's cham-
ber*):
The roof o' the chamber
With golden cherubins is fretted.

*PL* I.714 (*from the description of Pan-
demonium*):
Doric pillars overlaid
With golden architrave.

Knight (Variorum *Cymbeline*, ed. Furness, p. 77) sees in *PR* III.323–325, a possible reminiscence of *Cymbeline* I.vi.19–21, but Todd (V, 188) prints a closer parallel from Fletcher's *Purple Island*.

[171] Cf. Sonnet 29, "The lark at break of day arising." Commentators cite somewhat similar passages from Phineas Fletcher and John Lyly, but there can be little
doubt that Shakespeare's line was immediately in Milton's memory here.

(2)  IV.ii.258–281:

Fear no more the heat o' the sun . . .

*Ghost unlaid* forbear thee . . .

*Quiet consummation have,*

And renowned be *thy grave.*

*Comus* 434:

Stubborn *unlaid ghost.*– (T) [172]

*Epitaph on the Marchioness of Winchester* 47–48:

Gentle lady, may *thy grave*

*Peace and quiet ever have.*– (W)

### B.

(1) In his *History of Britain*,[173] Milton gives passing mention to "Kymbeline or Cunobeline," "the wise conduct of old Cassibelan" (Shakespeare's "Cassibelan, famous in Caesar's praises"[174]), and to the romantic fabrications of Geoffrey of Monmouth[175] concerning the "two sons of Cunobeline, Guiderius and Arviragus." This passage in itself does not prove that Milton also had Shakespeare's play in mind, but there can be no doubt that he had been impressed by the dramatic or epic possibilities of the *Cymbeline* material. This is indicated by the fact[176] that the name of Arviragus appears also in the famous lines of the *Epitaphium Damonis,*

Brennumque *Arviragum*que duces, priscumque Belinum . . . (164 ff.) ,

which allude to Milton's proposed epic upon the legendary history of Britain.

(2) In the disillusionment wrought by the supposed evil-doing of Imogen and the real perfidy of Dalila, Posthumus and Sam-

---

[172] See also *PR* IV.426–430:

        Till morning fair . . . *laid* the winds

        *And grisly spectres,* which the Fiend had raised,

with which Warton compares *Hamlet* I.i.147–149:

        And was about to speak, when the cock crew

        And then it started like a guilty thing

        Upon a fearful summons.

See above, *Hamlet,* B (1) (a), p. 155.

[173] *Prose Works,* V, 199–202.

[174] *Cymbeline* III.i.5–6.

[175] "Stuff . . . too palpably untrue to be worth rehearsing in the midst of truth."

[176] Noted by Masson (Milton's *Poetical Works,* III, 359).

son (and the Chorus) find relief by unpacking their hearts with words which score bitterly "woman's frailty"[177] and inconstancy.

II.v.20–32:

There's *no* motion
That tends to *vice in man*, but I affirm
*It is the woman's part*; be it lying, note it,
The woman's; flattering, hers; *deceiving*, hers . . .
All faults that may be nam'd, nay, that hell knows . . . .
For even to vice
*They are not constant*, but are changing still
One vice, but of a minute old, for one
Not half so old as that.

*Samson* 748–750, 1026–1040:

Out, out, hyaena! These are thy wonted arts,
And arts *of every woman false* like thee—
To break all faith, all vows, *deceive*, betray . . . .
. . . inward gifts
Were left for haste unfinished . . .
Of *constancy* no root infixed . . . .
. . . to *wisest men and best* . . .
Once joined . . . she proves . . . a thorn
Intestine . . .
A cleaving mischief, *in his way to virtue*
*Adverse and turbulent.*

(3) One of the most dramatic moments in *Paradise Lost* is that which pictures Satan's emotions when, bent upon consummating the fall of man, he sees Eve, who remains unconscious of his presence and whose beauty and innocence for a moment deter him from his evil purpose. In dramatic conception, and perhaps also in language, the passage seems to me to owe something to the very similar one in *Cymbeline* which describes Iachimo's equally malignant descent, equally delayed by stirrings of conscience, upon the sleeping Imogen. Satan, in other words, belongs to a dramatic tradition which includes Iachimo as well as Iago.[178]

II.ii.12–50:

Our Tarquin thus

*PL* IX.457–469:

*Her heavenly form*

[177] See above, *Hamlet*, B (5) (a), p. 158.
[178] See above, *Othello*, B (1), pp. 162–163.

Did softly press the rushes ere he waken'd
*The chastity he wounded.* Cytherea,
How bravely thou becom'st thy bed! fresh lily,
And whiter than the sheets! *That I might touch!*
But kiss; one kiss! . . . I lodge in fear.
*Though this a heavenly angel, hell is here.*

Angelic, but more soft and feminine,
Her graceful innocence . . . overawed
His malice, and *with rapine sweet* bereaved
His fierceness of the fierce intent it brought . . . .
*But the hot hell that always in him burns*
. . . Tortures him now more, the more he sees.

(4) In (3) immediately above, I called attention to the fact that Iachimo as well as Iago is included among the forebears of Milton's Satan. A passage from *Comus* should be added to the supporting evidence. Like Iachimo when he sees the sleeping Imogen, Satan (*PL* IX.457–469), literally hell-bent upon bringing ruin to the unsuspecting Eve, is genuinely moved, and, for a moment, deterred from his wickedness while gazing upon her helpless grace and innocence. So, too, is Comus, on seeing and hearing the Lady sing her Echo song.

II.ii.14–23, 49–50:

Cytherea,
How bravely thou becom'st thy bed! fresh lily,
And whiter than the sheets! That I might touch!
But kiss; one kiss! . . .
To see th' enclosed lights, now canopied
Under these windows white and azure, lac'd
With blue of heaven's own tinct!
. . . I lodge in fear.
Though this a heavenly angel, hell is here.

*Comus* 246–248, 262–264:
Sure something holy lodges in that breast,
And with these raptures moves the vocal air
To testify his hidden residence. . . .
. . . such a sacred and homefelt delight,
Such sober certainty of waking bliss,
I never heard till now. I'll speak to her,
And she shall be my queen.[179]

179 Cf. also below, pp. 218–219.

## 34. *The Winter's Tale.*
### A.[180]

(1) IV.iv.122–123:
    Pale *primroses*
That *die unmarried.*

*Lycidas* 142:
The rathe *primrose* that *forsaken*
   *dies.*— (W) [181]

## 35. *The Tempest.*
### A.[182]

(1) V.i.16–17:
    Winter's *drops*
*From eaves* of reeds.

*Il Penseroso* 130:
Minute *drops from* off the *eaves.*—
   (Malone)

(2) IV.i.62:
Thy turfy mountains where live *nib-bling sheep.*

*L'Allegro* 71–72:
Russet lawns and fallows gray,
Where the *nibbling* flocks do stray.
   — (W)

(3) I.ii.376–379:
Come unto these yellow sands,[183]
   And then take hands.
Curtsied when you have, and *kiss'd*
   *The wild waves whist.*

*On the Nativity* 64–65:
The winds with wonder *whist*
Smoothly *the waters kissed*
Whispering new joys to the mild
   ocean.— (M)

(4) IV.i.148–150:
    These our actors . . .
Are *melted* into air, *into thin air.*

*PR* I.497–499:
    Satan . . . disappeared,
*Into thin air* diffused.— (D)

(5) IV.i.44–47:
    Before you can say *'come'* and
*'go,'*
And breathe twice, and say 'so, so,'

*L'Allegro* 33–34:
*Come,* and *trip it* as you *go*
*On the light fantastic toe.*— (N)

---

[180] The phrase "forsake the court" occurs in *The Winter's Tale* I.ii.362, and in the ode *On the Nativity* 13 ("forsook the courts"); but this is a pastoral commonplace.

[181] "It is obvious that the general texture and sentiment of this line is from *The Winter's Tale* . . . especially as [Milton] had first written 'unwedded' for 'forsaken'" (Warton). Cf. Mark Pattison, *Milton,* p. 25.

[182] See also above, pp. 167–168, *Lear,* B (2).

[183] See also *A Midsummer Night's Dream* II.i.125–126: "She . . . sat with me on Neptune's *yellow sands,*" and *Comus* 117—"the *tawny sands.*" ("For *tawny* the Cambridge MS. has *yellow.*"—Verity.)

Each one, *tripping on his toe,*
Will be here with mop and mow.

(6) V.i.33–35:
Ye elves . . . that on the sands with
    *printless foot*
Do chase the ebbing Neptune.

*Comus* 897–899:
Thus I set my *printless feet*
O'er the cowslip's velvet head.— (W)

(7) I.ii.321–323:
As *wicked dew* as e'er my mother
    *brush'd*
With raven's feather from unwhole-
    some fen
Drop on you both!

*Arcades* 48–51:
. . . all my plants I save from nightly
    ill . . .
And from the boughs *brush* off the
    *evil dew,*[184]
And heal the harms of thwarting
    thunder blue.

### B.

(1) Thyrsis in *Comus* is, as Moody notes,[185] "manifestly akin to
Ariel." Both are spirits of air, and each serves as guardian and
attendant upon virtue and innocence. They resemble each other
in song as in deed.

V.i.88–94:
*Where the bee sucks, there suck I.*
    . . .
Merrily, merrily shall I live now
Under the blossom that hangs on
    the bough.

*Comus* 976–981:
To the ocean now I fly . . .
Up in the broad fields of the sky;
*There I suck the liquid air*
All amidst the Gardens fair. . . .—
    (Warburton)

Another line of Thyrsis' closing song is reminiscent of Prospero's epilogue.

Epilogue 1:
Now my charms are all o'erthrown.
    . . .

*Comus* 1012:
Now my task is smoothly done. . . .
    — (W)

(2) *The Tempest*'s airy voices re-echo through Paradise (before
Adam and Eve lose it) as well as through Comus' enchanted
wood.

---

184 "The expression and idea are Shakspearian, but in a different sense and application" (Warton, in Todd, VI, 163). See also above, p. 149, item B (1).
185 Page 37.

III.ii.144–149 [cf. III.iii.17, stage direction printed below, under (5)]:

> This isle is full of noises
> *Sounds and sweet airs,* that give de-
> light and hurt not.
> Sometimes a thousand twangling in-
> struments
> Will hum about mine ears, and
> sometimes *voices*
> That if I then had wak'd after long
> sleep,
> Will make me sleep again.

*PL* IV.680–682:
> How often . . . have we heard
> *Celestial voices* to the midnight air.
> — (D)

*Comus* 208:
> Airy tongues that syllable men's
> names.— (Br.)

*PL* V.547–548:
> Cherubic songs by night . . .
> Aërial music.

(3) Warton called attention long ago to the analogous use of magic paraphernalia on the part of Prospero and Comus; that is to say, to the implication that the magic powers of these two depend upon their books and glass, respectively.

III.ii.96–103:

> Thou mayst brain him,
> *Having first seiz'd his books,* or with
> a log
> Batter his skull. . . . *Remember*
> *First to possess his books;* for with-
> out them
> He's but a sot as I am, nor hath not
> One spirit to command. . . . *Burn*
> *but his books.*

*Comus* 650–653:

> With dauntless hardihood
> And brandished blade rush on him:
> *break his glass,*
> And shed the luscious liquor on the
> ground;
> *But seize his wand.*

(4) Comus' first greeting to the Lady is staged and written in the spirit of the dramatic romances, and probably with specific memories of Ferdinand's[186] first scene with Miranda. Ariel's song, and

---

[186] What appears to be an uncomplimentary allusion on Milton's part to another character of this play—the passage in the *Apology for Smectymnuus* in which Milton scores the "antic and dishonest gestures of *Trinculos,* buffoons and bawds"—has been thought to refer not to *The Tempest* but to the play of *Albumazor,* acted at Cambridge in 1614 (cf. Johnson's *Life of Milton, Works of Samuel Johnson,* London, 1825, VII, 70, n.); but this is an open question. (Cf. also Milton's *Prose Works,* III, 115, n.)

the Lady's, furnish a lyric setting, and then Comus, like Ferdinand, hails the Lady as a wondrous being and inquires whether she be mortal or goddess.

I.ii.421–427 *(after Ariel's song)*:
> Most sure, *the goddess*
> *On whom these airs attend.* . . . My prime request
> Which I do last pronounce, is, *O you wonder!*
> If you be maid or no?

Comus 244–268 *(after the Echo song)*:
> Can any mortal mixture of earth's mould
> Breathe such *divine inchanting ravishment?*
> . . . *Hail, foreign wonder!*[187]
> Whom certain these rough shades did never breed
> *Unless the Goddess* that in rural shrine
> Dwell'st here.

(5) The feast in *Paradise Regained*, prepared by Satan to tempt Christ, in its stage setting and in the final disposition made of it, distinctly resembles that prepared by Ariel for the shipwrecked mariners, according to the stage directions of the First Folio.

IV.I.35–41 *(the banquet is arranged by Ariel and his "meaner fellows")*:
> *Prosp.* . . . Go bring the rabble,
> . . . for I must
> Bestow upon the eyes of this young couple
> Some vanity of mine art . . .

PR II.236–239 *(in preparing for his banquet, Satan)*:
> Takes a chosen band
> Of spirits likest to himself in guile
> To be at hand and at his beck appear
> If cause were to unfold some active scene.

III.iii.17–19 *(and stage direction, ante, for the banquet scene)*:
> *Solemn and strange music* . . . Enter several *strange Shapes*, bringing in a banquet; and *dance about*

*Ibid.* II.340–367:
> A table richly spread in regal mode.
> . . .
> By the wine . . . in order stood
> Tall stripling youths rich-clad . . .

---

187 On revising this material for republication, I find that R. C. Browne (I, 287) had anticipated my point here to the extent of commenting upon this line, as follows: "Cf. Ferdinand's address to Miranda."

| | |
|---|---|
| *it* with gentle actions of salutations; and *inviting* the King etc., to eat, they depart. | Under the trees *now tripped, now* solemn stood<br>Nymphs of Diana's train . . .[188] |
| *Alon.* What *harmony* is this? . . .<br>*Gon.* Marvellous sweet music! | And all the while *harmonious airs* were heard.<br>. . . The Tempter now<br>His *invitation* earnestly renewed. |
| III.iii.52 (*as they try to eat—Stage direction*):<br>Thunder and lightning. Enter *Ariel, like a harpy*; claps his *wings* upon the table; and with a strange device the banquet *vanishes*. | *Ibid.* II.401–403 (*Christ refuses to eat*):<br>With that<br>Both table and provision *vanished* quite,[189]<br>With sound of *harpies' wings* and talons heard. |

Newton, it should be said, compares Satan's banquet with Armida's in *Jerusalem Delivered* (X.lxiv), and Todd reminds us that similar temptations appear frequently in the romances. Milton's stage setting, at all events (the music, dance, and the rest), is closer to Shakespeare than to Tasso, and Tasso says nothing of the disappearance of the banquet with the flapping of the harpies' wings at the end. *Jerusalem Delivered* and *The Tempest*, however, may each have contributed something, for both lived in Milton's memory.

## IV. THE NON-DRAMATIC POEMS

The commentators have not been able to accumulate many instances of probable contacts between Milton and Shake-

---

[188] Satan commends the gay attendants to Christ as "Spirits of air, and woods, and springs . . . who come to pay Thee homage" (*PR* II.374–376). "These spirits," says Dunster, "remind us of Shakespeare's 'Elves of hills, brooks, standing lakes, and groves,' " to whom Prospero bids farewell just before he abjures his magic. But Dunster, like virtually all the commentators, remains silent as to the stage management of the two banquet scenes.

[189] On this line, cf. R. C. Browne's note (*English Poems by John Milton*, II, 308).

speare's non-dramatic poems. I cannot add to their findings at present, but something may be gained by assembling them. So far as quantity goes, it may safely be said that these relationships are less important than those between Milton and the plays.

### 1. *Venus and Adonis.*

**A.**

(1) 453–456:
A red morn that ever yet betoken'd
. . .
*Gusts and* foul *flaws* to herdmen and to herds.

*PL* X.698:
Snow and hail, and stormy *gust and flaw.*— (N)

(2) 956–957:
She vail'd her eyelids, who like *sluices,* stopt
The *crystal* tide.

*PL* V.132–133:
Two other precious drops . . .
Each in their *crystal sluice.*— (T)

### 2. *Lucrece.*

**A.**

(1) 117–118:
Till sable night . . . *dim darkness* doth display.

*Comus* 278:
*Dim darkness,* and this leafy labyrinth.— (W)

(2) See above, n. 136.

### 3. *Sonnets.*

**A.**

(1) Sonnet 1:
*Thyself* thy foe, *to thy sweet self too cruel.*

*Samson* 784:
Ere I to thee, *thou to thyself* wast *cruel.* — (V)

*Comus* 679:
Why should you be so *cruel to yourself?*— (V)

(2) Sonnet 132:
That full *star that ushers in the even.*

*PL* IV.355:
The *stars that usher evening.*

(3) Sonnet 4:[190]

*Unthrifty loveliness,* why dost thou spend
Upon thyself thy beauty's legacy?
*Nature's* bequest gives nothing, but doth *lend,*
And being frank she lends to those are free.
Then, *beauteous niggard,* why dost thou abuse
The bounteous largess given thee to give?
*Profitless usurer,* why dost thou use
So great a sum of sums, yet canst not live?

*Comus* 679–687:

Why should you be so cruel[191] to yourself,
And to those dainty limbs, which *Nature lent*
For gentle usage and soft delicacy?
But you *invert the covenant of her trust,*
And harshly deal, *like an ill borrower,*
With that which you received *on other terms,*
Scorning the unexempt condition
By which all mortal frailty must subsist,
Refreshment after toil, ease after pain.

(4) See above, p. 212, n. 171.

## *4. The Passionate Pilgrim.*
## A.

(1) Number 10:

Sweet rose, fair flower, untimely pluck'd, soon vaded,
Pluck'd in the bud, and vaded in the spring!

*Death of a Fair Infant* 1–2:

O fairest flower, no sooner blown but blasted,
Soft silken Primrose fading timelessly![192]

I cannot here attempt a full analysis of the material assembled above, but it may be useful, with special reference to the purposes of this study as indicated at the outset, to point to certain conclusions which would seem to follow.

---

[190] "Steevens cited" this sonnet and the passage from *Comus,* "and the comparison is worth while" (Masson). See also above, notes 137, 160, and text. Masson compares also Sonnet 128 with Milton's *Elegia Sexta,* 39–48.

[191] See immediately above, *Sonnets,* A (1).

[192] Masson (Milton's *Poetical Works,* III, 147) sees here a likeness in rhythm, and adds that "Milton's taste in rhythm had by this time outgrown Sylvester's Du Bartas." Number 10 of *The Passionate Pilgrim,* however, is usually held not to be Shakespeare's.

1. If our materials may be trusted to prove anything, they prove conclusively that Milton did not forget Shakespeare in his later years. They show, in the first place, that about ten fairly definite Shakespearean reminiscences or allusions found their way into the most unpromising recesses of the controversial prose pamphlets of Milton's middle period. And a count of the totals reveals that two-thirds of the whole body of Milton's Shakespearean reminiscence[193] appears in *Paradise Lost, Paradise Regained,* and *Samson Agonistes.*

2. The evidence justifies the conclusion that the form and substance of Milton's work was significantly influenced by his Shakespearean memories—that they took deep impression upon the heart of his poetic fancy in youth, sustained and enriched his epic flights with an infinite variety of dramatic motifs and devices, and helped to establish in the unequalled masterpiece of his declining years a remarkable balance between Greek and Elizabethan dramatic forms. For the sum total of Shakespeare's recognizable influence upon Milton, whether by way of verbal and figurative recollection, or as a more or less immediate model in matters of dramatic technique, is surprisingly large. This conclusion seems to me inescapable, even though all reasonable discount be made for accidental or uncertain elements.[194] The thirty-five plays considered above include all those of major importance, with the possible exception of *Much Ado*; and of the whole Shakespeare canon only this play and *The Comedy of*

---

[193] Out of approximately 300 reminiscent passages in Milton here examined, almost 100 are from *Comus* and other early poems; almost 200 from *Paradise Lost, Paradise Regained,* and *Samson Agonistes* (some 135, 25, and 35 respectively); and about 10 from the prose pamphlets.

[194] Not all the illustrative material presented above may commend itself to every reader. On the other hand, some things that might be accepted without question have doubtless escaped me. Errors of omission—and perhaps of judgment—are inevitable in a study of this kind.

*Errors* are not represented in some way.[195] If from this list we subtract the eight or ten plays[196] which seem not to have yielded at least two or more fairly certain echoes, there remain twenty-five which Milton did not forget, and these include the greatest of the tragedies, histories, and comedies. Clearly, all three types made a strong impression upon him, but the influence of *Hamlet* and *Macbeth* is the most important of all. Next in order among the tragedies are *Lear, Othello,* and *Romeo and Juliet.* First among the histories stands the group of plays centering about Richard II, Henry IV, and Henry V, with *Richard III* scarcely less important. Among the comedies Milton drew most heavily upon *A Midsummer Night's Dream* and *The Tempest.*

[195] Professor G. C. Taylor, in the valuable paper frequently referred to above, held (p. 196) that it is "no longer necessary to throw *Much Ado* into the discard as a play not influencing Milton." To support his position he adduced, however, only the following passages (p. 193):

| | |
|---|---|
| *Much Ado* V.i.38: | *PR* IV, 469–470: |
| And made a *push at chance* and suffer- | But wilt prolong |
| ance. | All to the *push of fate.* |

This similarity—in the absence of definitely confirmatory evidence—seems to me too slight to establish a real claim for *Much Ado.* (I may add that Masson, to illustrate line 7 of *L'Allegro,* "The *night-raven* sings," quotes *Much Ado* II.iii.83–84: "I had as lief have heard the *night-raven.*" But this bird was a familiar of all the poets, from Peele and Spenser to Goldsmith. His singing in *L'Allegro,* therefore, does not materially help the case for *Much Ado.*) Some time after finishing this study I came upon another likeness which may just possibly alter the case:

| | |
|---|---|
| *Much Ado* II.iii.65: | *Lycidas* 165: |
| Sigh no more, ladies, sigh no more. | Weep no more, woeful shepherds, weep |
| (Cf. Arden ed., p. 101) | no more. (Cf. notes by Verity and |
| | Browne.) |

The passage in *Lycidas,* however, is very close also to the November eclogue (167–180) of *The Shepheardes Calender.*

[196] That is, *Titus Andronicus, The Merry Wives, Pericles, 1* and *3 Henry VI,* and possibly *The Two Gentlemen, Twelfth Night, The Taming of the Shrew* (but cf. above, p. 205, n. 149), *Timon,* and *Henry VIII.* (I do not include *2 Henry VI* and *The Winter's Tale* in this list of eliminations because one or two of the few echoes from these plays have been generally accepted as clear and unmistakable.)

It is evident, finally, that quantitatively as well as qualitatively the several plays contributed their quota of recollection or influence in various ways. In the case of *Measure for Measure*, for instance, one great passage impressed itself indelibly upon Milton's memory, whereas scarcely an act or a major theme of *Hamlet* and *Macbeth* escaped him.

3. Further study of the materials presented above may yield more definite conclusions as to the exact nature of Shakespeare's influence upon Milton than I have been able to formulate. The problem would necessarily present difficulties at any time. At best, perhaps, it admits of an estimate of general probabilities rather than of an exact analysis of facts.

For one thing, the reader will have observed that the two classifications under which I have grouped the material—like any that might have been adopted—overlap to some extent. I believe, however, that they have served to emphasize a distinction worth making. Two-thirds of Milton's Shakespearean recollection, to employ the quantitative test once more, is verbal or figurative. The remaining fraction, which is dramatic, though less in bulk is no less interesting in kind.

As regards the verbal and figurative material, one or two obvious remarks must suffice. In studying the evidence it is constantly to be remembered that the two poets drew upon a common stock of poetic diction and imagery, the heritage of the Renaissance. This fact, however, does not seriously diminish Milton's verbal indebtedness to Shakespeare. His borrowings vary in degree and kind. Some, especially his appropriations of descriptive nouns and adjectives, are as sharp and cleancut as "complete" steel, as sturdily obvious as clouted shoon treading upon this goodly frame, the earth. Others ("drowsy-flighted") steal upon the ear less obviously. These draw in their train shadowy recollections of a turn of phrase, a cadence, or modulation well loved though scarce remembered; and these have no less power to haunt and startle and waylay. Shakespeare's personifications—grim-visaged war, fiery expedition, and their kin—are Milton's familiars as much as Shakespeare's. Again, Shakespearean imagery is constantly recognizable in Milton's description of nature: of flowers, birds, and trees, dawn and night, moon and stars and tempest, and in the visible forms he gives to such abstractions as sleep and war, death and peace.

Of the probable or possible influence of Shakespeare upon Milton's dramaturgy I have given numerous instances in the body of this study. These may be said to fall into three categories. In the first place, there are many likenesses in dramatic theme—the *Paradise Lost* theme in *Othello* and *Macbeth*, the compound echoes of the *Hamlet* soliloquies in *Paradise Lost*, and the ideal of kingship as developed in the histories, in *Paradise Lost*, and *Paradise Regained*. Next, Milton is probably indebted to Shakespeare for certain details in his stage settings and backgrounds (the aerial voices and the magic shadow-shapes of attendant spirits in *Comus* and *Paradise Lost*, the *Tempest*-like banquet of *Paradise Regained*); and perhaps also for occasional hints of dramatic incident (Antony's challenge, and Samson's), and dramatic symbolism (the change of seasons in *A Midsummer Night's Dream*, *As You Like It*, and *Paradise Lost*, the storm in *Lear*, *Paradise Lost*, and *Paradise Regained*). Finally, the true inwardness as well as the outward appearances of Shakespeare's characters are reflected in Milton's. The majestic figure of the elder Hamlet rises again in the shape of Beëlzebub addressing his peers in Pandemonium; Hecate and the weird sisters cast their spells over the dark shades in which dwell Comus and Sin and Death; but Puck and Ariel lend their airy might to aid Thyrsis in undoing these charms. For the rest, besides finding Dalila as false as Cressid, we have seen that Eve, in *her* infinite variety, suggests Desdemona and Lady Macbeth and Cleopatra, and that Samson lives and dies with something of the same tragic intensity, disillusionment, and nobility as Macbeth, and Antony, and Julius Caesar. Adam, in rare moments, proclaims himself a worthy progenitor of Hamlet; and Satan, noblest of them all, holds in solution all the black malice of Iachimo, Iago, and Richard III, together with the indomitable strength and the lamentable human weakness of Henry IV, and King Claudius, and Macbeth.

# Index

The text of *Shakespeare and Our World* was set in Baskerville, an English type-face of the late eighteenth century. The designer, Helen Orton, complemented the text face with headings in Bell, a graceful type of the same family and period.

Heritage Printers, Inc., Charlotte, North Carolina, set the type and printed the book on Warren's Olde Style Antique Wove; Nicholstone Book Bindery, Inc., Nashville, Tennessee, bound it with a cloth manufactured by Arkwright-Interlaken, Inc.

THE UNIVERSITY OF TENNESSEE PRESS